# SAILING solo

# SAILING solo

**THE LEGENDARY SAILORS AND GREAT RACES**

NIC COMPTON

**Foreword by
Ellen MacArthur**

International Marine/McGraw-Hill
Camden, Maine

To my brother Simon
lost at sea off the Canaries
17 March 1980

"Of his bones are coral made:
Those are pearls that were his eyes:
Nothing of him that doth fade,
But doth suffer a sea-change
Into something rich and strange."
William Shakespeare, *The Tempest*

Although written alone, like any singlehanded campaign
there were many who helped. Special thanks to: Mary
Ambler, John Lewis, Ian McKay, Denis Horeau, Jean-
Michel Barrault, Colin Drummond, Mike Rangecroft,
Anne Hammick, François Mousis, Dwight Odom, Muffin
Dubuc, Vanda Woolsey & crew at Yachting World and
of course Vivien Antwi, Naomi Waters, and Nick Wheldon
back at MBHQ.

## SAILING SOLO
by Nic Compton

First published in Great Britain in 2003 by Mitchell
Beazley, an imprint of Octopus Publishing Group Limited.

First North American edition published 2003 by
International Marine/McGraw-Hill.

© Octopus Publishing Group Limited 2003
Text © Nic Compton 2003

ISBN 0071418458

A CIP catalog record for this book is available from the
Library of Congress.

While all reasonable care has been taken during the
preparation of this edition, neither the publisher,
editors, nor the authors can accept responsibility for any
consequences arising from the use thereof or from the
information contained therein.

Page 2: Florence Arthaud on *Pierre 1er* in the 1990 Route
du Rhum.
Page 5: Raphaël Dinelli on *Sodebo-Savourons la Vie* in the
1998 Route du Rhum.

Set in Minion, Helvetica, Bell Centennial and Bell Gothic

Printed and bound in China

# CONTENTS

# FOREWORD

**W**hen I was first asked to write this foreword I hesitated, not sure if I should be the one to do this in light of the far greater sailors that are included in this book. But when I read Nic Compton's book I felt a great empathy with my fellow sailors – past and present – and felt in some small way I could show my appreciation to those who have risked so much to achieve their dreams.

I have had a passion for the sea from the age of four – it consumed me. But I never consciously dreamt of being a solo sailor, I just wanted to be on the water to live my next adventure. It was only at the age of 18 when I sailed *Iduna* round Britain that I began to believe that I could have a career in sailing. Perhaps I had an inkling of my future solo career when I re-fitted *Iduna* with only one bunk – it was a conscious decision about going solo, it just felt the right thing to do!

But looking back I see I was always drawn to the stories of the solo pioneers. When I was a young girl at school in Derbyshire I would go into the library to read the only book it had on solo sailing, Francis Chichester's *Gypsy Moth Circles The World*. When I returned to my school recently, I searched for that book and it was still there – only one other kid had read it since I left eight years ago! Maybe that doesn't say a lot for kids' interest in solo sailing but, without doubt, the adventures of solo sailors have always captured the imagination regardless of one's age.

Even now, I am still completely amazed by the early pioneers of solo sailing. Imagine setting sail on a tiny boat with only the most basic of safety equipment, foul weather gear, and navigational aids. This is what Slocum, Chichester, Rose, Hasler and, to some extent, Sir Robin Knox-Johnston did. Even when Robin set the non-stop round the world record on Suhaili, he did so with few of the sophisticated aids and modern comforts we have now. Robin set his record of 313 days in 1968–69, seven years before I was born. Now, the monohull record stands at 93 days – a lot has been achieved in 26 years!

Today, solo sailors are racing across the oceans in the latest high-tech carbon racing machines costing millions. They have all the latest technology to help them – satellite communications, sophisticated auto-pilots, canting keels and masts, EPIRBS, gortex sailing gear, freeze-dried food, water desalinators – the list is endless! And this is demonstrated in the amazing records that are now being set by the modern day solo racer. But one thing will never change no matter what you have onboard – the ocean remains all powerful.

Nic effortlessly recounts many of the greatest solo stories demonstrating his understanding of the sea and the sailors who are prepared to sacrifice everything to compete on the world's oceans. These tales of great human endeavour leave you feeling in awe of the men and women who have attempted these incredible voyages.

One thing is for sure, there will be many, many more stories to tell as the sport of solo sailing continues to evolve. But the achievements of all those that have gone before will continue to live in the memories of those who follow.

*Ellen MacArthur, Skipper, Team Kingfisher*
*www.ellenmacathur.com*

# INTRODUCTION

Deep in the Southern Ocean, hundreds of miles away from human habitation, a small fleet of yachts is tearing its way across a bleak desert of sea in what seems like reckless haste. With triple-reefed mains and storm jibs set, they surf down 12m (40ft) waves at speeds of 20 knots and more, their wakes quickly erased by the screeching wind. Aboard, their radars scan the water ahead for icebergs, a satellite link to the race headquarters keeps them informed of their rivals' progress, and routing programmes help them decide the best route to take. These are efficient, state-of-the-art racers, costing up to £1million apiece. Their skippers are skilled professionals trained in the art of navigation, meteorology, nutrition and, above all, sleep management. They eat reconstituted food and sleep in 20 minutes naps. Each of them is embarked on what is one of the ultimate challenges known to man: to sail around the world singlehanded.

Meanwhile, on the other side of the world, another group of solo sailors is setting out on another yacht race in a very different setting. The TBS Grand Prix, Hungary's most hotly-contested singlehanded race, takes place in the foothills of the Alps, 160 miles from the sea, in an area more commonly associated with wine-making than sailing. Although just 77km (47.8 miles) long and 14km (8.7 miles) wide, Lake Balaton provides a sharp test of the competitors' skill and endurance, and every year about 20 skippers on an assortment of boats gather for this unique event. It takes all their stamina to race non-stop for most of the day, making the most of every wind shift and ensuring the boat is sailing at its optimum in order to steal a few valuable feet from their rivals. For, while the skippers strut their stuff in the Southern Ocean, these landlocked sailors are pursuing their own non-stop solo circumnavigation – around Lake Balaton.

Although literally a world away from each other, these two events are linked by a common passion: the desire to harness the elements of wind and water, alone, and without recourse to outside assistance. Whether it is in the wilds of the Southern Ocean or amid the vineyards of some Hungarian valley, it is a challenge that sailors the world over have responded to ever since man hoisted a sail on some rudimentary craft and set out to sea. Some do it of their own prompting and according to their own rules, including many of the great ocean navigators, from the "original" solo circumnavigator Joshua Slocum to the romantic individualists of the 1920s and 1930s, such as Alain Gerbault, and the latterday eccentrics such as Jon Sanders – the only man to have sailed three times around the world singlehanded and non-stop!

But an increasing number choose to pit their skills against other like-minded sailors, and combine the thrill of sailing alone with the rush of adrenalin that is a part of any race. The late 1970s were the high water mark of singlehanded racing, with up to 125 competitors taking part in the Observer's transatlantic race, while the advent of the Mini-Transat and Route du Rhum gave birth to a new generation of solo sailors in Europe. Likewise, across the Atlantic, the Newport to Bermuda One-Two and the Singlehanded TransPac generated new interest in the sport.

With the advent of the BOC Challenge and the Vendée Globe in the 1980s, the sport moved to a new, more professional level which has gradually become the norm across most of the sport. Singlehanded racing is now big money, with the top Around Alone campaigns costing around £2million. And it has, arguably, never been more popular. Depending on who you believe, between 50,000 and 200,000 people lined the entrance to Les Sables d'Olonne to welcome Ellen MacArthur back in 2000, while the year

before the Figaro race had the largest number of entries in its long history. Meanwhile, solo races are taking place from Hong Kong to Seattle to the Balearics and Lake Ontario, as well as on both sides of the Pacific.

It is this upsurge of interest in the sport that signalled the need for a publication that would provide a context for the many races that now make up the busy singlehanded calendar. Appropriately enough, thanks to the flexibility of

modern technology in the form of a laptop and a mobile phone, most of this book was written alone and on a boat — albeit up a muddy creek on the South Coast rather than on the ocean wave. I hope some salt has nevertheless crept through the keyboard and onto this page to convey the thrill of this most exhilarating of sports.

*Nic Compton, Newhaven*

**above** Singlehanded racing has come a long way since Francis Chichester won the first OSTAR in 1960 in 40 days. Lightweight catamarans such as *Fujicolor II* now sprint across the Atlantic in less than 10 days.

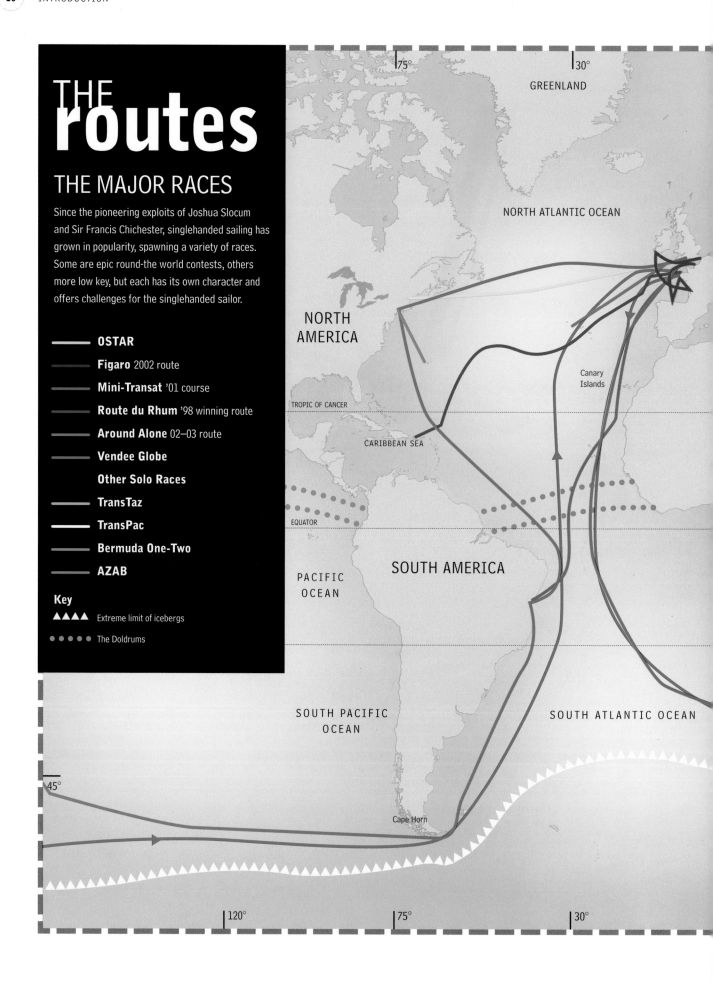

# THE routes

## THE MAJOR RACES

Since the pioneering exploits of Joshua Slocum and Sir Francis Chichester, singlehanded sailing has grown in popularity, spawning a variety of races. Some are epic round-the world contests, others more low key, but each has its own character and offers challenges for the singlehanded sailor.

- **OSTAR**
- **Figaro** 2002 route
- **Mini-Transat** '01 course
- **Route du Rhum** '98 winning route
- **Around Alone** 02–03 route
- **Vendee Globe**
- **Other Solo Races**
- **TransTaz**
- **TransPac**
- **Bermuda One-Two**
- **AZAB**

**Key**

▲▲▲▲ Extreme limit of icebergs

● ● ● ● ● The Doldrums

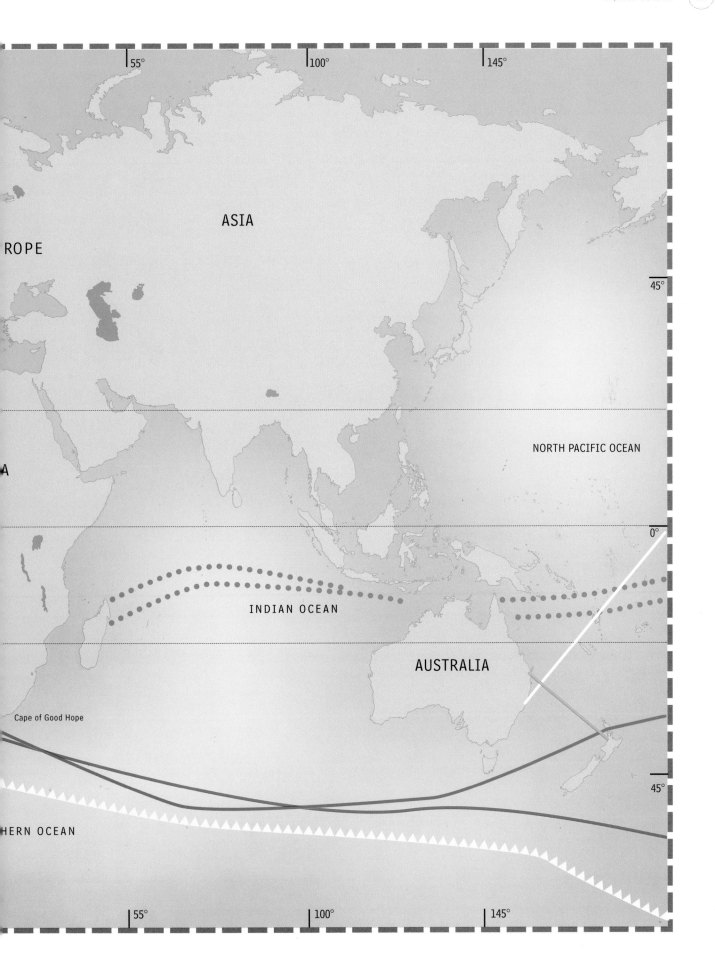

ROPE

ASIA

A

45°

NORTH PACIFIC OCEAN

0°

INDIAN OCEAN

AUSTRALIA

Cape of Good Hope

45°

HERN OCEAN

55° 100° 145°

55° 100° 145°

**left** Robin Knox-Johnston's
*Suhaili,* in which he completed the
first ever solo round-the-world
race in 1968–9.

# THE **routes**

## PIONEERING SOLO CIRCUMNAVIGATIONS

What used to be an exceptional achievement accomplished by only a small handful of individuals has, since the advent of round-the-world races in the 1980s, become an increasingly common occurrence. There are, however, a few notable sailors who forged the way for all those to come.

**Joshua Slocum**
First solo circumnavigation on *Spray*, 24 April 1895–27 June 1898

**Francis Chichester**
First fast solo circumnavigation on *Gipsy Moth IV*, 28 August 1966–28 May 1967

**Robin Knox-Johnston**
First non-stop solo circumnavigation on *Suhaili*, 14 June 1968–22 April 1969

**Chay Blyth**
The "impossible route". First non-stop solo circumnavigation the "wrong way" round on *British Steel*, 18 October 1970–6 August 1971

**Bernard Moitessier**
The "long way" solo circumnavigation, on *Joshua*, 22 August 1968–21 June 1969.

### Key
▲▲▲▲  Extreme limit of icebergs
● ● ● ●  The Doldrums

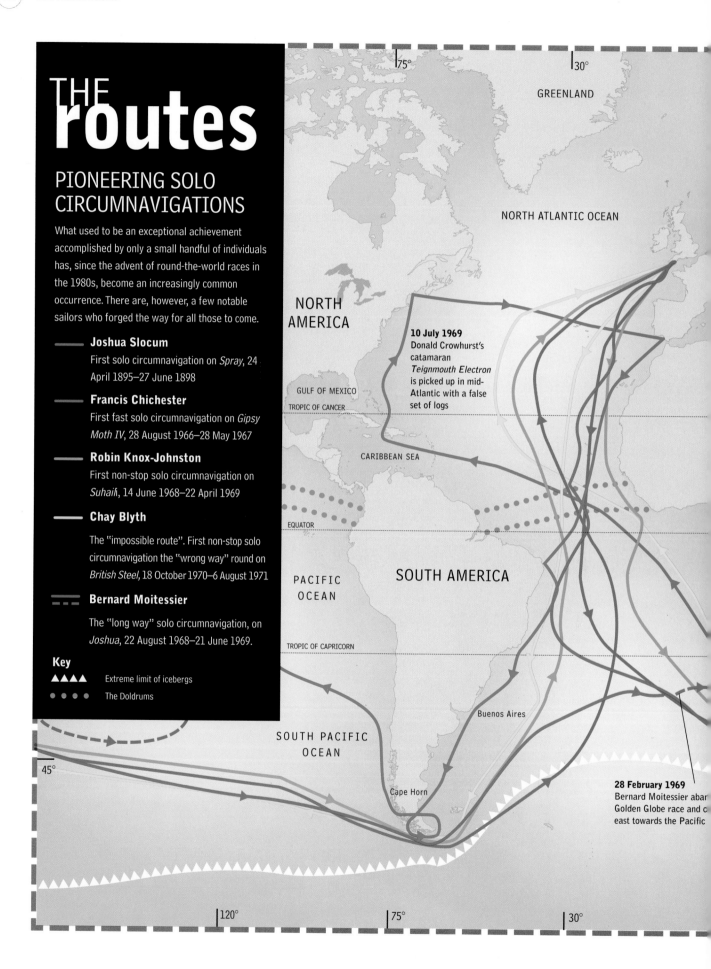

GREENLAND

NORTH ATLANTIC OCEAN

NORTH AMERICA

GULF OF MEXICO

TROPIC OF CANCER

CARIBBEAN SEA

EQUATOR

PACIFIC OCEAN

SOUTH AMERICA

TROPIC OF CAPRICORN

Buenos Aires

SOUTH PACIFIC OCEAN

Cape Horn

**10 July 1969**
Donald Crowhurst's catamaran *Teignmouth Electron* is picked up in mid-Atlantic with a false set of logs

**28 February 1969**
Bernard Moitessier abar
Golden Globe race and c
east towards the Pacific

75°  30°

45°

120°  75°  30°

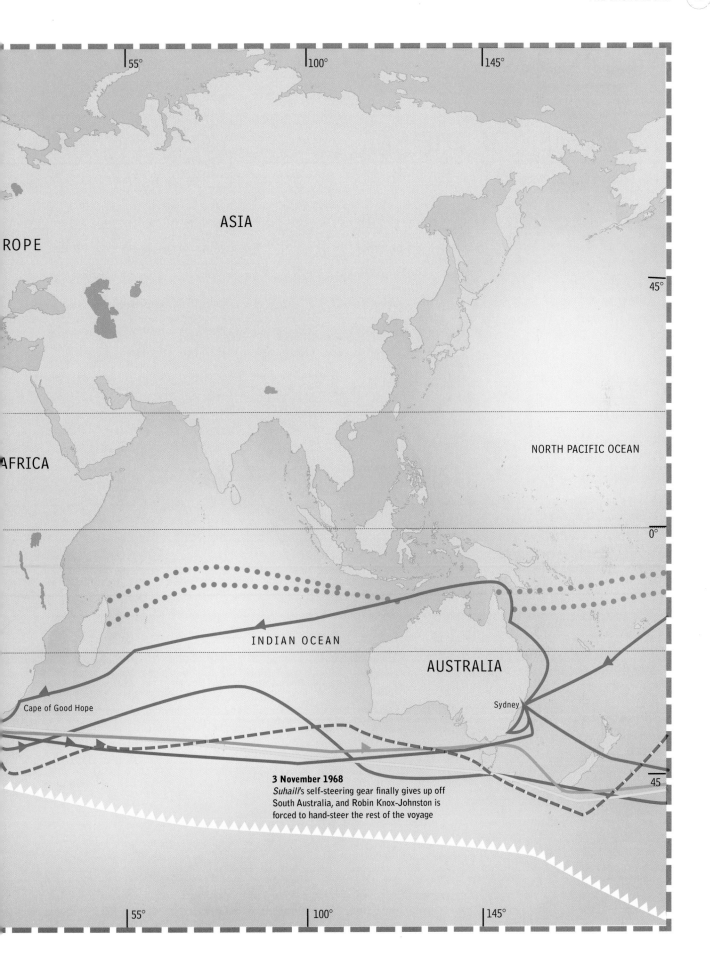

55°    100°    145°

ASIA

EUROPE

45°

AFRICA

NORTH PACIFIC OCEAN

0°

INDIAN OCEAN

AUSTRALIA

Cape of Good Hope

Sydney

**3 November 1968**
*Suhaili's* self-steering gear finally gives up off
South Australia, and Robin Knox-Johnston is
forced to hand-steer the rest of the voyage

45

55°    100°    145°

# GREAT MEN OF THE SEA

**"** After four gales my hands are worn and cut about badly and I am aware of my fingers on account of the pain from skin tears and broken fingernails. I have bruises all over from being thrown about. My skin itches from constant chafing with wet clothes, and I forget when I last had a proper wash, so I feel dirty. I feel altogether mentally and physically exhausted and I've been in the Southern Ocean only a week. It seems years since I gybed to turn east and yet it was only last Tuesday night, not six days, and I have another 150 days of it ... I feel that I have had enough of sailing for the time being... **"**

*A World of my Own*, Robin Knox-Johnston

## THE GOLDEN GLOBE CONTENDERS

**Robin Knox-Johnston**
*Suhaili* (UK) finishes in 313 days

**Bernard Moitessier**
*Joshua* (Fr) sails on to Tahiti

**Chay Blyth**
*Dytiscus* (UK) retires at Port Elizabeth, South Africa

**John Ridgeway**
*English Rose IV* (UK) retires at Recife, Brazil

**Bill King**
*Galway Blazer* (UK) retires at Capetown

**Nigel Tetley**
*Victress* (UK) boat breaks up off Azores

**Donald Crowhurst**
*Teignmouth Electron* (UK) lost at sea, possible suicide

**Loïck Fougeron**
*Captain Brown* (Fr) reaches St Helena under jury rig

**Alex Carozzo**
*Gancia Americano* (It) retires off Lisbon

The date is 9 September 1968, and Robin Knox-Johnston is 87 days out of Falmouth, England on his way back to Falmouth, via New Zealand. His purpose: to be the first man to sail singlehanded, non-stop around the world. He has already suffered one serious knockdown which almost forced him to retire: his self-steering system is badly damaged and will eventually break irreparably off Australia, forcing him to make do with rope lashings or steer the boat himself; his yacht's cabin has been bodily shifted by the force of the breaking seas and will leak for the rest of the voyage. Despite these setbacks, and many more to come, he continues the journey and, although not sailing the fastest boat, is the only person to complete the course. He arrives back in Falmouth 313 days after he left, having sailed a distance of over 48,000km (30,000 miles). He has not only won a race but he has earned himself a place in history.

In many ways the race for the Golden Globe trophy was the greatest challenge of them all. It came after Englishmen Francis Chichester's and Alec Rose's epic circumnavigations, and Frenchman Eric Tabarly's triumphant victory in the second OSTAR; suddenly singlehanded voyages were in the news, and the sailing world was looking for old records to break and new records to set. Chichester's journey had proven that a lengthy non-stop voyage was possible (he put in only in Sydney, Australia to modify his keel and fix his self-steering, but although exhausted was otherwise in a fit state to continue) and the general sentiment, most notably expressed by the father of the Golden Globe's eventual winner, Robin Knox-Johnston, was: "There's only one more thing left to do…"

Chaired by Francis Chichester and sponsored by the *The Sunday Times*, the rules of the Golden Globe were simple: to sail alone and unassisted around the world via the three capes: Cape of Good Hope, Cape Leeuwin, and Cape Horn. The start time was any time between 1 June and 31 October 1968, leaving from any English port and returning to the same place. A Golden Globe trophy was to be presented to the first finisher and a prize of £5000 to the fastest.

In the end nine boats set off: five never made it past the Cape of Good Hope; one boat broke up in mid-ocean; one skipper probably committed suicide; only one completed the course.

One finisher out of nine is not a very auspicious record, but it proves how close to the edge of the contemporary technology and

**left** Although the slowest of the nine boats that challenged for the Golden Globe trophy, Robin Knox-Johnston's *Suhaili* was rugged and reliable. She was the only entrant to complete the first ever solo round-the-world race, returning to Falmouth after 313 days at sea.

endurance the contest was. Those skippers were truly pushing the limits. Nowadays, some 15 boats usually set off on the Vendée Globe solo round-the-world race and about half complete the course; the completion rate is even higher for the Around Alone (ex-BOC) race, whose stopovers greatly improve the chances of finishing in one piece.

Knox-Johnston had wanted a new sailing yacht to be built for the voyage but, unable to raise the finance, had settled for the dumpy little cruising boat he had had built in India a few years earlier. But, of course, *Suhaili* was never intended for a such a voyage. Knox-Johnston and two merchant navy colleagues had had her built for a bit of fun and possibly to sell at a profit back in Europe. Yet she had two distinct advantages over the "longer and faster" boat he dreamed of. First, the 9.8m (32ft) William Atkin-designed ketch was based on the Colin Archer rescue boat-types from Norway, well known for their ability to survive the very worse the North Sea could throw at them – albeit not with any particular thought to speed. Secondly, after buying his partners out, Knox-Johnston had sailed the vessel

from India back to the UK with his brother Chris and a friend. Consequently, by the time he left Falmouth on 14 June 1968 he already knew his boat intimately and had ironed out many of the problems often associated with new, untried craft – unlike several of his rivals.

Although the Golden Globe was not a proper "race", in that there was no set place or time for the start, the build-up to each boat's departure must have felt every bit like one. The only chance for the smaller boats of winning the trophy was to get away first and put as many miles under their keels as they could before the bigger boats started. The great Atlantic rowing combination of British paratroopers Chay Blyth and John Ridgway were away first in small, almost identical production boats. Knox-Johnston was next, followed by Bernard Moitessier, Loïck Fougeron, Bill King, Nigel Tetley, Donald Crowhurst, and Alex Carozzo.

Much of the competition was wiped out early on. Blyth was the first, pulling in at Recife in Brazil; then Ridgway and King at Capetown. Carozzo headed to Lisbon with a stomach ulcer while Fougeron gave up after a knockdown in the Roaring Forties, deep in the wild Southern Ocean. As one by one the boats were knocked out of contention, it became a battle between Knox-Johnston and Moitessier, with Tetley following gamely in his trimaran *Victress*. Crowhurst, sailing his identical trimaran *Teignmouth Electron*, was thought to be on his way too.

## The unflappable versus the philosophical

There could hardly have been a greater contrast between the two front runners: Knox-Johnston, the down-to-earth, unflappable Englishman, and Moitessier, the earnest, philosophical Frenchman. At the start of the race Moitessier already had a reputation as an experienced ocean yachtsman, having sailed his 11.9m (39ft) steel yacht, *Joshua*, around the world two years earlier. His boat was a rugged, no-nonsense ketch designed for ocean cruising ("Solid, simple, sure – and fast on all points of sail," as he himself describes her) and Moitessier had spent several months getting her ready for this challenge.

So, while Knox-Johnston battles with broken windvanes, leaking planking seams, fouled drinking water, and dodgy electrics, Moitessier contemplates the phosphorescence, measures the weather by the stiffness of his tea towel and talks to his "eldest brother" (or what Knox-Johnston might know as "God"). So in tune does he become with his boat and the elements that he reaches "a kind of indefinable state of grace". He also gradually gains ground on Knox-Johnston and, while being too far behind to overtake his rival, seems assured of winning the £5000 for the fastest circumnavigation. Not that he knows any of this, having turned down the offer of a radio from *The Sunday Times* – keen to have regular reports from all the competitors to run in its pages – opting instead for a sling-shot and film containers to shoot messages onto the decks of passing ships.

But rather than head home for glory, he does an extraordinary thing. After nearly four months in the Southern Ocean, instead of heading for home and the waiting crowds, he decides he can't face going "back to the snake pit". As he puts it: "Leaving from Plymouth and returning to Plymouth now seems like leaving from nowhere to go nowhere." Or, more positively expressed in a sling-shot message to his agent: "I am continuing non-stop towards the Pacific Islands because I am happy at sea, and perhaps also to save my soul."

So he simply keeps going, sailing east to Capetown, past Tasmania and New Zealand again, eventually stopping at Tahiti, 10 months after leaving Plymouth and four months after rounding Cape Horn. He has in effect sailed one-and-a-half times around the world in less time Knox-Johnston took to go round once. By crossing his outward longitude on 25 February 1969 (two months before Knox-Johnston's return to Falmouth), he can also technically claim to be the first non-stop solo circumnavigator. His book of the voyage, *The Long Way*, becomes a maritime classic and Moitessier is heralded as the spiritual leader of singlehanded sailors. It is a status he enjoys to this day, nearly a decade after his death.

Unperturbed by such abstract considerations, the man who prided himself on being described by a psychiatrist as "distressingly normal" both before and after his voyage plods on, tortoise-fashion, for his finish at Falmouth. Knox-Johnston arrives there on 22 April 1969 to well-deserved acclaim. For a short while at least, Britannia rules the waves once more.

But while Knox-Johnston may have won the Golden Globe trophy, the race for the fastest circumnavigation is still on, with *Victress* and *Teignmouth Electron* battling it out in the Atlantic. As reports reach him of Crowhurst coming back into contention after a long radio silence, Tetley pushes his boat to the limit and on 21 May, 1920km (1200 miles) from home, his trimaran breaks up and sinks. Tetley is lucky to

> **" I AM CONTINUING NON-STOP TOWARDS THE PACIFIC ISLANDS BECAUSE I AM HAPPY AT SEA, AND PERHAPS ALSO TO SAVE MY SOUL "**
>
> Bernard Moitessier in the Golden Globe, 1968

**right** Although Bernard Moitessier, in *Joshua*, abandoned the Golden Globe race to "save his soul", in crossing his outward longitude before Knox-Johnston completed his voyage, Moitessier technically became the first non-stop solo navigator. He went on to achieve fame for his philosophical writings.

be picked up by a passing ship. Although she has lost the race, *Victress* is the first trimaran to be sailed singlehanded around the world non-stop, and the first to sail around Cape Horn. *The Sunday Times* eventually awards her skipper a "consolation prize" of £1000 with which he builds himself another trimaran.

## Fraud on the high seas

More drama is to come. Crowhurst, the struggling electronics-company boss from Teignmouth, looks on track to win the £5000 prize. His performance so far has been mercurial, recording some of the fastest and slowest passages of the group. The press is euphoric; race chairman Francis Chichester expresses his reservations. Then, on 10 July 1969, *Teignmouth Electron* is picked up by the mailship *Picardy*. There is no sign of Crowhurst on board and initial reports assume he must have fallen overboard on his way to certain-seeming victory. The truth is much, much stranger. Closer

inspection of his logbooks reveals that *Teignmouth Electron* never left the Atlantic.

Just six weeks into his intended circumnavigation, Crowhurst realises he doesn't stand a chance. His boat is ill-prepared and his start rushed. As small problems develop, he seems unable to act – unlike Tetley who overcame far greater damage on *Victress* – and convinces himself that the boat is unfit to continue. Unable to face the humiliation of giving up, however, he dawdles off the coast of South America for four months, keeping two parallel logs: one truthful, showing his actual position day by day, another fraudulent, showing the position he would claim to be in. He radios back his false positions for a few weeks, then, to mask any inconsistent radio signals, shuts down for three months while he "sails around the world". He only resumes contact once (according to his bogus log) when he is "HEADING DIGGER RAMREZ" – theoretically just about to round Cape Horn. In fact, he is hovering off the Falkland Islands, still very much

**right** A launch from the RMV *Picardy* approaches the *Teignmouth Electron,* discovered ghosting in mid-Atlantic with no-one on board.

on the "right" side of the Horn, getting ready to rejoin his imagined trail and head home.

His duplicity is in its way an act of genius. As the chroniclers of his "strange voyage" put it: "To calculate backwards from an imagined distance to a series of daily positions, and from them via declination and other tables to the correct sun-sightings is a formidable and unfamiliar job, far harder than honest navigation." Crowhurst is not really criminal material, however. All the months at sea and the strain of his forgery gradually drive him insane. On 1 July 1969 he writes a final entry in his logbook: "Now is revealed the true nature and purpose and power of the game offence I am. I am what I am and I see the nature of my offence … It is finished. It is finished. IT IS THE MERCY."

Many theories have been offered for what happened next. It is thought probable that he threw himself off the back of his boat and drowned, though some of a more imaginative disposition suggest that he somehow escaped to South America and may be living there still. Either way, the Crowhurst legend had been established – albeit not quite in the way he had hoped.

## Early pioneers

But of course the history of singlehanded sailing goes back much further than the Golden Globe. Fishermen have been setting out on sometimes unintentionally long solo voyages for centuries. The Pacific islanders in particular are famed for their great navigational expertise, which enabled them to achieve improbably long voyages as a matter of course, and often singlehanded. Few, though, have been quite as far off course as the "copper-skinned" sailor who is said to have washed up in a dug-out on the Spanish coast during the Middle Ages – supposedly one of Europe's first sightings of a native American, or "red Indian", fresh from a very early crossing of the Atlantic. Unfortunately he was unable to make himself understood and died soon after. But such exploits go largely unrecorded or are dismissed as "folklore" – predictably, the only documented early record-holders are all white, Western and, usually, American.

One of the busiest periods for solo "firsts" was the end of the 19th century, when a flurry of pioneers established new records on both sides of the American continent. It all started with Alfred Johnson and the first centenary of the American Revolution. Keen to prove the supremacy of US sailors on this symbolic anniversary, on 25 June 1876, this Newfoundland fisherman set off to visit his relatives in Liverpool in a cutter-rigged 6m (20ft) dory. He had taken the precaution of fitting a canvas deck over *Centennial* and loading some ballast, but essentially the boat was little more than an overgrown dinghy. Despite capsizing just 480km (300 miles) from Ireland, he completed his crossing in 64 days, from Gloucester, Massachusetts to Abercastle, Wales, thus becoming the first man to sail across the Atlantic singlehanded. His average speed was just two knots.

Although the modest Johnson himself made little mileage out of his extraordinary feat, it was widely discussed, and soon other, equally brave – or foolhardy – sailors attempted the challenge. But how to better Johnson's achievement? There were only two ways: either do it faster or do it in a smaller boat. Thus was born the cult of the solo record-breakers which continues to this day, with increasingly small boats being pressed into service.

In fact, although no-one could take away Johnson's claim to an Atlantic "first", his records for speed and size were soon broken. It began in 1880, with Frederick Norman and his 4.9m (16ft) *Little Western*, just a few inches shorter that *Centennial*, who swiftly laid claim to have sailed "the smallest boat to cross the Atlantic". Then, in 1891, William Andrews set about to break the record again – and this time it would be a race. Andrews and his brother Asa had already beaten the two-handed transatlantic record in 1878, in the 5.5m (18ft) *Atlantic*, and, in 1888, he made his first, abortive attempt to beat the singlehanded record. Having failed the first time, three years later he challenged his long-time rival Josiah "Si" Lawlor to race for it.

Both gentlemen sailed 4.6m (15ft) vessels, though Andrews's *Mermaid* had a centreboard, while Lawlor's *Sea Serpent* had a conventional keel. Andrews headed south for the more moderate weather, while Lawlor, like Johnson

above Donald Crowhurst went to extraordinary lengths to cover up his cheat, creating a whole set of false logs to support his pretence of having sailed around the world. In fact, he never left the Atlantic, and is presumed to have committed suicide.

## HOWARD BLACKBURN

The legend of this indestructible dory fisherman was established in 1883 when he and his fishing partner lost sight of their base ship off the Newfoundland coast. Blackburn rowed for five days and four nights through icy gales without food or water to reach land, losing all his fingers and most of his toes to frostbite in the process. His partner died after two days. Despite this experience, in 1899 he built himself the 8.8m (29ft) sloop *Great Western* in which he crossed the Atlantic in 61 days. Two years later he attempted to set a new transatlantic record with his 7.3m (24ft) sloop *Great Republic*, crossing from Boston to Lisbon in 39 days.

before him, took the shorter but more dangerous northern route. In the end Lawlor's gamble paid off, and while Andrews crept towards Spain, running out of food and eventually being picked up half-dead by a passing steamer, Lawlor reached the Cornish coast in just 45 days. Although he rather disingenuously describes his journey as "without incident", contemporary reports reveal his boat suffered at least one knockdown and was on one occasion attacked by a rampant shark, and that he himself was twice thrown over the side. Despite all this, Lawlor had convincingly won the first ever singlehanded transatlantic race.

Unperturbed by almost dying during his 1891 Atlantic race against "Si" Lawlor, William Andrews set off three years later and set a new record for sailing the smallest boat across the Atlantic Ocean in the 4.4m (14ft) *Sapolio*. His record would stand for 71 years until, in 1965, it was challenged by American journalist Robert Manry, who successfully crossed to Falmouth on his 4m (13ft) *Tinkerbelle*. This record in turn only lasted a few years as in 1968 the American Hugo S Vihlen crossed from Casablanca to Fort Lauderdale in *April Fool* – measuring all of 1.8m (6ft). That seemed to have them licked, until tom McNally turned up in 1993 with his 1.6m (5ft 4½in) *Vera Hugh*. McNally is now trying to secure an even safer record with a high-tech nutshell measuring just 1.2m (3ft 11in).

Meanwhile, on the other side of the North American continent, one Bernard Gilboy was preparing to set another record: the first documented solo crossing of the Pacific Ocean. His choice of craft was the 5.8m (19ft) *Pacific*, which he had specially built for the journey. Setting off on 11 August 1882, he made slow progress, and after four months was still 2400km (1500 miles) from Australia when his boat capsized. Despite losing his compass and rudder and most of his food, he refused to pull in at any of the nearby islands. Instead, surviving on a diet of sea birds and flying fish, he sailed on under jury rig for another six weeks. He was eventually picked up by a passing ship 800km (500 miles) from Brisbane having sailed 10,400km (6500 miles) in 164 days – an average of just 40 miles a day.

## Old man and the sea

But in the history of singlehanded sailing there is one name than looms infinitely larger than all others; one man who achieved what was then thought impossible and inspired sailors over the next 100 years to attempt to follow him: Joshua Slocum, the first man to sail solo around the world. His 76,600km (46,000-mile) voyage aboard the boxy oyster boat *Spray* was remarkable not just because it was a "first" but because of the skill Slocum displayed in managing his 11.3m (37ft) craft with only rudimentary equipment in often extreme situations. As well as being seemingly fearless, he was also a great sailor.

Slocum has become a legendary figure not only because of his pioneering voyage, however, but also because he was able to set his experiences down on paper. *Sailing Alone Around the World*, the book he wrote about his circumnavigation, has become one of the classics of maritime literature, reprinted in countless editions and translated into dozens of languages. It has also ensured that the image of Slocum that survives is the one that he himself created: the austere, hardy man "born in the breezes" who "studied the sea as perhaps few men have studied it, neglecting all else".

By all accounts, Slocum was indeed a natural sailor. Born in Nova Scotia "in a cold spot, on coldest North Mountain, on a cold February 20" in 1844, Slocum left home at 16 and soon found himself on a full-rigged ship bound for Dublin. It was the start of a career which would take him to ports around the world and around the Horn several times. Aged 25, he was given his first command, and by the time he was 38, he owned shares and was captain of the 1800-tonne *Northern Light*, "the finest American sailing-vessel afloat". Then, in 1884, he decided to go his own way and bought the *Aquidneck*, "a little bark which of all man's handiwork seemed to me the nearest to perfection of beauty". It was the beginning of his troubles.

His wife Virginia – whom he had married in Australia in 1871 and who, along with their three sons and one daughter, accompanied him on all his trips – died soon after he bought the *Aquidneck*. A year and a half later he set off with his new wife Henrietta, but disease, mutiny and finally shipwreck befell the unfortunate captain and his family. He eventually found himself on the coast of Brazil, paying off his crew from the proceeds of what could be salvaged of the wreck of his once-proud ship. Undaunted, he built a curious 10.7m (35ft) junk-rigged "canoe" – half-dory, half-sampan – called *Libertade* on which he sailed the 8800km (5500 miles) back to Boston.

The age of sail had by then passed, however, and even a skipper of Slocum's experience found it hard to find work on anything other than a steamer, something the 45-year-old sailor could not bear to contemplate. Instead, he turned writer. His first book, *Voyage of the Libertade*, was published in 1890 and was followed four years later by *Voyage of the Destroyer* from New York to Brazil – the latter an account of an escapade piloting a torpedo boat for the Brazilian government during a naval rebellion. Both books were printed at his own expense and made little, if any, money for him, but they no doubt provided useful training for the greater oeuvre yet to come.

Meanwhile, Slocum had been given an old sloop by a friend who warned him that "she wants some repairs". In fact, he spent 13 months rebuilding the *Spray*, though by the time she was launched she had cost him just $553.62 and, as he

## I FELT THAT THERE COULD BE NO TURNING BACK, AND THAT I WAS ENGAGING IN AN ADVENTURE THE MEANING OF WHICH I THOROUGHLY UNDERSTOOD

proudly reports, "she sat on the water like a swan". His wife now living with her sister and his children having all grown up, Slocum was free to set off on his great adventure.

As he left Boston, on 24 April 1895, he seemed aware of the significance of what he was attempting – though he could surely never have guessed what long-standing impact his voyage would have. "A thrilling pulse beat high in me," he writes. "I felt that there could be no turning back, and that I was engaging in an adventure the meaning of which I thoroughly understood."

After stopping off in Nova Scotia, and buying his badly-needed chronometer for $1, Slocum crosses the Atlantic in a respectable 29 days, arriving in Gibraltar on 4 August. There he is warned off his intended route through the Mediterranean for fear of pirates and instead heads back west towards Brazil – thus becoming the first person to sail across the Atlantic singlehanded from east to west.

Joshua Slocum at the start of his epic journey

**left** On 24 April 1895, Joshua Slocum left Boston to become the first man to sail around the world singlehanded. He returned three years and two months later, and subsequently wrote a book about his voyage which would become a bible for all solo sailors.

**above** Slocum's yacht, the
*Spray*, was a "very antiquated"
11.2m (36ft 9in) ex-oyster boat
which a friend gave him as a
joke. He spent 13 months
rebuilding her before setting
off on his epic adventure.

During his epic circumnavigation, Slocum has all manner of adventures, from fighting off pirates to violent gales and even a beaching on the coast of Uruguay. It takes him three months just to negotiate the tricky waters of the Straits of Magellan, the inland passage just north of Cape Horn. There he has his first encounter with "savages" and, after being forced back into the straits a second time after a storm, is struck by hail which "cut my flesh till the blood trickled over my face".

On clearing the Horn, he wrote, "One wave, in the evening, larger than others that had threatened all day … broke over the sloop fore and aft. It washed over me at the helm, the last that swept over the *Spray* off Cape Horn. It seemed to wash away old regrets. All my troubles were now astern; summer was ahead; all the world was again before me. … Then was the time to uncover my head, for I sailed alone with God."

He finally makes it back to Boston on 27 June 1898, three years and two months after he set off. Slocum's narrative of the journey was first published as a series in *The Century Illustrated Monthly Magazine* from September 1899 to March 1900. The book version followed in March 1900. In these memoirs, Slocum describes the effect such prolonged loneliness had on him: "During these days a feeling of awe crept over me. My memory worked with startling power. The ominous, the insignificant, the great, the small, the wonderful, the commonplace – all appeared before my mental vision in magical succession. Pages of my history were recalled which had been so long forgotten that they seemed to belong to a previous existence. I heard all the voices of the past laughing, crying, telling me what I had heard them tell many corners of the earth."

After completing his voyage, Slocum settled down at Martha's Vineyard, a small town on the US eastern seaboard, for a couple of years, buying a farm and attempting to grow hops. It seems to be a troublesome time for this man who, by his own admission, found it hard to settle on land, "the customs and ways of which I had finally almost forgotten." Perhaps not surprisingly, it was not long before he was on the high seas again, making several solo trips to the West Indies from

**❝ ALL MY TROUBLES WERE NOW ASTERN; SUMMER WAS AHEAD; ALL THE WORLD WAS AGAIN BEFORE ME… THEN WAS THE TIME TO UNCOVER MY HEAD, FOR I SAILED ALONE WITH GOD ❞**

Joshua Slocum on clearing Cape Horn

1905 onwards. He set off on his final voyage in 1909, at the age of 65, apparently intending to sail up the Orinoco river and on to the Amazon. He was never seen again and was declared legally dead some months later.

Curiously, Slocum's voyage and the publication of his book did not launch an immediate armada of boats sailing around the world in his wake. He remained a one-off, an American eccentric, for over two decades. Perhaps his description of pirates and storms on the high seas were a little too vivid and put others off, or perhaps the world was just too busy adjusting to the new century to contemplate ocean voyages.

### Quiet American; fiery Frenchman

It was not until 1921 that the next solo circumnavigation took place, and it was once again by a fellow American. Harry Pidgeon made an unlikely ocean navigator. Born in land-locked Iowa to a farming family, he developed a passion for canoeing in his 20s and later built himself a houseboat, but otherwise had little experience of nautical matters. It was not until he was in his late 40s that he decided to build his first seagoing yacht. Lengthened and adapted by Pidgeon from plans published by the popular *Rudder* magazine, the 10.4m (34ft) *Islander* was a shallow-draught yawl designed for amateur construction. Instead of a gently rounded shape, each side of the hull was built in two relatively flat sections joined at a "chine", or sharp angle.

Pidgeon's voyage has been described as "the most perfect circumnavigation". Leaving Los Angeles on 18 November 1921, he arrived back home nearly four years later. Apart from briefly running aground in South Africa and a minor scrape with an errant steamer while in harbour, almost nothing of any consequence befell the "amateur navigator". In part this was no doubt due to his easy-going nature; what others might have considered dire hardship, he accepted as par for the course. He extended this attitude to people he met on his voyage, tending to be non-judgmental and open-hearted towards people who only a few years earlier Slocum had described as "savages". A keen photographer and amateur anthropologist, he documented his 14 "stops" meticulously and later wrote a book about his voyage. Yet seven years later, Pidgeon was off again, sailing almost exactly the same route, only on this occasion going via Hawaii instead of Tahiti and taking a year longer to complete the loop, to become the first man to circumnavigate the globe alone, twice.

Aged 75, Pidgeon married Margaret Gardner and set off on a honeymoon cruise in April 1948. Before long, however, *Islander* was wrecked off the New Hebrides and the couple abandoned ship. Unperturbed, Pidgeon built a new yacht, *Sea Bird*, to the original design and sailed it happily off Los Angeles until his death in 1954 at the age of 96. He was above all a man who sailed far but left little wake.

Pidgeon's modest approach was the very opposite of that other great singlehander of his era, Alain Gerbault, whom he met briefly in Panama. War hero, tennis champion, ocean voyager, best-selling author, human rights activist, womanizer, egotist – Gerbault has been described as many things. And indeed he achieved much in his lifetime, though perhaps not in quite the heroic manner he liked to portray. But then, as with Alain Colas, the great self-publicist of the 1970s, the myth surrounding Gerbault overshadows his genuine achievements.

Born to a wealthy French family (his first mistake, some of his detractors seemed to think) in 1893, Gerbault had his first brilliant career as a fighter pilot during World War I. Claims for his success vary wildly – he shot down between six and 23 German planes, depending which source you accept – but in any case he was decorated and left the air force with honours. At war's end he resumed his old obsession with tennis and became a rising star of the French tennis circuit. But after the thrill of the chase at high altitudes,

such a genteel sport is not enough for this ambitious polymath. As he puts it: "Every man needs some goal, some mountain-top or distant isle of his choosing that he must attain by his own efforts, alone and in his own good time."

So Gerbault looks to the sea for a challenge. Visiting his friend Ralph Stock (author of *The Cruise of the Dream Ship*) in Great Britain, he spots the graceful-looking *Firecrest* moored nearby. Designed by the great British yacht designer and author Dixon Kemp in 1892, the 11m (36ft) gaff cutter was designed for sailing to windward. Her narrow beam and heavily-ballasted keel was the cutting edge of contemporary racing technology – but not intended for ocean passages.

## An inauspicious start

Ever the young man in a hurry, Gerbault buys *Firecrest* and spends two years sailing around the Mediterranean before really going to sea. His aim is to be the first person to sail singlehanded across the Atlantic from east to west to north America (Slocum sailed from Gibraltar to South America in 1895). But Gerbault is not only inexperienced, he is also ill-prepared. The 101-day voyage is a catalogue of disasters, from his badly-cured meat going off to his fresh water supply being contaminated, the mainsail boom fitting shearing, halyards breaking, and sails ripping. At one point he is even swept off the bowsprit and only just manages to clamber back on board by grabbing hold of the bobstay.

Arriving in New York on 15 September 1923, he is greeted with much fanfare and awarded the newly-conceived Blue Water Medal. After a visit to France by liner, he returns to the refurbished *Firecrest*, complete with new bermudan sails (which, bizarrely, he sets off with, before even trying them out), and resumes his journey. Entering the Pacific via Panama, he visits the Galapagos, the Marquesas, Tahiti, and Keeling Cocos island – losing anchors and breaking mooring lines all along the way. He loses his yacht's lead keel on an uncharted coral reef at Wallis Island, but luckily the French navy is on hand to help repair the damage and he sails on none the worse for his scrape with the seabed. Gradually,

## EDWARD MILES

The first man to sail around the world travelling from west to east, Miles interrupted his journey in the Red Sea to go home to the United States and build a new boat after his 10.97m (36ft) *Sturdy* was destroyed by an engine fire. As well as spreading The Word during his travels in 1928–32, he also remarried twice en route.

however, he is seduced by the beauty of the islands and their gentle way of life. It's an attraction that many more singlehanded sailors will succumb to – especially French ones – including, most famously, the great Bernard Moitessier.

It has a profound effect on Gerbault, and he views his homecoming with increasing alarm: "As my journey neared its end I felt a growing sense of dejection," he writes. "My voyage was almost done and the happiest years of my life were almost over."

He arrives back in Le Havre on 26 July 1929, after 64,000km (40,000 miles) at sea, to a euphoric welcome. He is awarded the Légion d'Honneur on the deck of a warship and is fêted at both the Yacht Club de France and the Roland-Garros tennis championship. Already well known because of his exploits in the air and on the tennis court, he suddenly acquires celebrity status. At this point it seems that everything he touches turns to gold - though it seems that it brings along its share of envy too. His critics seize on the melodramatic language of his books *Alone Across the Atlantic* and *In Search of the Sun*, and in particular his insistence on referring to *Firecrest* as his "ship", rather than simply "boat" or "yacht", infuriates some of his detractors.

He donates *Firecrest* to the French Naval Academy – although she unfortunately sinks en route to her new moorings – and builds a new 10.5m (34ft) yacht which, with characteristic modesty, he christens *Alain Gerbault*. On 28 September 1932 he sets out on his last voyage: back to the Pacific. There he becomes an outspoken supporter of the traditional Polynesian way of life – sometimes more so than the indigenous population – and writes several more books about the islands, including an impassioned plea for his "dying paradise". He eventually dies of malaria in Timor, on 16 December 1941, and is buried without ceremony in a cemetery in Dili. His boat is pillaged and disappears. Finally, in 1947, the French navy exhumed his body and reburies it, with full military honours, at one of his favourite spots on the island of Bora-Bora.

Despite his ignominious end, Alain Gerbault's acclaimed circumnavigation and the

success of his books raised the profile of singlehanded sailing in France and accounts in part for the country's subsequent fascination with the sport.

In the 1920s and 1930s, the number of solo voyages gradually increased, although it remained a trickle compared to the explosion that would take place in the 1960s and '70s. It is estimated that about 160 sailors set off on their own up to the mid-1970s – of which only 34 were before 1945. Understandably, apart from the eccentric Argentinian Vito Dumas, none were recorded during the war years. A few notable trips were made during the 1950s, including the relentless chef-turned-sailor Jean Gau, who completed two circumnavigations and at least 10 Atlantic crossings, and Marcel Bardiaux, who made an estimated 300 passage stops and became the first man to round Cape Horn singlehanded from east to west.

**above** Despite his relative inexperience as a sailor, Alain Gerbault shot to fame in France when he completed the first east-to-west transatlantic crossing to America in 1923. His glamorous lifestyle and reputation as a tennis player no doubt helped.

## Across the pond, alone

The event that ultimately turned a rather misanthropic occupation practised mainly by loners and misfits into the mainstream sport it has become today took place with little pomp or ceremony. In fact, it passed virtually unnoticed. The start of the first OSTAR (Observer Singlehanded Transatlantic Race), on 10 June 1960, was a major watershed for sailing as a whole. Only five boats took part in the first race – including its founder Blondie Hasler on his 7.6m (25ft) *Jester* and Francis Chichester on his "oversize" 11.9m (39ft) *Gipsy Moth III* – but within 16 years that number would swell to 125, including Alain Colas on his 72m (236ft) monster *Club Méditerranée*. Eric Tabarly's dramatic win in 1964 turned the heat up on what had been regarded as more of an endurance sport than a test of speed. In the 20 years that followed the first OSTAR, virtually all of the records for solo sailing were either challenged or set for the first time – and then usually immediately broken again. It was, in many ways, the golden age of singlehanded sailing.

What the OSTAR proved was that fast, long-distance, solo passages were now a viable possibility. This was partly made possible through technological developments, such as self-steering mechanisms which enabled skippers to sleep knowing the boat would stay on course; powerful winches which enabled them to handle large sails without depleting their energy; and generally improved materials which could withstand a sustained battering at sea. As the limits of what yachts were capable of expanded, it became increasingly just a question of how far their skippers could push themselves.

One man who was always ready to rise to such a challenge was Francis Chichester. After finally achieving his goal of sailing across the Atlantic in under 30 days in the 1964 OSTAR – by three minutes, and even then he was beaten by Tabarly's astonishing 27-day crossing – he was ready for a new adventure. What he came up with was essentially a round-the-world solo speed challenge, although it was nicely dressed up as a retrospective race against that great 19th century clipper the *Cutty Sark*. To achieve his goal the 65-

year-old enlisted the support of sponsors and had a powerful new 16.3m (53ft) ketch built, drawn by the leading British design team of the day, Illingworth and Primrose.

At the same time a similar voyage was being planned with little publicity and no sponsors by the "Southend greengrocer" Alec Rose, himself 58 years old. Once invalided out of the Navy because of stress, Rose was only known for the bit part he played in the second OSTAR in 1964, when he appeared out of nowhere to take fourth place. His boat was the 18-year-old Fred Shepherd-designed

**left** By the 1930s, Alain Gerbault had turned his back on the high life and gone to live on his boat in the Pacific. He wrote several books on the Polynnesian way of life.

**below** Although never as high-profile as Francis Chichester, Alec Rose captured the heart of the British nation when he circumnavigated the world on *Lively Lady* in 1967–8.

## THE GIPSY KING

Francis Chichester came to sailing late. By then he had already made himself a fortune in New Zealand, farming, prospecting for gold and setting up an aircraft company. Returning to the UK in 1929, he set off to break the Croydon–Sydney record – flying solo in his biplane *Gipsy Moth*. He didn't quite manage it within the necessary 15 days, but his exploit made headline news around the world. He subsequently set a new record flying from New Zealand to Australia and later flew solo from New Zealand to Japan, almost losing his life on taking off when overhead cables snared his plane. Chichester was already 59 and recovering from lung cancer when he won the first OSTAR in 1960. Yet in the following decade he would earn himself a place in history with his various *Gipsy Moth*s as one of Britain's most accomplished sailors.

**right** Francis Chichester's swift circumnavigation on *Gipsy Moth IV* in 1966–7 astonished the world and set the scene for the Golden Globe trophy the following year. He was unhappy with the boat's design, however, and shortly after his return, donated her to the National Maritime Museum in Greenwich, London, where she still resides.

*Lively Lady*, re-rigged as a yawl and pretty to the eye, but hardly the fastest boat on the water. The modest "everyman" captures the public's imagination, however, and the contest soon develops into a David and Goliath-type battle, with Chichester seeming to have everything going for him and the underdog Rose winning the heart of the nation.

Chichester sets his departure date for 27 August 1966, and Rose, knowing that his boat is smaller and slower, rushes to leave on 7 August. But fate seems to be against him. First his self-steering and his engine play up then, as he heads off once more for Australia, he has a night-time collision with a ship in the English Channel. Worse, while he is making repairs in Plymouth, *Lively Lady* falls over at low tide and cracks several frames. His journey is postponed for a year.

Chichester, meanwhile, is well on his way. Despite grumbles about his new boat, *Gipsy Moth IV*, both in the design and her unprepared state, he beats all the singlehanded records by arriving in Sydney on 12 December 1966 after 107 days at sea. He has not beaten the *Cutty Sark*, however, which would have been there a month before him. After 47 days of repairs and reprovisioning, he sets off again and arrives back in Plymouth on 28 May 1967, after a further 119 days at sea. Again he has broken the singlehanded record, but again he is notionally behind the Cutty Sark. It is nevertheless the fastest solo circumnavigation yet, and Chichester is greeted with euphoria at Plymouth before being knighted by the Queen – using, to the amazement of all foreign correspondents, the very sword that Elizabeth I used to knight Francis Drake.

Part of the reason for the enormous interest in Chichester's achievement was that for the first time the public was able to follow his progress through the regular reports he sent home via his radio. As a result, photographers were able to fly out by helicopter to meet him as he rounded Cape Horn, providing some of the most memorable images of the 1960s – much to his sponsor the Wool Marketing Board's delight. The age of modern communications and, inexorably entwined, media hyperbole had dawned on the yachting world.

But the public hadn't forgotten their folk hero. Alec Rose set off again in *Lively Lady* on 16 July 1967 and, after a month's stopover in Melbourne, continued on his loop. Forced to put into Bluff in New Zealand for a week to repair his rig, he arrived back in Portsmouth on 4 July 1968. His 318-day circumnavigation was 92 days slower than Chichester's, but you would not have known it. *Lively Lady* was escorted into Portsmouth by the Royal Navy and 250,000 people gathered on shore to meet him. In a popular, egalitarian gesture, the people's hero was soon knighted by the Queen also.

### Around without a break

Both Chichester's and Rose's voyages were landmark achievements and rightly celebrated around the world, but they did beg one question: why stop? Why not go around in one, beautiful uninterrupted loop? No sooner than *Gipsy Moth IV* was tucked in harbour (keen to rid himself of his unruly charge, Chichester swiftly donated her to the National Maritime Museum) than thoughts began to turn to the big one, and so the Golden Globe was born.

One of the first skippers to drop out of that "race" was Chay Blyth, who pulled into Capetown after his 9.15m (30ft) glassfibre production boat *Dytiscus* performed a spectacular backward somersault. As adulation was poured over Knox-Johnston, Moitessier, Chichester and Rose, the ex-paratrooper became increasingly disgruntled. His record-breaking row across the Atlantic with John Ridgway had given him an appetite for a challenge – but what was there left to do? A passing comment by his wife gave him the idea: "Why not sail around the other way?" Blyth would attempt the "impossible journey", circumnavigating singlehanded from east to west – traditionally the "wrong way" because it goes against the usual course of the trade winds and ocean currents – via the Roaring Forties.

He persuaded British Steel to underwrite the construction of a new steel (of course) ketch designed by Robert Clark. The aptly-named *British Steel* ingeniously managed to be reasonably light, fast and very, very strong.

Leaving the Hamble River, near Southampton, on 18 October 1970, Blyth's voyage took him 292 days, bringing him home on 6 August 1971. He had not only become the first man to sail the "wrong way" round singlehanded non-stop, but he had also done it in 21 days fewer than Knox-Johnston and 26 days fewer than Rose, who both went the "right way" round.

## Women first

That, it seemed, was that. It would now just be an on-going matter of whittling time off each record as boats became faster and sailors more knowledgeable. Except for one significant omission: in fact, half the human race. Yes, it was the women's turn. For while women had let men set all the endurance records at sea, the race was now on to set their own "firsts".

In fact, although Ann Davison was the first woman to cross the Atlantic singlehanded as long ago as 1952–3, the challenge to circumnavigate solo was taken up rather more slowly – and even then it was somewhat inconclusive. Momentum began to gather in the late 1970s, with several women almost simultaneously planning a challenge (no trophy from *The Sunday Times* this time, though, nor even *Cosmopolitan* magazine for that matter). On paper the award should have gone to the Polish naval engineer Krystina Chojnowska-Liskiewicz, who set off from Las Palmas on 28 March 1976, returning some 755 days later on 21 April 1978.

Perhaps it was because of the intrusive state support of her voyage (her yacht was shipped to Las Palmas from Poland and Polish naval vessels lent her assistance frequently along the route), or perhaps because she took the "easy" route via Panama, or perhaps simply because the Cold War was at its peak just then and she was on the "wrong" side – whatever the reason, her achievement is usually sidelined by that of the more photogenic (and easier to spell) Naomi James. Never mind that both Harry Pidgeon and Alain Gerbault both went via Panama and Gerbault himself had reason to be thankful to the French Navy…

Ten months after Chojnowska-Liskiewicz left Las Palmas, two French women set off on two

**above** The Polish naval engineer Krystina Chojnowska-Liskiewicz became the first woman to sail around the world singlehanded in 1976–8. She received considerable outside assistance along the way, however.

**left** Having dropped out of the Golden Globe, the great Atlantic rower, Chay Blyth, took up a new challenge: to sail non-stop around the world the "wrong way".

### ANN DAVISON

Despite losing her husband while the couple were attempting to cross the Atlantic, in 1952 Davison sailed again in the 6.7m (22ft) *Felicity Ann*. Stopping off at the Canaries, the Windward Islands and Antigua, she reached New York on 25 November 1953, becoming the first woman to sail across the Atlantic singlehanded.

**above** Naomi James was the first woman to circumnavigate the world via Cape Horn. She took 272 days, and stopped at Cape Town and the Falkland Islands.

very different circumnavigations: Brigitte Oudry from the French mainland and Yannick Le Nénaon from Martinique. Oudry would return home after 18 months, while Le Nénaon would take a leisurely six years to complete her voyage.

Last in the women's fleet was New Zealander Naomi James. Despite her late introduction and having taken up sailing only two years earlier, James had had an auspicious start to her new career. A chance encounter in St Malo with Rob James (then skipper of Chay Blyth's old *British Steel*) led to a double marriage: to the man and the sea. Before long Blyth had agreed to lend her *Express Crusader* – a 15.95m (52ft) cutter which as *Spirit of Cutty Sark* had already notched up a fourth place in the 1968 OSTAR – and was helping her prepare for her historic circumnavigation.

Thus, as her husband Robert sailed off on *Great Britain II* in the fully-crewed Whitbread Round the World Race in August 1977, Naomi followed a few weeks later, alone. She had never even spent a night at sea. Despite this, and despite losing her beloved cat Boris over the side, she managed to complete her loop on 8 June 1978 in just under nine months. Crucially, according to the record-makers of the time, James sailed via Cape Horn and received no outside assistance. As a result, she is still widely credited as being the first woman to sail around the world – though strictly speaking the phrase "via Cape Horn" should be appended to that.

As with the men, the next logical development was a solo loop non-stop. It was to be another ten years before that was finally achieved by Australian Kay Cottee, who managed it in 1988 in a cool 189 days – faster than Chichester, Knox-Johnston and Blyth. Then, in July 1996, Blyth's own record was eclipsed by Samantha Brewster in *Heath Insured II*, a 20.4m (67ft) steel cutter. Although her feat is officially recorded as "round the world, assisted, westabout", due to the help she received after damaging her rig, she demolished Blyth's time by around 45 days to become the first woman to sail around the world "the hard way". It took her a little over 247 days.

## ROBIN LEE GRAHAM
The first "child" to sail around the world singlehanded was just 16 when he sailed *Dove* from Los Angeles in September 1965. It took six years and much encouragement from his enthusiastic father and their National Geographic sponsors for the young man to complete his voyage, which was subsequently made into a film. Australian Jesse Martin became the youngest person to circumnavigate solo non-stop in 1999. He was aged 18.

## JON SANDERS
One of the great unsung heroes of singlehanded sailing, Jon Sanders, has the distinction of having sailed five times around the world. Impressive? Even more so when you realise that two of his circumnavigation were sailed concurrently without stopping in 1981–2, while the other three were sailed concurrently without stopping in 1986–8! The first journey took him 420 days for 76,800km (48,000 miles) while the second took 658 days for 128,000km (80,000 miles). The Australian decided to sail his fifth and final circumnavigation from west to east 'to break the monotony'.

Ten months solitary confinement with hard labour" is how the winner of the first non-stop singlehanded round the world race described his ordeal. "That he had the fortitude to endure it and carry on says a lot about his strength of character, for the Golden Globe was, as much as anything, a psychological battle. Of the four final contenders, only Nigel Tetley failed due to boat failure – Moitessier went off in search of his soul, while Crowhurst went mad and committed suicide. Although probably sailing the slowest

## ❝GOD AND COUNTRY❞

boat, Knox-Johnston had the right psychological make-up to maintain his sanity through 313 days alone at sea and to take on the mantle of "hero" at the end of it.

This can in part be attributed to his strong belief in "God and country" combined with the discipline learned during his time on merchant ships. He sums up his approach in the phrase, "the Lord helps those who help themselves" and explains: "The rules are there, the physical laws that we have slowly learned. If we obey them we have a chance of survival. It is no use knowing that your boat is heading towards the eye of a storm and praying to God to see you through it safely. That's not his job. It's your task to steer the boat away from the eye, and you are asking too much if you expect the boat to survive when you deliberately ignore the rules."

William Robert Patrick Knox-Johnston was born in Putney on 17 March 1939 and nicknamed "Robin". He built his first boat at the age of four – an orange-box raft which sank as soon as its proud builder attempted to board it. His second boat, a 3m (10ft) canoe he built when he was 10, fared little better: it sank on launching, although he later patched it up enough to get a picture of himself in

it in the *Junior Express* newspaper. A clear sign of things to come.

Aged 17 and having failed the entrance exam for the Royal Navy, Knox-Johnston joined the Merchant Navy. His career with the British India Steam Navigation Company took him first to East Africa, then the Persian Gulf and India. Based in Bombay with his new wife and their daughter Sara, he decided to make the most of cheap labour and materials and build a small cruising yacht. *Suhaili* was launched at the Colaba Workshop, Bombay, on 19 December 1964.

On the journey to the UK the sturdy 9.8m (32ft) ketch proved her seaworthiness, being particularly well "balanced" under sail – ie steering herself with little attention needed to the helm. This would prove crucial in Knox-Johnston's round-the-world bid, and enable him to carry on when his self-steering broke down, unlike so many other singlehanders before and after him.

Far from being damaged by his spell of "solitary confinement", Knox-Johnston immediately swung into a successful racing career – albeit almost entirely in crewed boats. Just two years after winning the Golden Globe, he won the Round Britain race with 1968 OSTAR competitor Leslie Williams, and won again in 1974 with Jerry Boxall on the catamaran *British Oxygen*. He sailed around the world again in 1977, this time as co-skipper of the 24m (79ft) *Heath's Condor*, which won the final leg of the Whitbread despite losing her carbon fibre mast early in the race.

Off the race course, Knox-Johnston sailed to Greenland with mountaineer Chris Bonington to climb the 2,660m Cathedral and completed a transatlantic in *Suhaili* sailing without modern navigation instruments. In 1994, he sailed on board the catamaran *ENZA* to win the Jules Verne Trophy for the fastest ever circumnavigation. Not bad for a man who had suffered two sinkings by the age of 10.

# ROBIN
# knox-johnston

# europe 1
## NEW MAN STAR

**left** The 18.2m (60ft) trimaran *Banque Populaire* is typical of the new breed of lightweight ocean flyers which now dominates the transatlantic races. Unfortunately, she capsized off Newfoundland while in the lead in the 1996 Europe 1 Star.

# THE routes

## EUROPE 1 NEW MAN STAR (EX-OSTAR)

When the first OSTAR was raced in 1960, it was considered an endurance test for one sailor to sail a boat singlehanded across the Atlantic. Now the 4828km (3000 mile) crossing is treated as little more than a sprint by the lightweight trimarans that make the crossing in less than ten days.

**Northern route**
5037km (3130 miles)

**Great circle**
4522km (2810 miles)

**Rhumb line route**
4699km (2920 miles)

**Azores route**
5681km (3530 miles)

**Tradewind route**
6759km (4200 miles)

**- - - Fujicolor II**
Winning route 1992

### KEY

▲▲▲    icebergs

| 10% | Fog Hazard |
| 20% | percentage of time when |
| 30% | visibility is less than 1/4 mile |

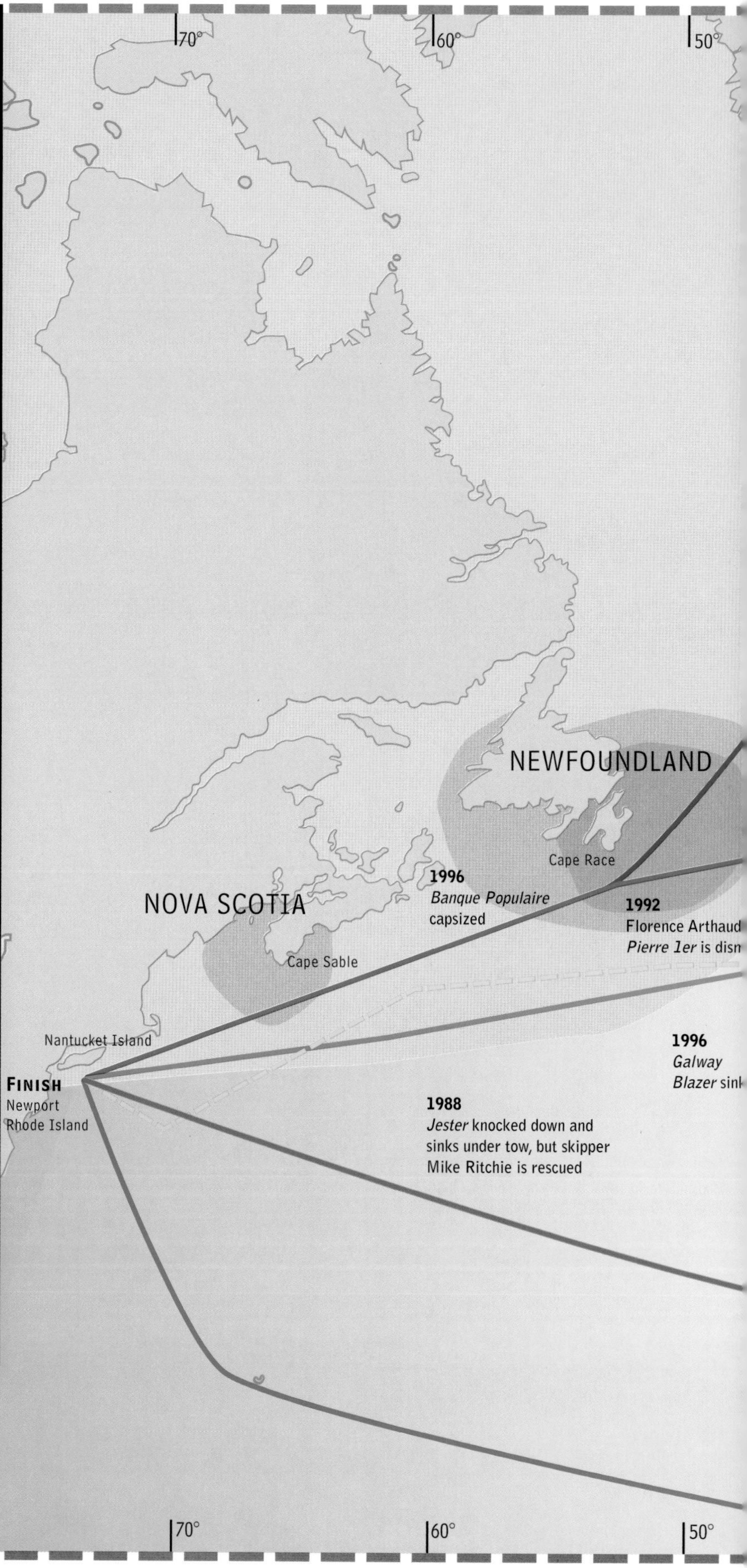

NEWFOUNDLAND

Cape Race

NOVA SCOTIA

**1996**
*Banque Populaire*
capsized

**1992**
Florence Arthaud
*Pierre 1er* is disn

Cape Sable

Nantucket Island

**1996**
*Galway
Blazer* sink

**FINISH**
Newport
Rhode Island

**1988**
*Jester* knocked down and
sinks under tow, but skipper
Mike Ritchie is rescued

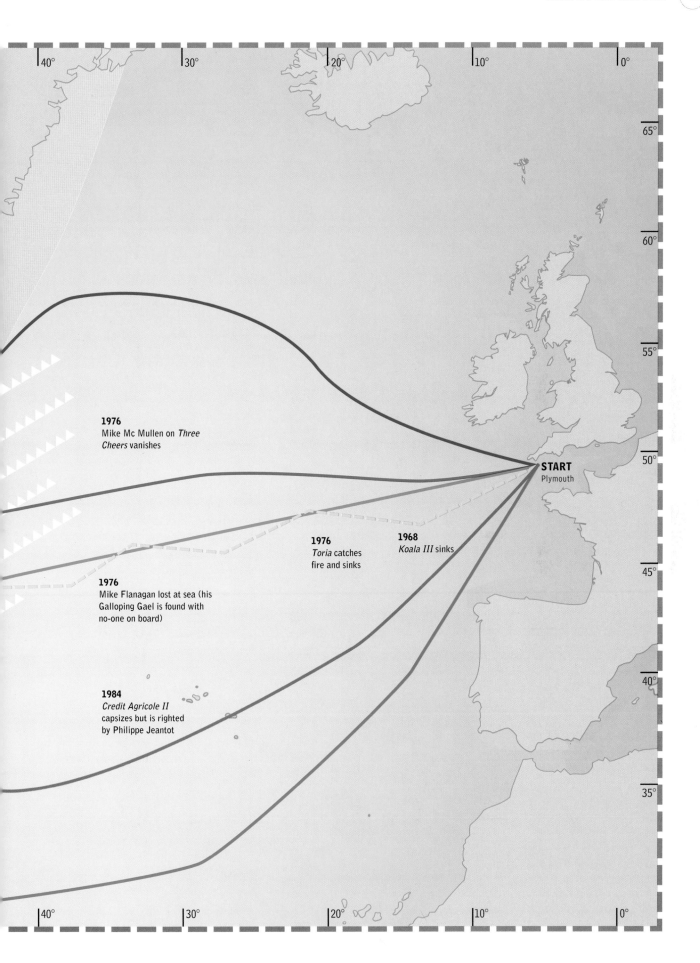

40°    30°    20°    10°    0°

65°

60°

55°

**1976**
Mike Mc Mullen on *Three Cheers* vanishes

50°
**START**
Plymouth

**1976**
*Toria* catches
fire and sinks

**1968**
*Koala III* sinks

**1976**
Mike Flanagan lost at sea (his
Galloping Gael is found with
no-one on board)

45°

**1984**
*Credit Agricole II*
capsizes but is righted
by Philippe Jeantot

40°

35°

40°    30°    20°    10°    0°

# ONE MAN, ONE BOAT, THE SEA

**"** The bows lifted in the air and smashed down 10 feet to dash a hose of water over my back. Flashes of lightning made the fog brightly luminous. There was no sound of thunder above the sail's own thunderclaps as it flogged in the wind. The rain was a deluge but I didn't notice that or didn't distinguish it from the sea-water hitting me. The ship lurched, pitched, rolled, trying every trick to throw me from my hold... **"**

Francis Chichester on the first OSTAR

**above** Four of the five competitors that set out on the first OSTAR in 1960, from left to right, Francis Chichester, Blondie Hasler, David Lewis, and Val Howells.

**right** Francis Chichester's *Gipsy Moth III* was the largest yacht in the first race, and won convincingly. Chichester was particularly proud of the self-steering gear attached to the rear of the boat, which he designed himself, and nicknamed Miranda.

It is the mother of all singlehanded ocean races; the original contest that pitted one sailor on one boat against the sea; a 4506km (2800-mile) crossing that has sunk several yachts, and claimed its own share of lives as well. It has provided the training ground for most of the world's greatest sailors, and has been a testbed of technological innovation. Its roll of honour is long and distinguished: Francis Chichester, Eric Tabarly, Alec Rose, Clare Francis, Alain Colas, Naomi James, Mike Birch, Florence Arthaud, Yves Parlier, Giovanni Soldini, Philippe Poupon, and Ellen MacArthur, to name but a few. For many years it was simply *the* race to win. Not surprising then that, although other, more demanding, races have since been conceived, the OSTAR (now the Europe 1 New Man STAR) holds a unique place in the pantheon of ocean racing.

A quick look at the 11 winners shows graphically how much ocean racing has evolved over the past 40 years: from Francis Chichester's elegant 11.9m (39ft) sloop *Gipsy Moth III*, winner in 1960, to Francis Joyon's lightweight 18.3m (60ft) trimaran *Eure et Loire*, winner in 2000 – and everything in between. Indeed many of yachting's great ideological battles have been fought in the waters between the race's startline in Plymouth and its finish in Newport, RI. Some were resolved, such as the conclusive victory of multihulls over monohulls, while others remain running sores which have carried over to other races, one such being the controversial role of boat sponsorship.

Yet it had all seemed so simple to start with. "One man, one boat, the sea." That was the principle on which the OSTAR's founder Blondie Hasler initiated the first singlehanded transatlantic race. Hasler was a former lieutenant-colonel in the Royal Marines who had achieved some fame through his daring wartime exploits in kayaks, notably the courageous but costly raid on the German naval base at St Nazaire. After the war he had built himself a fully-decked Folkboat with an unusual junk rig, fully controlled from his helming position inside a small round hatch. He named her *Jester*, because she was "such a bloody joke", but determined to try out her seakeeping abilities in that ultimate test: an ocean race.

Not that there were many takers. Hasler's challenge stood pasted to the noticeboard of the Royal Ocean Racing Club in London for nearly three years before Francis Chichester finally responded. Chichester had yet to make his name

at sea and was better-known for his air-borne adventures on board his bi-plane *Gipsy Moth*. Hasler's transatlantic race caught his imagination, however, and once fired up he was a man to be reckoned with. Little did those two men know how their half-crown wager would transform the face of yachting history.

As for the logistics, the Slocum Society in America was the only organization to offer its (largely symbolic) backing at first. Eventually, *The Observer* newspaper was persuaded to sponsor the race – thanks largely to personal contacts with its editor, and former Royal Marine, David Astor – but most yacht clubs were wary of getting involved. Many regarded singlehanded racing as fundamentally unsafe since by definition it contradicts one of the basic rules of the sea: always having someone on lookout to prevent collision. After being turned down by several clubs, the Royal Western Yacht Club in Plymouth

finally agreed to take on the organization and running of the event. At long last, Hasler had his race.

## The famous five

The fleet that assembled on the start line at Plymouth on 11 June 1960 was hardly impressive. Out of 50 enquiries, only eight boats signed up for the race, and of those only four made it to the line on the day, with a fifth following a few days later. Chichester's 12.1m (39ft) sloop *Gipsy Moth III* was easily the largest boat there – if anything, she was considered too big for singlehanded sailing. The other competitors were Hasler with his *Jester*, Valentine Howells (described by Chichester as "the black-bearded Viking") with his 7.6m (25ft) Folkboat *Eira*, David Lewis and his 7.6m (25ft) Vertue class *Cardinal Vertue* and, the first in what would become an unstoppable challenge from across

**below** By the start of the 1984 race, the battle between monohulls and multihulls had already been decided in favour of the latter. Now it was only a matter of whether catamarans or trimarans would triumph.

the Channel, the Frenchman Jean Lacombe and his 6.4m (21ft) *Cap Horn*.

Chichester's finishing time of 40 days, 12 hours and 30 minutes seems positively leisurely by today's standards – Francis Joyon blasted across the Atlantic in a record-breaking 9 days, 23 hours and 21 minutes in the 2000 transatlantic – but it was a good eight days ahead of the second-placed Hasler and a full 39 days ahead of Lacombe. With his 79 days at sea, the Frenchman held the record for the slowest crossing until 1972 when Peter Crowther held out for 88 days on the gaff cutter *Golden Vanity*.

Generally, the enormous increase in speed over the race's history has not been achieved in great leaps and bounds, but incrementally, with successive winners shaving one to three days off each previous race, the three notable exceptions being 1964, 1980 and 1988.

The first dramatic change to the race came in its second running, in 1964, and it came in the shape of one man: Eric Tabarly. A serving naval officer, Tabarly was enthused by reading accounts of the first OSTAR and decided to build a boat to win the second race. Whereas the 1960 competitors seemed mainly concerned with getting across the Atlantic in one piece, Tabarly was focused on one thing alone: winning the race. His 11.9m (39ft) *Pen Duick II* was as big a boat as one man could reasonably manage on his own, with a light displacement to require less sail area for maximum speed. The price he paid was having a less forgiving boat which needed more frequent sail changes and adjustments. Being young and immensely fit, however, that was ultimately a price worth paying.

## The dark horse

Chichester, back with *Gipsy Moth III* and determined to better his 33-day "trial" crossing of two years before, was all-too aware of the threat the unknown French sailor posed, writing: "Tabarly is the dark horse in this race and I think I can hear him galloping through the night. If my senses tell me right I can make him out 120 miles to the north." It was a prescient remark – Tabarly was by then about 100–150 miles ahead of him.

Tabarly's spectacular win on *Pen Duick II* in just 27 days, 3 hours and 56 minutes, after weeks of tantalising radio silence, did much to raise the profile of the race on both sides of the Atlantic – most notably, of course, in France, where his triumph and subsequent award of the Legion d'honneur by President Charles de Gaulle was greeted with undiluted euphoria. It was the start of France's love affair with sailing in general and, until its sailors devised alternatives of their own, with the OSTAR in particular. It was also the start of another enduring legend: Tabarly the mighty.

But Tabarly's win was crucial not only in raising interest in the race – the number of entries more than doubled in 1968 from 15 to 35 – but also in defining an approach to the race. Whereas other competitors had chosen boats from existing designs, *Pen Duick II* was the first yacht specifically designed to win that race. From there on, that would become increasingly the norm, while "low-budget" entries from standard yachts would become increasingly rare and race victories for such yachts virtually impossible.

Tabarly's personal approach stood him apart from the others too. As 1968 winner Geoffrey Williams would later put it: "He did not regard the crossing as a long and arduous cruise, but had a fiercely competitive outlook which helped him keep the boat going fast… His sleeping habits and his constant sail changing all reflected his determination to win the race." It was nothing less than the birth of "professional" singlehanded

**above** Eric Tabarly transformed the face of singlehanded racing when he entered *Pen Duick II* in the 1964 OSTAR. Despite his self-steering breaking in mid-Atlantic, he won the race by a large margin, thereby igniting France's love affair with the sport.

racing – though of course Tabarly still hung on to his day job with the navy.

Along with the spiralling costs of building yachts to order came an increasing dependence on sponsorship, so that by the third OSTAR in 1968 several yachts bore their sponsor's names, albeit covertly, most notably Williams's high-tech winner, the 14.9m (49ft) *Sir Thomas Lipton*. Other sponsored boats in the race were *Spirit of Cutty Sark* (whisky), *Golden Cockerel* (Courage brewery), *Startled Faun* (Watney's Brewery) and *Gancia Girl* (Italian wine) – it would take a few more years for sponsors to realise that sailors were interested in more than just alcohol and tea. But these quaint attempts to dress up the sponsor's name in a maritime style were abandoned over the following two OSTARs, with such unboatmanlike names as *Cap 33*, *British Steel*, *Robertson's Golly*, *ITT Oceanic*, *FT,* and *Gauloises* finding more favour with their sponsors.

It was just the start of an issue which would continue to dog the OSTAR, as well as many other ocean races, with attempts at keeping the race "pure" gradually eroded by the practical reality of attracting well-funded and well-equipped boats to the start line. Today's "no holds barred" approach to sponsorship is the result of the 1970s' hard-fought battles between idealism and pragmatism.

### Electronic teapot

*Sir Thomas Lipton* brought to the fore another important issue. Known disparagingly by some as the "electronic teapot", the yacht was filled with the latest navigation and communication equipment including, most controversially, a weather routing link with a computer back home in London. Thanks to an elaborate link up with the Met Office weather station at Bracknell and daily position updates from *Sir Thomas Lipton*, the computer could work out the best routes for Williams to take. In the event, this information

may have won the Cornishman the race. Ten days into the race, a deep depression hit the fleet with high seas and 60-knot winds, stopping the yachts in their tracks. All except Williams' yacht. His shore-bound computer had warned him of the approaching storm and he had simply headed north to avoid it. While most of the fleet were thrashing about under bare poles, *Sir Thomas Lipton* was sailing into an unassailable lead.

Under the minimal rules of the race at this time such action was entirely legal, although it clearly gave the advantage to boats able to afford such sophisticated technology. The following year it was banned under the principle that it constituted "outside assistance", and therefore went against the ethos of the race. Even now, when modern racing yachts are crammed with the latest technology, receiving assistance from shore-based routing experts is specifically banned and will lead to penalties or even disqualification.

It was all a long way away from Hasler's original concept of "one man, one boat, the sea". For the 1968 OSTAR, he handed over his beloved *Jester* to Mike Ritchie and went trout fishing in Scotland instead. As he later said: "I would hate to be sponsored and paid for… For me it would be horrible to start on a Transatlantic race knowing that I had to do well to give my sponsor his money's worth." It was the end of the Hasler era, but Ritchie proved himself a worthy successor and would go on to sail *Jester*, and then her replica, in almost every OSTAR up until 2000, when he sailed his last race at the age of 82.

The advent of the multihulls was, perhaps surprisingly, a gradual affair. Two catamarans and one trimaran took part in the second OSTAR, with only David Lewis's *Rehu Moana* managing to break the 40-day barrier to give her a seventh place out of 15 entrants. Multihulls fared better in other races, however, and by 1968 the tide was unstoppable. Thirteen of the 35 entries for that year's OSTAR were multihulls, including Tabarly's awesome 20.4m (67ft) trimaran *Pen Duick IV*, described by *Yachting World* as "this fearsome tin trimaran [whose] crossbeams look like the innards of an oil refinery". Lack of preparation and a collision at the start forced Tabarly to retire, but other multihulls succeeded

> **FOR ME IT WOULD BE HORRIBLE TO START ON A TRANSATLANTIC RACE KNOWING THAT I HAD TO DO WELL TO GIVE MY SPONSOR HIS MONEY'S WORTH**

Blondie Hasler on the new era of sponsored racing

**above** After Blondie Hasler's retirement, Mike Richey took on the much-loved *Jester,* taking part in almost all the transats until his last race, aged 82, in 2000.

**right** *Vendredi 13* introduced the concept of the "jumbo yacht" in 1972.

that year, taking third, fifth, and seventh places. Tom Follett turned up with an innovative design by up-and-coming American designer Dick Newick: a 12.2m (40ft) long proa called *Cheers*. Based on traditional Melanesian craft, a proa is basically a hull with a single float on one side – instead of going about in the conventional manner, it simply stops, resets its sails and heads off in the other direction. Follett was lucky and took the southerly route that year, enjoying warmer weather and avoiding a depression which slowed most of the other competitors and gaining third place in a very respectable 27 days.

## The tin trimaran

But 1972 was the year the multihulls really started to show their mettle, despite being reduced to just eight out of 54 starters. The 'tin trimaran' *Pen Duick IV* was back, but without Tabarly at the helm this time. Financial difficulties had forced Tabarly to sell his yacht, despite her by-then successful race record, and one of his former crew members Alain Colas snapped her up. Colas had had two years' experience sailing her with Tabarly and knew the vessel intimately.

But all eyes that year were on the extraordinary 39m (128ft) three-masted schooner sailed by Jean-Yves Terlain, *Vendredi Treize*. Ever since Chichester had won the first OSTAR on *Gipsy Moth III*, each race had been won by the largest boat in the fleet. It is one of the basic rules of naval architecture that the longer the waterline length, the faster a boat is capable of sailing, and the transatlantic race had proven true to that dogma. The idea with *Vendredi Treize* was to design as big a hull as possible with relatively small sail area that could be handled by one person. Her three masts were therefore rigged with just three boomed staysails – in fact she proved under-

**below** The man the media loved to hate. Alain Colas became a legendary figure on the racing scene, partly thanks to his larger-than-life personality.

canvased sailing in light airs or off the wind, and Terlain added three light genoas. Although there were grumbles ashore that such a boat was not in the spirit of the original race, there was nothing in the rules to stop her.

Despite the hype, after 20 days of radio silence, the "ghost ship", as some were calling *Pen Duick IV*, confounded the bookmakers and appeared in Newport 16 hours ahead of the gigantic *Vendredi Treize*, smashing the previous record by five days. Another trimaran, Jean-Marie Vidal's *Cap 33*, grabbed third place while Tom Follett's *Three Cheers*, designed by Dick Newick, was placed fifth. Not only did trimarans dominate three out of the top five places, but the French held all three top positions – a sure sign of what was to come.

Chichester sailed his last race in 1972, aged 70. His final OSTAR challenge ended in tragedy, however, when a French weather ship sent out to rescue him (despite his pleas to be left alone) collided with an American yacht killing seven people. Chichester died in hospital later that year.

The French set a different kind of record in 1972 when Marie-Claude Faroux became the first woman to complete a singlehanded transatlantic race. The first attempt by a woman in 1968 had not lasted long: Edith Baumann's *Koala II* sank soon after the start and Baumann had to be picked up by a French naval vessel. Faroux fared rather better in the following race, finishing in 14th place in 32 days and 22 hours. Her time was cut back by Clare Francis in 1976, who finished 13th on *Robertson's Golly* in just over 29 days, and then by Naomi James in 1980, who finished 24th in 25 days and 19 hours. Women were beginning to make their mark in an overwhelmingly male-dominated sport.

## *Club Méditerranée*

Despite the success of the multihulls in 1972, the monohulls were to have one last stand, and the only way to go to get the extra speed to beat the multihulls, it seemed, was to go ever bigger. That's what Alain Colas believed, anyway. His verdict on *Vendredi Treize* was that Terlain's theory had been correct, but he just hadn't gone far enough. His solution was to build a colossal

72m (236ft) four-masted schooner, crammed with the latest technology – including satellite navigation, radar, weatherfax, and air conditioning – for the 1976 race. Closed circuit TV cameras were targeted on each sail so that Colas could check on their set. It was a veritable "Cathedral of the Seas", as he himself described it, and cost over one and a half billion old francs to build. This "floating laboratory", named *Club Méditerranée* after its principle sponsors, symbolised just how far technology had come in the previous 16 years or so. Whereas in 1960 observers had wondered how Chichester would be able to manage his 11.9m (39ft) yacht on his own, here was someone tackling something six times as long. Tabarly's opinion of Colas's vision was however damning: "His boat adds nothing new to naval architecture. It is quite uninspired, being merely an enlarged version of *Vendredi Treize*, with all her defects as well, multiplied by two."

It was a tribute to Colas's powers of persuasion that he managed to raise the funds to build his megalithic fantasy – yet ironically an elementary sailing accident nearly prevented him sailing at all. A coil of rope on the anchor line of his *Pen Duick IV*, by then renamed *Manureva*, nearly severed his foot and put him in hospital for six crucial months. It took yet more of his powers of persuasion to convince the OSTAR race committee that he was truly fit to enter the 1976 race a few months later.

Terlain was back at that startline too, but whereas Colas had switched from a multihull to an outsize monohull, Terlain did the opposite: he abandoned *Vendredi Treize* in favour of the 21.3m (70ft) trimaran *Kriter III*, the renamed *British Oxygen* in which Robin Knox-Johnston had won the 1974 Round Britain Race. Meanwhile, *Vendredi Treize* had been renamed *ITT Oceanic* and returned with Yvon Fauconnier at the helm. And there was the greatest French sailor of them all: Tabarly, this time in a monohull, the 22.3m (73ft) ketch *Pen Duick VI*, fresh from completing the Whitbread Round the World Race. Normally manned by a crew of 18, Tabarly was going to sail her across the Atlantic solo having made few concessions for singlehanded sailing, other than fit self-steering. Many doubted he would make it.

The 1976 OSTAR was in many ways the pinnacle of the race – or, for some, its nadir. There were more boats entered than ever before, 125 in all, including the largest entry ever, the 72m (236ft) *Club Méditerranée*, and one of the smallest, the 7.6m (25ft) *Jester* with Mike Ritchie on board once again.

## David and Goliath

It was also the worst weather ever encountered, with seven full gales hitting the boats on the shortest, "great circle", route. More than one third of the fleet either retired or was sunk; Mike Ritchie on *Jester* decided to opt for a cruise around Ireland instead, and Terlain's *Kriter III* broke up in mid-Atlantic. Mike Flanagan's *Galloping Gael* was discovered mid-Atlantic with

**below** The monstrous *Club Méditerranée* was 72m (236ft) long, cost one and a half billion old francs to build, and was almost beaten by a 9.5m (31ft 2in) dismantlable trimaran in the 1976 race.

no-one aboard, the skipper presumed lost overboard. The most poignant loss, however, was Mike McMullen on *Three Cheers*. Just a few days before the start of the race, his wife was electrocuted while working to prepare *Three Cheers*. McMullen decided to do the race in her memory but was never seen again. Only a small fragment of *Three Cheers* eventually turned up in a fisherman's net off Iceland.

The race itself turned into a stalking game between Colas on *Club Méditerranée* and Tabarly on *Pen Duick VI*. While Colas, the ultimate in self-publicists, broadcast daily updates on how his race was going, Tabarly maintained characteristic radio silence. It drove the media into a frenzy of speculation. In fact, *Pen Duick*'s self-steering had broken and an exhausted Tabarly was enduring agonising self-doubt, even turning back for home at one stage. Meanwhile, Colas had had to pull in at Newfoundland to make repairs to his rig, losing precious hours. For the press, it had all the making of a David and Goliath story. Eventually a yacht turned up in the early hours at Newport, tacking up and down the harbour waiting for someone to notice her. It was Tabarly, a full seven hours ahead of his rival.

It was a devastating blow to Colas who had staked his reputation on his "jumbo yacht". To add insult to injury, the committee penalised him 58 hours for having received "outside assistance", relegating him to fifth place. But perhaps the most astonishing result came after *Club Méditerranée* crossed the finish line, when the Canadian delivery skipper Mike Birch turned up with his 9.5m (31ft) trimaran *The Third Turtle*, winning his class and third overall. His modest little craft, designed by Dick Newick, had taken just 17 hours longer than Colas's multi-million franc techno-monster. Three hours later the Pole Kazimierz Jaworski crossed the line on his 11.6m (38ft) sloop *Spaniel*. Suddenly the accepted laws of length versus speed were thrown out of the porthole. For, although three of the first four boats were monohulls, the success of *The Third Turtle* signalled the end of an era. *Pen Duick VI* would be the last monohull to win the race and henceforth multihulls would increasingly dominate the results.

It was also the end of the "no holds barred" era of the OSTAR. Apart from the controversy surrounding *Club Méditerranée*, there were some that questioned the safety of sending so many singlehanded yachts, with their inevitable periods of sailing "blind", across increasingly busy waters. Hasler's assertion that any singlehander who got into trouble "should be prepared to drown like a gentleman" was not being heeded, perhaps unsurprisingly, and some asked why others should risk their lives (and spend taxpayers money) going to the rescue of those who did not make it.

## The French pull out

The Royal Western's response was to restrict the number of entries to 110, with a maximum size limit of 17.1m (56ft) overall – that would later be increased to 18.3m (60ft). All boats entered would be fitted with an Argos transponder, which would transmit daily position fixes via satellite to monitoring centres in Britain, France, and the United States. In addition, since 1972, all competitors had to complete a 800km (500 mile) singlehanded voyage on their vessel in order to qualify for the OSTAR.

It was all too much for the French, who suspected the race organisers were trying to loosen their stranglehold on the event. Within days of the finish of the 1976 OSTAR, they were planning their own "no holds barred" solo race from St Malo to Guadeloupe, the now famous Route du Rhum. The impact was almost immediate: only 90 boats made it to the start of the 1980 OSTAR, well below the maximum set by the organizers.

While the French were off doing their own thing, the Americans made hay. The 65-year-old newspaper owner Phil Weld, the oldest sailor in the fleet, set a new record of 17 days 23 hours and 12 minutes on his trimaran *Moxie*. It was a long-awaited win for *Moxie*'s American designer Dick Newick, who also claimed a fourth place with *Olympus Photo* helmed by Mike Birch – both fresh from winning the first Route du Rhum. Americans Phil Stegall (third) and Walter Greene (fifth) and Englishman Nick Keig (second) made up the rest of the top five.

## THE CLASS SYSTEM

Originally devised as a free-for all regardless of size, three classes were introduced in 1976. Each class was named after a notable and appropriately-sized OSTAR veteran: *Jester* (under 11.6m/38ft), *Gipsy Moth* (11.6–19.8m/38–65ft) and *Pen Duick* (over 19.8m/65ft). A handicapping system was operated by the Royal Western Yacht Club, but the rules were kept secret to prevent rule bending. This lasted until 1984 when it was replaced by a five-class system – this time simply named Classes 1–5 for: 18.3–15.2m (60–50ft); 15.2–12.2m (50–40ft); 12.2–10.7m (40–35ft); 10.7–9.1m (35–30ft) and 9.1–7.6m (30–25ft) – with competitors racing boat-for-boat. The 15.2–12.2m (50–40ft) class has since been split in two and, to many people's chagrin, the 9.1–7.6m (30–25ft) class was dropped altogether in 2000.

**left** By 1976, Eric Tabarly had achieved almost iconic status in France. He solidified his reputation by winning that year's OSTAR on *Pen Duick VI*. Once again, his self-steering gave up in mid-Atlantic and he had to hand steer much of the way.

Weld would be the last non-French sailor to win the race – and one of only three non-French winners in 11 starts. The French returned in force the following race and, from then on, the event would turn increasingly into a "Franco-French" duel, with the gallic fleet fighting it out amongst themselves at the head of the fleet.

With their hull length now limited, the monohulls stood little chance of making the top rankings. The first five boats in 1984 were all multihulls – and all finished well within the 1972 record set by Alain Colas. Despite being the first monohull to break the 20-day barrier, Kazimierz Jaworski and his 17.1m (56ft) *Spaniel II* arrived in Newport nearly two days after the first multihulls had finished.

## Tabarly shows the way

Meanwhile, Marc Pajot had taken Tabarly's place on his revolutionary foil trimaran *Paul Ricard*, the French hero having to pull out because of an old skiing injury. With no time to complete the required 500-mile qualifying sea time on *Paul Ricard*, Pajot raced as an "unofficial entry" and took an early lead before being knocked back by a depression and eventually having to pull into Newfoundland for repairs. He finished a disappointing "unofficial" fifth. But although she

failed to shine during that year's OSTAR, *Paul Ricard* soon proved herself on the trip back to France. Tabarly screamed across the Atlantic in 10 days, breaking by two days the mythical record set by the schooner *Atlantic* in 1905. Ahead of the game as always, Tabarly was showing the way, and the point was not lost on his fellow sailors.

With the battle for speed now convincingly won by multihulls, the debate shifted to the relative merits of catamarans and trimarans. Increasingly, trimarans would find favour with singlehanders, being less likely to capsize, while catamarans seemed to have the edge for speed, although being harder to handle. Beyond that, it was all down to technology, with the next decade or so being marked by rapid development in the design and construction of multihulls. The advent of hydrofoils, wing masts, and moulded sails went hand-in-hand with the introduction of materials such as Kevlar and carbon fibre. The result was boats capable of sailing at twice the speed of the apparent wind.

The first major technological leaps took place in time for the 1984 OSTAR. After winning the second Route Du Rhum with the innovative catamaran *Elf Aquitaine*, Marc Pajot had her successor built using the best materials money could buy. The result: a 4.7-tonne catamaran constructed entirely of pre-pregnated carbon fibre, making her lighter and stiffer than any wooden or GRP equivalent. *Elf Aquitaine II* also boasted a revolutionary "balestron" rig, where the main boom overlaps the mast to take the tack of the jib, and "X" shaped crossbeams. Her sails were of Kevlar. It was the most credible challenge mounted by a catamaran for years, although in the end Pajot would only finish a close third.

New trends were emerging among the trimaran designs, too, with Yvon Fauconnier's *Umupro Jardin V* incorporating floats with buoyancy of around 200 per cent of the boat's total displacement. Unlike Tabarly's *Pen Duick IV*, which had small floats to allow the boat to be knocked down rather than capsizing, the new generation of trimarans used the floats to 'lift' the main hull, sometimes even sailing with the both windward hulls out of the water! Later

> **"OCEAN RACING IS LIKE A RELIGION IN FRANCE, AND SINGLEHANDED YACHTSMEN ARE LIKE THE HIGH PRIESTS "**
>
> Tony Bullimore on the French love of sailing

**below** Tom Grossman's chances of winning the **1980** OSTAR came to an end when his trimaran *Kriter VII* collided with a fellow competitor at the start of the race.

**left** The oldest man to win the OSTAR. Phil Weld was 65 when he beat all comers on his dainty trimaran *Moxie* in 1980. He was the first American and the last non-French skipper to win the race.

trimarans would raise the floats' buoyancy up to 300 per cent.

And there was innovation in the monohull fleet too. Warren Luhrs's *Thursday's Child*, designed by Lars Bergstrom, was the first OSTAR boat to feature water ballast, not to mention a pendulum rudder. She set a remarkable monohull record that would survive even the challenge of BOC-hardened monohulls for eight years.

## Tears at the finish

But while technology was the order of the day for the boats, the eventual result on the 1984 race was decided by a human gesture. For while Poupon and his state-of-the-art John Shuttleworth-designed trimaran *Fleury Michon VI* were first over the line, in a record-breaking 16 days, 12 hours and 25 minutes, he was not to win the race. Midway across the Atlantic, Yvon Fauconnier had stood by Philippe Jeantot while he righted his capsized catamaran *Credit Agricole*. Despite arriving 10 hours after Poupon, he was awarded a 16-hour time allowance for his act and clinched first place. Poupon broke down in tears when the decision was announced.

It was the last race to be sponsored by *The Observer* newspaper. From then on, the race

would go through a number of guises – with more or less cumbersome names, depending on its sponsors – starting with the Carlsberg STAR in 1988 followed by the Europe 1 STAR in 1992 and 1996, before settling for the Europe 1 New Man STAR in 2000. Not surprisingly, with so many titles to choose from, many people still refer to it as the OSTAR, while the French have always called it "le Transat anglais" – or simply "le Transat".

Trimaran development continued apace, with the 18.3m (60ft) Adrian Thompson-designed *Paragon* and the 18.3m (60ft) Nigel Irens-designed *Apricot* setting the pace in the 1985 Round Britain race. *Apricot* not only won that race, with the doughty Tony Bullimore at the helm, but went on to beat the French 80 and 85ft (24.3 & 26m) multihulls. The result was a flurry of Irens-designed 18.3m (60ft) tris at the start of the 1988 Carlsberg STAR (or C-STAR), as the OSTAR was then called, with Mike Birch on *Fujicolor*, Olivier Moussy on *Laiterie Mont St Michel*, and Philippe Poupon on *Fleury Michon IX*. Tony Bullimore was back with the Barry Noble-designed *Spirit of Apricot*, the original *Apricot* having been wrecked during the last Route du Rhum. The new boat boasted a 30.5m (100ft) tall wing mast and should have

**above** As well as being an exceptional sailor, Eric Tabarly continuously pushed the limits of yacht design. His revolutionary foil trimaran, *Paul Ricard*, came a disappointing "unofficial" fifth in the 1980 OSTAR with Marc Pajot at the helm, but proved herself by beating the transatlantic record on the way back.

performed well in the light weather which prevailed, but a late start and lack of preparation handicapped her performance.

## Whale of a time

But once again all the technology in the world was no match for nature – and this time it was not the weather but the whales that caused havoc. David Sellings reported a pod of whales molesting and eventually sinking his yacht *Hyccup*. And the intrepid Birch smashed the centreboard case of his flyer *Fujicolor* on the back of a whale, forcing him to limp back home to La Trinité. He apparently ran out of food three days from home and took his mind off his stomach by reading Reed's Nautical Almanac from cover to cover. The wonders of literature.

The were tears for *Jester* fans too, as the boat that started it all suffered a knockdown and water poured in through an errant hatch. Skipper Mike Ritchie (by then aged 66) was rescued, but the boat sank while on tow. Remarkably, a trust was set up shortly after the race which raised enough funds to build a replica in time for the next race. The spirit of *Jester* lived on.

It was ideal weather for the new generation lightweight multihulls, with a high pressure system over the North Atlantic offering ideal reaching conditions instead of the usual string of depressions. As Phil Steggall, on the extreme trimaran *Sebago*, put it: "It just didn't feel like an OSTAR – the bread didn't even go mouldy!"

The cats (and tris) lapped it up. Leaving nothing to chance this time, Poupon pulverized his own previous record, finishing some 150 miles ahead of the next boat with a time of just 10 days 9 hours and 15 minutes. It was a record that would stand for 12 years, despite the arrival of potentially even faster trimarans. The French had themselves a new sailing hero. And there was triumph in the lower ranks too, with Nic Bailey finishing 12th overall in 16 days and 17 hours, setting a new Class 4 record and beating all the Class 2 and 3 boats into the bargain.

The proliferation of singlehanded races, especially in France, certainly contributed to the improving standard of yachts entered in the transatlantic. With the Route du Rhum finally adopting a 18.3m (60ft) size limit in 1990, many of the stars of that race could simply appear with the same boats in Plymouth two years later. Thus, in 1992, Florence Arthaud entered her Route du Rhum winner *Pierre 1er*, while Laurent Bourgnon brought *Primagaz*, in which he would win the next "French transat".

## Swifter than the wind

By then the Open 60 trimarans had reached the proportions which would be sustained for the rest of the decade: over 15.2m (50ft) wide, with 30.5m (100ft)-tall wingmasts and displacement of six tons or less. In five knots of wind, they exceeded wind speed, and in 10 knots went more than double the wind speed. In over 15 knots they were in the high 20s and probably scooting along on one hull! It seemed as if the fundamental proportions had reached their optimum for singlehanded racing, and it was then a matter of tweaking with the details, such as the shape of the foils and construction materials. By 2000, French designer Marc Lombard would be experimenting with "J" shaped foils and carbon fibre/Nomex construction.

Among the monohulls, the confluence of the Vendée Globe later in the year meant that many Open 60s began using the transatlantic to test their boats and/or qualify for the round-the-world contest. No surprise then that Yves Parlier, who went on to a fourth place in the 1992–3 Vendée, should set a new monohull record of 14 days and 16 hours in his souped up *Cacolac d'Aquitaine* in 1992.

But it was the Mike Birch/Nigel Irens creation *Fujicolour II* that was to dominate the next two Europe 1 Stars, as the race was then called, giving Loïck Peyron a rare double win in 1992 and 1996. Only Tabarly had succeeded in winning the race twice before then. Peyron had tuned up Birch's trimaran, giving it foils and a wing mast, and managed to avoid the dismasting he suffered in the 1994 Route du Rhum. Arthaud wasn't so lucky and capsized off Newfoundland in 1992, while after taking an early lead Bourgnon had to retired with a broken mainsheet track.

> ## "IT JUST DIDN'T FEEL LIKE AN OSTAR – THE BREAD DIDN'T EVEN GO MOULDY!"
>
> Phil Steggall on the 1988 race (in *Yachting World*)

## ICEBERGS VERSUS FLYING FISH

With unpredictable Atlantic weather systems, the opposing currents of the Gulf Stream, icebergs, and fog to contend with, it's no wonder the singlehanded transatlantic race is such a challenge. Choosing the right course can and will win or lose a race. The most direct route is to follow the Great Circle 4,500km (2,810 miles) or the Rhumb Line 4,600km (2,920 miles), which both usually carry the risk of head winds and/or icebergs. Alternatively, the Northern Route 5,000km (3,130 miles) carries an even higher likelihood of icebergs but has more favourable current and winds. Blondie Hasler fared poorly on this route in 1960, while Francis Joyon almost won on it in 1996. The gentler route, with more favourable, lighter winds and flying fish, is the Southern Route 5,600km (3,530 miles) – it is also the longest. Most STAR winners have taken a path somewhere between the Great Circle and the Rhumb Line.

**far left** Development continued in the monohull classes too, with the advent of the Open 60s. One of the most experimental was Yves Parlier's *Aquitaine Innovations*, with her wing mast, and spider-like stay booms.

**left** After her triumphant win in the Route de Rhum, Florence Arthaud attempted to make it a double by entering *Pierre 1er* in the 1992 "English transat", only to be dismasted off Newfoundland.

1996 was not much kinder, with two 18.3m (60ft) trimarans capsizing. The surprise of that year's race was Francis Joyon, who almost won by taking the northern route, the first serious contender to use the route since Blondie Hasler on *Jester* back in 1960. Joyon sailed over the depressions affecting most of his rivals and reached the Newfoundland Banks with a 480km (300 mile) lead. It was all to no avail, however, as a sudden gust of wind off Nova Scotia capsized his trimaran *Banque Populaire*.

But while the big-name sponsors stole the limelight at the start of the 2000 Europe 1 New Man STAR (yes, new sponsors, new name), it was a relative outsider who stole first prize. After coming third in 1992 and capsizing in 1996, Francis Joyon was dropped by his sponsors *Banque Populaire* in favour of Lalou Roucayrol. Undaunted, Joyon cobbled together a new boat, buying the platform of the old *Banque Populaire* and stepping the 10-year-old rig from Arthaud's *Pierre 1er*. With partial funding from the department of Eure et Loire, he prepared his campaign virtually on his own. Despite sailing one of the oldest boats in the fleet, he was the first to break the race's 10-day barrier, finishing in nine days, 23 hours, and 21 minutes – nearly 10 hours faster than Poupon's 1988 record. Quite remarkably, three more trimarans finished inside that record. Ironically, Roucayrol managed to capsize the new *Banque Populaire*, giving the sponsors their second bloody nose in a row.

## Mighty MacArthur

An even bigger surprise awaited the monohull fleet. With many of the round-the-world superstars limbering up for the Vendée Globe, it was the largest gathering of Open 60s ever. Around Alone winner Giovanni Soldini was there, as were Yves Parlier, Michel Desjoyeux, Thierry Dubois, Catherine Chabaud, and Mike Golding. Then there was up-and-coming British newcomer, Ellen MacArthur, at 23 years old the youngest of the Open 60 skippers. Having won her class in the 1998 Route du Rhum, MacArthur had secured sponsorship to build *Kingfisher* in New Zealand, and had just brought the boat back to the UK, sailing on her own from Cape Horn onwards. During the 2000 STAR, Ellen survived a depression which dismasted three of her rivals, collided with a whale which then wrapped itself round the boat's keel, and fell head first down her forehatch. She arrived in Newport with two black eyes and a large cut on her forehead having won first place in the monohull division. It was a remarkable achievement which boded well for the Vendée later that year.

Once again "le Transat" had proven itself as the breeding ground of another great name in ocean racing. To its credit, however, it has done this not at the expense of the amateurs and newcomers, but in conjunction with them. It may not entirely be the race Blondie Hasler envisaged, but much of that original spirit remains. For that reason it still remains *the* race to win.

## THE CORINTHIAN SPIRIT

While high-tech professionals have dominated the top end of the fleet, the rest of the classes are filled with so-called "Corinthians", amateurs who sail without seeking the blaze of publicity required by the sponsors of the high-profile race machines. The list of entries for 1996, for example, included a book seller, a lawyer, a policeman and a vet – not forgetting, of course, pub landlord Peter Crowther with his lug-rigged *Galway Blazer II*. Many enter with no real hope of winning but simply for the personal satisfaction of having completed the course, of having been "one man [or woman], one boat, one sea". For this reason they are often felt to represent the true spirit of the race.

## CAREER PROFILE

**1931** Born in Nantes, France, on 23 July

**1952** Joins French navy as pilot and serves in Asia

**1964** Wins OSTAR on *Pen Duick II* and awarded Légion d'Honneur by Charles de Gaulle

**1967** Wins Fastnet on *Pen Duick III*

**1968** Retires from OSTAR on *Pen Duick IV* after collision

**1969** Wins San Francisco-Tokyo singlehanded race on *Pen Duick V*. Sets new record on *Pen Duick IV* in Los Angeles-Honolulu race

**1972** *Pen Duick IV* wins OSTAR with Alain Colas at helm

**1973** Twice dismasted on *Pen Duick VI* during first Whitbread Round the World Race

**1976** Wins OSTAR on *Pen Duick VI*

**1980** Breaks *Atlantic*'s 1905 transatlantic record by nearly two days on *Paul Ricard* in 10 days, 5 hours

**1984** Fourth over the line in OSTAR *Paul Ricard*. Marries Jacqueline; daughter Marie is born

**1986** Rescued by *Pen Duick VI* when *Côte d'Or II* breaks up during Route du Rhum

**1987** Rescued with brother Patrick when trimaran pitchpoles during La Baule – Dakar double-handed race

**1989** Rescued after pitchpoling during the Lorient-St Barth-Lorient double-handed Transat

**1993** Skippers *La Poste* in Whitbread Round the World Race

**1997** Crew on *Aquitaine Innovation*, winner of Le Havre-Cartagena transatlantic race

**1998** 13 June, lost at sea off Milford Haven, UK. Body recovered five weeks later

Tabarly the mighty, Tabarly the invincible – this is the image that France's most famous sailor conjures up. Yet the photos of Tabarly taken at the end of the 1976 OSTAR, when he emerged from the mist after 23 gruelling days at sea to win his second transatlantic, tell a different story. They show a shrunken, almost emaciated man, his eyes barely hiding the excruciating toll of steering his ship through the roughest OSTAR on record.

So excruciating that, when his self-steering broke just four days from the start, even the great Tabarly contemplated giving up and set a course for home. Instead, after a few hours' sleep, he reset his course for Newport and went on to achieve a much-heralded win against the 72m (236ft) "Jumbo yacht" Club Méditerranée. It was the pinnacle of his career, and sealed his already awesome reputation, but his victory was achieved at a high personal price. The famously taciturn Tabarly was human after all.

Eric Tabarly was born in Nantes in 1931 and started sailing almost as soon as he could walk – albeit mainly in a land-locked pond. He joined the naval air arm in 1952, and soon acquired a passion for racing on board his father's 8-Metre and cruising their classic 1898 cutter *Pen Duick*, designed by the great Scottish designer William Fife III. It was aboard *Pen Duick II*, named after the family yacht, that Tabarly had his first OSTAR win in 1964. Within a few days of crossing the finish line at Newport, he was being given a ticker-tape parade through the Champs Elysée to receive his Légion d'Honneur from President Charles de Gaulle. It was a meteoric rise for the man that a few months earlier was struggling to find the finance to build his first challenger. The next 12 years continued at the same, frenetic pace. Not only would Tabarly sail a series of famous boats to great victories, he would also be deeply involved in the design and construction of each vessel.

First came *Pen Duick III*, a 19.7m (65ft) wishbone schooner which won all the main RORC races in 1967. She was followed by *Pen Duick IV*, the distinctive, bare aluminium trimaran which Tabarly crashed at the start of the 1968 OSTAR but which went on to win the 1972 OSTAR with his protegé Alain Colas at the helm. Then, after winning the singlehanded San Francisco-Tokyo race on *Pen Duick V*, he began planning the next and last in the series. *Pen Duick VI* suffered two dismastings during the 1973

## "THE MIGHTY... THE INVINCIBLE "

Whitbread Round the World Race, but ultimately sealed Tabarly's reputation in the Atlantic three years later.

The man his mainly younger rivals liked to called "Pépé" married Martinique-born Jacqueline Chartol in 1984 and their daughter Marie was born that year. By then, Tabarly's star had begun to wane. His revolutionary trimaran *Paul Ricard* was no longer competitive and the two *Côte d'Ors* which followed never fulfilled their potential. In 1993, he announced his retirement, though the same year he skippered the French Whitbread entry *La Poste*, and in 1997 he crewed on board *Aquitaine Innovation*, winning the Le Havre-Cartagena transatlantic race. In the summer of 1998, a wonderful fleet of yachts gathered at Tabarly's home port of Bénodet to celebrate the 100th anniversary of his beloved *Pen Duick*. The event was followed by a unique gathering of Fifes at their birthplace on the Clyde – but Tabarly never made it to Scotland. En route from Bénodet, the man who took pride in never wearing a life jacket or harness fell over the side during the night and drowned. France had lost its brightest sailing star.

# ERIC tabarly

# SOLITAIRE
## du figaro

**left** Up to 58 boats take part in the annual Solitaire du Figaro, sailing four legs of up to 1062km (660 miles) each. It has been described as the "Olympics of singlehanded sailing".

# UNIVERSITY OF CHAMPIONS

" Suddenly I heard a loud clunk and the boat shuddered. I threw myself into the cockpit to discover that my spinnaker was well and truly wrapped around the forestay! I fought in the darkness to untwist the sail, and as soon as it filled, the boat began veering from side to side which sent her into a broach. ... Soaking legs, halyard in teeth, sail in arms, I prayed that the wind would not catch the spinnaker and send the lot – with me – overboard. ... and after all that's happened, it seems like magic that there are three dolphins with me right now. "

Damian Foxall on a stormy night during the 2001 Figaro

Anyone wondering why so many of today's top singlehanded sailors are French need look no further than the Figaro. Originally set up as a simple annual race, it has grown into a national championship incorporating a series of Grand Prix-style races culminating in the four-legged 2400km (1500 mile) Solitaire. There's a special Figaro school to train the skippers in the dark arts of solo sailing and there's a one-design yacht specially designed for competing in the series. More than just a race, the Figaro has become an institution – a fantastically successful institution which turns out some of the best sailors in the world.

he Solitaire itself is one of the most gruelling races of any sport: 15 days of flat-out racing in near-identical 9.1m (30ft) sailboats in some of the most challenging waters in Europe. It's been compared to running a marathon – except that you have to run the whole thing as if it were a sprint: flat out, with every tack and every sail change performed as fast as possible. For every minute counts in a race that sometimes sees 30 boats finishing within an hour of each other after three days' racing. Not only that, but no weather routing or outside assistance of any kind is allowed – so it's up to the skipper to keep an eye

on the weather, decide on tactics, and make sure the boat is on course. If they have time, they might eat a little and, if they are lucky, even sleep a bit. Often, the winner is the skipper who manages to sleep best – as well as getting all the other practical stuff right. Franck Cammas, who won the 1997 race, sums up the most important psychological attitude needed to win. "In the Figaro, you learn to be patient, to be measured, to be cunning, and to be modest. You can never definitely say, 'I am going to win this race.'"

The Figaro is the ideal training ground for a career in singlehanded racing, and nearly 600 skippers have taken part in the 33 Solitaires organized so far. There have been up to 58 boats on the start line. Not surprisingly the list of winners of the race reads like a roll call of the most famous French solo sailors, including Philippe Poupon (1982, 1985 and 1995), Christophe Auguin (1986), Alain Gautier (1989), Yves Parlier (1991), Michel Malinovsky (1971), Laurent Bourgnon (1988), Jean Le Cam (1994, 1996 and 1999), Jean-Marie Vidal (1972 and 1987) and Michel Desjoyeaux (1992 and 1998). Even the list of past losers is pretty impressive, including the likes of Clare Francis, Mike Birch, Isabelle Autissier, Jean-Yves Terlain, Loïck Peyron,

# THE routes

## SOLITAIRE DU FIGARO

Since its inception, the length of the Figaro has increased from 1046km (650 miles) in 1970 to 2721km (1691 miles) in 2002. A new, faster, one-design boat launched in 2003 could change all that.

— 1970 route

— 2002 route

**1 1973**
10 out of 14 boats abandon race due to bad weather

**2 1978**
Pierre Saint Jalm's boat breaks up off the Lizard

**3 1979**
36 out of 46 boats abandon race – Pierre Follenfant rescued

**4 1985**
Jean le Cam loses race when he falls asleep at the helm

**5 1985**
Luc Berthillier found drifting in liferaft

**6 1996**
Alain Gautier falls over the side and is picked up by Nicolas Bézenger

**7 2001**
Christophe Le Bas only skipper to finish 3rd leg

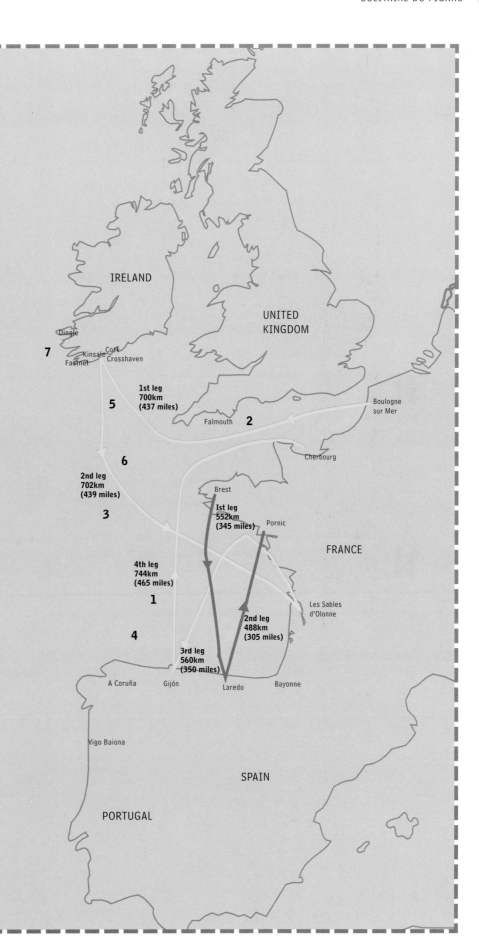

IRELAND

UNITED KINGDOM

ATLANTIC OCEAN

Dingle

7    Kinsale  Cork
Fastnet     Crosshaven

**1st leg
700km
(437 miles)**

5                      2

Falmouth

Boulogne sur Mer

6

**2nd leg
702km
(439 miles)**

Cherbourg

3

Brest

**1st leg
552km
(345 miles)**

Pornic

**4th leg
744km
(465 miles)**

FRANCE

1

Les Sables d'Olonne

4

**2nd leg
488km
(305 miles)**

**3rd leg
560km
(350 miles)**

A Coruña    Gijón    Laredo    Bayonne

Vigo Baiona

SPAIN

PORTUGAL

Catherine Chabaud… well, you get the picture. No wonder Ellen MacArthur describes it as "the Olympics of singlehanded sailing".

### Try, try again

Not only that, but they keep coming back. Philippe Poupon sailed in the race 15 times, winning three, before announcing he was hanging up his oilskins up in 2001. Only Jean Le Cam has raced in more, notching up 16 starts and three wins. As co-founder Jean Michel Barrault puts it: "While hundreds of sailors have taken part in it and it has helped form most of the winners of the great ocean races, the Solitaire du Figaro retains a fascination that keeps them coming back – for the pleasure of suffering, for its conviviality. It's a tribute to the race that sailors as well-known as Philippe Poupon, Alain Gautier, Jean Le Cam, and Florence Arthaud, who have nothing to prove, come back to take on the keen young things, their motivation simply being: 'I like this race.'"

> **❝THE SOLITAIRE DU FIGARO RETAINS A FASCINATION THAT KEEPS [PEOPLE] COMING BACK❞**
>
> Jean Michel Barrault on the popularity of the racce

Twelve boats lined up for the start of the first Aurore, as it was then called, on 6 August 1970. The course was made up of just two legs: from Brest in Brittany to Laredo in Spain back to Pornic on the west coast of France. The entrants were a mixture of cruisers and racers built or adapted to fit the IOR Half Ton rule. Navigation was by sextant and compass, communication was via HF radio, and autopilots were banned. The line-up included Jean-Yves Terlain, who two years later would rock the OSTAR establishment with his three-masted *Vendredi Treize*, future Route du Rhum near-winner Michel Malinovsky, and the only non-French entry, British 1968 OSTAR winner Leslie Williams.

Terlain set the tone of many future races when his brand new yacht was wrecked on the Spanish coast, while Joan de Kat gave early proof to what would soon become a incontrovertible rule: that good sleep control is more often than not the key to victory. He had picked up a few tips while he was traveling in Asia and used them to good effect, finishing 15 minutes in front of Malinovsky. The latter would come back to win the following year and later become a race director. Meanwhile the race itself, originally named after its principal

**right** Up to 58 skippers compete to win France's most adrenalin-charged solo race. And since 1991, they have all raced on identical boats.

**above** Despite becoming a superstar on the ocean racing circuit, Philippe Poupon still returns to the Figaro year after year, clocking up 15 starts and three wins over 22 years.

sponsor the *Aurore* newspaper, was renamed when the *Aurore* became part of the Figaro group in 1980.

One of the great challenges of the Figaro, and no doubt one reason why so many skippers keep coming back to it year after year, is that unlike most yacht races the course changes every year. To make matters more complicated, the race was bumped up to three legs in 1972 and then to the current four legs in 1976. It is a logistical nightmare for the organizers and a constantly shifting navigational puzzle for the skippers, but it keeps the race fresh and helps put newcomers on a more level footing with the race diehards.

The usual pattern is to start and finish on the west coast of France, heading north to either England or Ireland and/or south to Spain, as well as the occasional foray up the Channel. Each leg is generally about 400–480km (250–300 miles) long, although as the boats have got faster so the legs have gradually got longer – the longest in the 1970s was 865km (540 miles), from Kinsale to Laredo, but by 1995 this had crept up to the current record of 1056km (660 miles), from Arcachon to Kinsale via the Fastnet Rock off the south west tip of Eire.

The English stopover was brought into the equation when the third leg was introduced in 1972, with Falmouth chosen as the cross-Channel destination to complete the square course up the east side of the Atlantic. That was changed to Kinsale in Ireland in 1974, which since then has proven to be the overwhelming favourite, occasionally replaced by Howth and Falmouth or, in 2001, Dingle. A Coruña and more recently Gijón have tended to be the most regular stopovers in Spain, though the fleet has made it as far south as Baiona, near the border with Portugal.

These constantly changing vistas clearly appeal to the race's best known ambassador: "I like the rhythm of this race. You get to go sailing and discover new places," says Philippe Poupon. "It's always good to explore new stopovers. It's one of the attractions of the race."

## Les Figaristes

Apart from giving an opportunity for a little tourism (when you're not catching up on sleep) the stopovers are also important for the social spirit of the race. They provide an opportunity

## THE COURSES OF THE SOLITAIRE DU FIGARO

| Year | Course |
|------|--------|
| 1970 | Brest (Fr) – Laredo (Sp) – Pornic (Fr) |
| 1971 | Brest (Fr) – Santander (Sp) – Pornic (Fr) |
| 1972 | Perros-Guirec (Fr) – Falmouth (UK) – A Coruña (Sp) – Pornic (Fr) |
| 1973 | Perros-Guirec (Fr) – Falmouth (UK) – Laredo (Sp) – Pornic (Fr) |
| 1974 | Perros-Guirec (Fr) – Kinsale (Eire) – Laredo (Sp) – Pornic (Fr) |
| 1975 | La Baule (Fr) – Perros-Guirec (Fr) – Kinsale (Eire) – Le Croisic (Fr) |
| 1976 | La Baule (Fr) – Perros-Guirec (Fr) – Falmouth (UK) – Kinsale (Eire) – Port du Crouesty (Fr) |
| 1977 | Perros-Guirec (Fr) – Crosshaven (Eire) – Quiberon (Fr) – Laredo (Sp) – Port du Crouesty (Fr) |
| 1978 | Perros-Guirec (Fr) – Kinsale (Eire) – Pornichet (Fr) – La Baule (Fr) – Laredo (Sp) – Quiberon (Fr) |
| 1979 | Les Sables d'Olonnes (Fr) – Laredo (Sp) – Quiberon (Fr) – Kinsale (Eire) – Concarneau (Fr) |
| 1980 | Perros-Guirec (Fr) – Kinsale (Eire) – Les Sables d'Olonnes (Fr) – Pornic (Fr) |
| 1981 | Perros-Guirec (Fr) – Crosshaven (Eire) – Brest (Fr) – A Coruña (Sp) – Concarneau (Fr) |
| 1982 | Arcachon (Fr) – A Coruña (Sp) – Falmouth (UK) – Quiberon (Fr) |
| 1983 | Perros-Guirec (Fr) – Kinsale (Eire) – Crozon/Morgat (Fr) – A Coruña (Sp) – Pornichet (Fr) – La Baule (Fr) |
| 1984 | Granville (Fr) – Kinsale (Eire) – La Rochelle (Fr) – A Coruña (Sp) – Concarneau (Fr) |
| 1985 | Granville (Fr) – Kinsale (Eire) – Presqu'île de Crozon (Fr) – Bayona de Vigo (Sp) – La Rochelle (Fr) |
| 1986 | Perros-Guirec (Fr) – Kinsale (Eire) – A Coruña (Sp) – Pornic (Fr) |
| 1987 | Arcachon (Fr) – A Coruña (Sp) – Bénodet (Fr) – Sainte Marine (Fr) – Pornichet/La Baule (Fr) |
| 1988 | Port Bourgenay (Fr) – A Coruña (Sp) – Brest (Fr) – Kinsale (Eire) – Quiberon (Fr) |
| 1989 | Perros-Guirec (Fr) – Kinsale (Eire) – Lorient (Fr) – A Coruña (Sp) – La Trinité (Fr) |
| 1990 | Port Bourgenay (Fr) – Vigo (Sp) – Bénodet (Fr) – Kinsale (Eire) – La Rochelle (Fr) |
| 1991 | Cherbourg (Fr) – Kinsale (Eire) – Concarneau (Fr) – Gijón (Sp) – Lorient (Fr) |
| 1992 | Arcachon (Fr) – Kinsale (Eire) – Pornichet (Fr) – Gijón (Sp) – Port la Forêt (Fr) |
| 1993 | St Malo (Fr) – A Coruña (Sp) – Douarnenez (Fr) – Kinsale (Eire) – St Quay Portrieux (Fr) |
| 1994 | Brest (Fr) – Kinsale (Eire) – Gijón (Sp) – Perros-Guirec (Fr) – Port Bourgenay (Fr) |
| 1995 | Arcachon (Fr) – Kinsale (Eire) – La Rochelle (Fr) – Gijón (Sp) – Brest (Fr) |
| 1996 | Perros-Guirec (Fr) – Howth (Eire) – St Nazaire (Fr) – Gijón (Sp) – Port du Crouesty (Fr) |
| 1997 | Arcachon (Fr) – Gijón (Sp) – Brest (Fr) – Kinsale (Eire) – St Quay Portrieux (Fr) |
| 1998 | Cherbourg (Fr) – Howth (Eire) – Ile de Groix (Fr) – Gijón (Sp) – Concarneau (Fr) |
| 1999 | Brest (Fr) – Falmouth (UK) – Brest (Fr) – Bayona (Sp) – Douarnenez (Fr) |
| 2000 | Arcachon (Fr) – Gexto-Bilbao (Sp) – St Nazaire (Fr) – Falmouth (UK) – Cherbourg-Octeville (Fr) |
| 2001 | La Rochelle (Fr) – Gijón (Sp) – St Quay Portrieux (Fr) – Dingle (Eire) – Hendaye (Fr) |
| 2002 | Boulogne sur Mer (Fr) – Cork (Eire) – Les Sables d'Olonnes (Fr) – Gijón (Sp) – Cherbourg (Fr) |

for the skippers to get to know each other and to feel part of the bigger family of Figaristes – a welcome relief after days of isolation afloat. It's useful networking for up-and-coming sailors and a chance for the race veterans to share their experience, not to mention forge lifelong friendships with like-minded people. As a result, not unlike its multi-legged big sister the round-the-world Around Alone (BOC), the Figaro has acquired a reputation as one of the more sociable races – something of a paradox for an event which is all about doing it alone.

This distinctive combination of intense racing and cross-Channel forays produces a pace that has nevertheless flummoxed many of the champions of longer races such as the OSTAR and Route du Rhum, more used to building up a regular rhythm over weeks or even months. For many, sleep deprivation is the main problem, with most skippers only snatching a few minutes' sleep at a time during the three to four-day laps. Even that may be too long, as Jean Le Cam discovered in 1985. He and Poupon were neck and neck for the first two-and-a-half legs, until halfway into the third leg when Le Cam fell asleep for an hour while waiting for a breeze to arrive. The snooze cost him the race. By the time he woke up, Poupon had caught the breeze and was already several miles ahead, securing overall victory. But Le Cam was lucky – other sailors have found themselves waking up on the rocks.

The 2001 winner Eric Drouglazet claims to have only slept one and a half hours during the 87-hour final leg from Dingle to Hendaye. It took Drouglazet (or "Drouglouglou" as some call him) nine attempts to triumph in what he described as his "bad love affair" with the race, a reference to the love/hate feelings that many skippers seem to feel towards it: "It's a big chunk of race that used to make me dream when I was a kid," he said. "But it's all about pain, loss of sleep, and bad food. I had to push myself the whole time so as not to regret not winning." Or, as two-times winner Jean-Marie Vidal put it: "You don't do it in order to suffer. But you have to know you are going to suffer." However, the 1972 and 1987 winner does not see the race simply as a rite of passage. "While for some the Figaro is an

obligatory passage in their career, I take part for the purely sporting aspect, for a personal challenge. It's part of the charm of the event. It's a race which is played on a more or less level playing field and is made up of several legs, which allows one to rest, to make repairs, but also for the competitors to get to know each other. It's an important factor in the success of the race. And then there is that tough element, its difficulty, the challenge that every competitor takes up."

## Calms and hallucinations

Calm weather is usually worse than windy weather as skippers have to make the most of every wind shift to stay ahead of the opposition, and on top of that what would normally be a three-day leg can stretch out up to six days, such as during the calm years of 1986 and (for the first leg anyway) 1998. Exhaustion is commonplace, as are hallucinations. After several day's catnapping it's not unusual for the sea to turn into a field of green grass and the fleet of boats sailing across it to change into a herd of cows – a very disconcerting vision several hundred miles away from land.

For Christophe Auguin, 1986 winner and five-time Solitaire competitor, that's all part of the race's interest. Despite winning an unprecedented three round-the-world races, France's most successful solo sailor still finds the Figaro a challenge: "The length of each leg makes it fascinating, because three days is hard to manage. From the point of view of sleep, the Solitaire is much harder than a round-the-world race."

Inevitably, the race has had its share of drama and accidents – more often than not due to bad weather rather than bad seamanship. The same year that 15 people died during the 1979 Fastnet race, the Figaro fleet was battling its way across the Irish Sea from Kinsale to Concarneau when the storm struck. A record number of boats abandoned the race – 36 out of 46 – although miraculously no-one was killed. Pierre Follenfant had a close shave, however, when his boat broke up during the night. Bobbing about in his lifejacket amid the wreckage, he grabbed a waterproof light that was miraculously floating

**❝IT'S A BIG CHUNK OF RACE THAT USED TO MAKE ME DREAM AS A KID❞**

Eric Drouglazet explains his motivation for entering the Figaro

**left** Jean le Cam had to wait 16 years before his first Figaro win in 1994. He holds the record as the most frequent participant: 16 starts and three wins.

**above** Sleep deprivation is the toughest obstacle. The 2001 winner Eric Drouglazet claims to have only slept for one and a half hours during the final three-day leg from Ireland to Spain.

past him and was able to attract the attention of fellow competitor Olivier Moussy. Without it, he would almost certainly have drowned.

Likewise Alain Gautier who fell over the side in the Irish Sea during the 1996 race while checking to see if his hull was clean. His boat sailed on without him, and he was left clinging to a piece of wood until Nicolas Bérenger happened to spot him paddling about in the clear blue sea under a clear blue sky. Although Gautier's mid-ocean swim became the butt of many a joke, everyone knew that comedy could so easily have turned to tragedy. They knew too, that it could so easily have been them.

Not so lucky was Pierre Saint Jalm, hit by Force 6 winds during the first leg of the 1978

race. Three other boats retired, but Saint Jalm fell ill and collapsed in his cabin. His boat was driven onto the rocks on the Lizard in Cornwall and he was eventually airlifted to hospital after a walker spotted him. Or Luc Berthillier. He was presumed dead when he disappeared after his yacht sank, along with one other sinking and four dismastings, on the way to Kinsale in 1985. He was eventually picked up five days later by a Spanish trawler drifting about on his semi-inflated raft.

Most recently, a whole leg of the race had to be abandoned in 2001 due to bad weather, the first time such an extreme measure has been taken. It was an ambitious course from the very start, criss-crossing from La Rochelle to Gijón then back up to Brittany before crossing to Ireland and finishing with one of the longest legs ever, 1038km (649 miles) from Dingle to Hendaye in the French Basque country. A total of 2790km (1744 miles). As usual, however, the problems started in the Irish Sea, when 50–60 knot winds were forecasted as the fleet approached the Fastnet. No doubt fearing a repetition of 1973, when 10 out of 14 boats were abandoned due to severe weather between England and Spain, the organizers diverted the fleet to Crosshaven from where they cruised around the coast to Dingle for the final leg. One sailor, however, carried on regardless. Christophe Le Bas managed to slip past the Fastnet ahead of the bad weather and made it in to Dingle at 3:40 the following morning, none too happy that his excellent performance would count for nothing.

## The chick's race

It's all a long way from the image presented by that celebrated singlehander Olivier de Kersauson, who has never taken part in the race, but once disparagingly described it as "une course de gonzesses" (a chick's race). Six hundred Figaro skippers would surely disagree. Thanks to its relatively short legs, however, and the fact that the fleet does tend to sail close together, there have been no fatalities in the Solitaire so far.

Under the Half Ton rule, production boats such as the Super Challenger, the Super Arlequin, the Mallard, and the First 30 all fared consistently well in the race. But while there was room within the rule for development and innovation, it also meant that skippers were not playing on an altogether level playing field. Everything changed in 1990, however, with the appearance of a new one-design boat specifically created for the race and intended to focus on the sailor's performance rather than on the ingenuity of the boat builder.

The Figaro Solo, or Figaro Bénéteau as it was later named, was designed by Groupe Finot and Jean Berret very much in the vein of the 18.3m (60ft) "Southern Ocean surfers" starting to find favour among BOC and Vendée Globe sailors. Very beamy, with flat-bottomed hulls and deep, narrow keels, they were little more than overgrown dinghies – albeit with rather more sophisticated

rigs and ballasting arrangements. *Generali Concorde*, sailed by Alain Gautier in the 1988–9 Vendée Globe and 1990–1 BOC, paved the way among the bigger boats, while the Figaro adopted a 9.44m (31ft) version as its one-design class.

It was a bold step and one which cemented the future of the race. Even during the changeover year, when the Solos raced alongside the old Half Tonners, most skippers had already converted to the new boats. And, no doubt much to the association's satisfaction, they immediately proved their worth by beating the old boats. By keeping the cost of the boats down to around 350,000 francs, participation was kept within reach of any reasonably well-sponsored skipper. Even 10 years later the total cost of a Figaro campaign, including the hire of a boat, was estimated at between 300,000–335,000 francs.

Over the years, however, the boats' specifications varied slightly and boats were subtly – or not so subtly – altered by their skippers. Some are said to have gone as far as recasting the boats' keels to put the ballast where it is most useful, doing away with the internal lead pigs favoured by the rule-makers. Others have simply ground into the steel keels and plastered them with lead to lower the centre of effort. One way and another, the result was that after 10 years the boats began to lose their conformity and – even worse – to look outdated.

## New blood

A new design was commissioned from designer Marc Lombard which was launched in time for the 2003 season. At 10m (33ft) LOA, it is almost a metre longer than its predecessor, with carbon fibre mast, twin rudders, and an updated interior (including a chic inclined double chart-table, à la Vendée Globe). "Seaworthy, modern, fast, fun, lively, and of good quality" is how the designer described it. Such improvements do not come without a cost, however, and inevitably the price of the boat has risen to around 650,000 francs.

The hope is that having a more exciting, up-to-date class will bring some new blood into the race and stem the recent ebb of "bizuths", as the

> **"SEAWORTHY, MODERN, FAST, FUN, LIVELY AND OF GOOD QUALITY"**
>
> Marc Lombard on his new 2003 Figaro design

"freshers" or newcomers are called. With an estimated extra one knot of speed, longer courses should also be possible, helping towards the ultimate aim of making the class more international. And this time the plan is to keep the boats strictly within class, so no modifications will be allowed. That's the plan anyway, though history suggests than canny sailors will always find ways of adapting their steeds to squeeze that crucial extra 0.1 knot of speed out of them.

Along with new boats, the navigational equipment has gradually improved over the years. Whereas in 1970 the boats were equipped with compass and sextant, plus RDF (radio direction finder) for cloudy weather, nowadays most boats have on-board computers linked to a GPS (global positioning system), digital compass, digital barometer (reading to within half a hectopascal), speedometer, and anometer (for wind speed and direction). A sophisticated navigation programme means paper charts are barely needed other than as emergency backup or for outdoor use (being more waterproof than most computers).

Since 1983 electronic autopilots, as opposed to mechanical windvane pilots, have been allowed and are now even capable of anticipating the boat's movement and adjusting the helm accordingly; useful while you're tapping at your computer below decks, but most skippers still prefer to take the helm themselves to make the most of every little shift of wind and errant wave. There are some things that humans still do better than computers, and steering a sailboat is one of them.

## The importance of weather

Unlike several other of the singlehanded races, routing by a shore-based adviser is strictly forbidden. In the early days, this meant skippers were limited to listening to the weather forecast on the radio (Radio-France and the BBC being the main sources) and relying on their own meteorological know-how to interpret what was happening around them.

Even the advent of weatherfaxes change things little, as the technology was initially banned from Figaro boats for fear of encouraging a technology race. Instead, skippers were provided with detailed weather forecasts before the start of each leg and with daily updates radioed by a chase boat. Weatherfaxes were finally allowed in 2001, although the computer programmes which could use the information to predict a boat's optimum route were still banned and skippers were made to sign an affidavit promising not to use them.

Communication on board is limited to VHF, since that replaced HF in 1975, with a special frequency (P4) being designated for the Figaristes to overcome the problem of overcrowding on the main channels. Mobile phones, understandably, are banned to prevent skippers receiving any secret outside assistance.

With competitors all sailing almost identical boats, the racing is usually very close. Unlike the great ocean races where the fleet is likely to be spread over hundreds if not thousands of miles, the Figaro boats tend to race as a pack. And with entry levels of up to 58 (the 1999 record), that's a lot of boats. It makes for dramatic photography and may in part account for its close following amongst the French media – that and the fact that it is sponsored by a national paper, of course.

With such close competition, it is rare for one skipper to completely dominate a race – Gilles Le Baud is the only person to have won every lap, and that was back in 1973. And rare indeed are skippers such as Patrick Eliès, who recorded a 14-hour advantage over his nearest rival in 1979. It's more common for winners to perform averagely well across all the legs – in fact, several skippers have won the race without winning a single leg, including 2002 winner Christophe de Pavant. For the secret to winning the Solitaire, as 2000 third-placed Gildas Morvan explains, is "being very consistent over all the legs, without trying to be spectacular, but also to always get a placing without doing any bad legs".

There are always exceptions, however, and for some the race has brought instant stardom. Laurent Bourgnon, for instance. When he entered

# "...BEING VERY CONSISTENT OVER ALL THE LEGS, WITHOUT TRYING TO BE SPECTACULAR..."

Gildas Morvan reveals the secret behind a successful Figaro race

**right** Damian Foxhall celebrates a rare win for a "foreigner". In 1998, the Irishman became only the second non-French skipper to win a leg of the race since Claire Francis in 1975.

**above** The Figaro is the breeding ground of stars. The latest crop of up-and-coming sailors includes Karine Fauconnier, winner of the 2000 two-handed transat.

the race for the first time in 1988 at the age of 22 he came from three races down to snatch overall victory from Alain Gautier in the final race. Gautier, who had to get special dispensation to join the race when he first entered as a minor in 1980, had to wait until the following year (and his tenth attempt) for glory. Bourgnon summed up what the race meant for him in terms every Figariste would recognize: "The Figaro is a great race which gives you a definitive measure of your performance, with immediately visible results. I've learnt a lot and gained a great deal of pleasure thanks to its genuine spirit of camaraderie."

## The extraterrestrial

Another quick learner was Yves Parlier. He entered as a bizuth in 1990 and by the following year had already earned the nickname of

"l'extraterrestre" (the extraterrestrial) for his uncanny ability to read the weather. Refusing to join the flock, he went off and did his own thing and left the rest of the fleet behind, claiming a well-deserved first prize. The prize for sheer dogged persistence, however, must go to Le Cam, who had to wait 16 years for his first win in 1994.

Not surprisingly, as the all races start and finish in France, the vast majority of Figaro competitors are currently French – although in 1998 the Irish sailor, Damian Foxall, became the first non-French skipper to win a leg of the race since Claire Francis in 1975 and the Dutchman Hans Bouscholte in 1993. His experiences on a wild and windy night nearly turned him from victor into casualty. "Suddenly I heard a loud clunk and the boat shuddered. I threw myself into the cockpit to discover that my spinnaker was well and truly wrapped around the forestay! I fought in the darkness to untwist the sail, and as soon as it filled, the boat began veering from side to side, which sent her into a broach. I was hanging on to the foot of the sail as the boat lay over and waves broke onto the foredeck – life sometimes doesn't feel fair! With a wrap of sheet around the forestay still and the boat surfing at 14 knots, it took me several attempts of running between foredeck and cockpit to get the spinnaker down without broaching. Soaking legs, halyard in teeth, sail in arms, I prayed that the wind would not catch the spinnaker and send the lot – with me – overboard. I could feel my heart beating – gees, I'm almost shaking… Well what a night number one is turning out to be. The kite is back up, I'm doing about 12–13 knots, and after all that's happened it seems like magic that there are three dolphins with me right now."

Curiously, the latterday English heroine Clare Francis remains the only woman to have won a leg of the race - way back in 1975.

But French sailors have an automatic advantage over their overseas rivals thanks to the infrastructure that supports the Solitaire. The starting place for many is the solo sailing training centre at Port la Forêt, nicknamed "la vallée des fous" (the valley of the mad) by that old antagonist Olivier de Kersauson. The centre runs courses for a dozen aspiring Figaristes in navigation, meteorology, tactics, and that all-important subject: sleep control. After that, they are ready to tackle one of the many inshore and short offshore races that count towards the title of *Champion de France Solitaire* – from the Porquerolles in the south to Perros-Guirec in the north. And if you can't make it to Port la Forêt, short courses are run at other centres such as Concarneau and Marseilles.

It is a comprehensive program which not only ensures that Figaro sailors are by and large safe sailors, but also that they are successful sailors. Most recently Thomas Coville, Gilles Chiorri, and Sébastien Josse have all come up through the Figaro ranks to start promising singlehanded careers, while Karine Fauconnier has been tipped as the latest rising female star. The daughter of Yvon Fauconnier (who reinvented the infamous *Vendredi Treize* into the luxury yacht *ITT Océanic*) went through the entire Figaro formula before winning the two-handed Transat in 2000.

They are just the latest crop in a seemingly endless flow of talented singlehanded sailors to come out of this most testing of races. It's a tried-and-tested approach which has helped ensure France's worldwide domination of the sport for the past three decades. No wonder the French love the Figaro.

**below** Some 38 boats took part in the 2002 Figaro, which saw some of the closest racing in the history of the race. It was the last year for the "first generation" Figaro class, before a new design was introduced in 2003.

You couldn't help but sympathize with the 30-year-old French sailor as he broke down in tears when the result of the 1984 OSTAR was announced. First in with his *Fleury Michon* in a record-breaking time of 16 days and 12 hours, he went to bed content in the knowledge that he had won the race. He was to be cruelly deceived.

Yvon Fauconnier was eighth over the line when he arrived early the next morning, 10 hours after Poupon. On the way over, however, he had stopped to assist Philippe Jeantot whose catamaran *Credit Agricole II* had capsized 200 miles off the Azores. After examining Fauconnier's log, the race committee awarded him a 16-hour compensation and, by the time Poupon awoke the next morning, he had been relegated to second place. No wonder he felt a little misty-eyed.

Poupon had his revenge, however. At the next OSTAR, four years later, he tore across the Atlantic in his trimaran *Fleury Michon IX*, smashing his previous record by an astonishing six days. Suddenly the transatlantic race it had taken Chichester 40 days to complete in 1960 had been whittled down to a 10-day sprint. Poupon's record would stand for 12 years.

Like several other successful French sailors, Poupon (or "Philou" as he is affectionately known) started his professional sailing career crewing for that icon of ocean racing, Eric Tabarly. Unlike most of this privileged group, however, Poupon was entrusted with one of the great man's boats and sailed *Pen Duick III* (renamed *St Malo – Pointe-à-Pitre*) in the 1978 Route du Rhum. His creditable seventh place signaled the arrival of a bright new talent.

The following year he started what was to be the most enduring love affair of his life: with the Figaro singlehanded race. Over the next 22 years he would take part in 15 Figaros, winning three – a record only beaten by his friend Jean Le Cam,

who took has taken part in 16 and won three. Part of the reason for Poupon's success has been his long-standing relationship with his sponsors, Fleury Michon, who have funded a long line of memorable boats bearing their name, from an 8m (26ft) monohull to a 26m (85ft) multihull. One of the most successful was the trimaran *Fleury Michon VIII*. Regarded as relatively small when she entered the 1986 Route du Rhum against one of the biggest fleet of giant multihulls ever seen, she nevertheless went on to trounce them all, setting a new course record of 14 days and 11 hours.

But while Poupon has triumphed on the Atlantic and on the Figaro circuit, he has fared

## THE MOST ENDURING LOVE AFFAIR OF HIS LIFE

less well in his round-the-world challenges. In the first Vendée Globe in 1989–90 his boat capsized off the Cape Good Hope and he had to be rescued by Loïck Peyron, while his second attempt in 1992–3 also nearly ended in disaster when he was dismasted 2414km (1500 miles) from the finish. Undaunted, he carried on under jury rig, finishing an impressive third, just seven days behind leader Alain Gautier.

Now more inclined to go cruising in the Caribbean with his family, Poupon announced in 2001 that he was racing in the Figaro for the last time, boasting that despite his age he still "frightened the young". He was forced to eat his words by the end of the race when, for the first time in 22 years he finished outside the top ten in a poor 19th place. Was it the end of a legend? Not if "Philou" has anything to do with it. "It pisses me off to leave on a bad note," he said later. "The love this race inspires means you always give it your all. I will have to have my revenge!"

# PHILIPPE poupon

**left** Sailing across the Atlantic
in a 6.4m (21ft) sailing boat is a
risky business, as the death toll
of the Mini-Transat testifies.
The 2001 race was no exception.

# DANGER ZONE

**"** Life aboard a 6.5m (21ft) sailboat in the big ocean can be very miserable. There are no accommodations below deck. In order to keep the weight down, I probably won't even be installing a bunk to sleep on. I will be navigating with the chart on my lap and using a bucket for my nature calls. … The salt water will attack my skin and I will more than likely have salt water sores to contend with. Sleep will come in 10 to 15 minute catnaps …. I will be battling autumn gales in the Bay of Biscay and flat calm seas in the doldrums interspersed with severe thunderstorms and high winds. **"**

Gale Browning on racing conditions in the Mini-Transat

**below** The living space on a Mini is not much larger than a double bed, but with only a fraction of the normal headroom! It is not likely to stay this horizontal or this dry either.

Gale Browning wrote this description of crossing the Atlantic on a 6.5m (21ft) Mini months before she took part in the 2001 Mini-Transat. The only US competitor in that race, she knew from all her pre-race training what she would be facing – her disappointing 48th place overall suggests she got everything she bargained for, and a good deal more besides. For these beamy little boats, with bulbous topsides and masts almost twice their length, may look like toys but sailing them is anything but child's play. In the 25 years since the Mini-Transat was founded, more than half a dozen people have died in the race, countless boats have been dismasted, and several have sunk. One survivor spent 76 days at sea in his liferaft before reaching land.

It's clearly not a race for the faint-hearted. For a start, look at the boats: 6.5m (21ft) is the length of an average sized living room, but with a maximum 3m (10ft) beam, they are half the width. With their flat bottoms and minimal cabintops, you're lucky if you've got decent sitting headroom, and as for standing, that's purely an outdoor activity. Plenty of legroom in the cockpit, but the streamlined deck design means you are exposed to every wave that comes over the plumb bow – and with a minimum freeboard of just 750mm (30in), that's likely to be most of them. Living on a Mini has been compared to living inside a washing machine, except that the soap has been replaced by salt.

Once you're out there, the race rules ban satellite systems, so the only form of communication you're going to have is by VHF radio, which has a range of just 30 miles. No weather routing here, no reassuring chats with

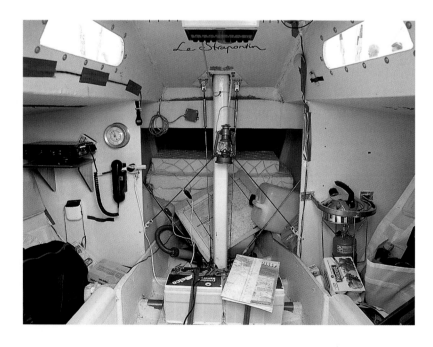

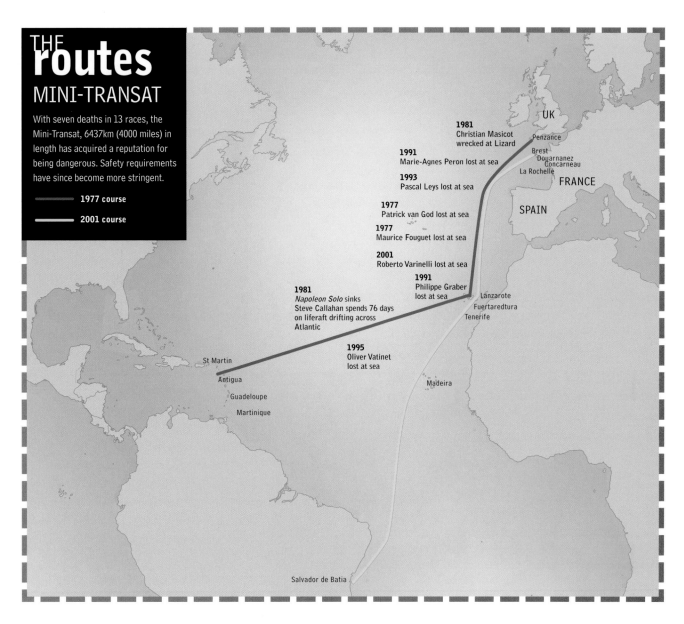

## THE routes
### MINI-TRANSAT

With seven deaths in 13 races, the Mini-Transat, 6437km (4000 miles) in length has acquired a reputation for being dangerous. Safety requirements have since become more stringent.

— 1977 course
— 2001 course

**1981**
Christian Masicot wrecked at Lizard

**1991**
Marie-Agnes Peron lost at sea

**1993**
Pascal Leys lost at sea

**1977**
Patrick van God lost at sea

**1977**
Maurice Fouguet lost at sea

**2001**
Roberto Varinelli lost at sea

**1991**
Philippe Graber lost at sea

**1981**
*Napoleon Solo* sinks
Steve Callahan spends 76 days on liferaft drifting across Atlantic

**1995**
Oliver Vatinet lost at sea

UK

Penzance
Brest
Douarnanez
Concarneau
La Rochelle
FRANCE
SPAIN

Lanzarote
Fuertaredtura
Tenerife

St Martin
Antigua
Guadeloupe
Martinique

Madeira

Salvador de Batia

the family back home, just a twice-daily log-in with the nearest chase boat. If you're lucky, you might pick up race positions from a French radio station, but it's quite likely that you won't have any idea where you stand in the fleet until you arrive in harbour. Dominique Bourgeois summed up the feeling of isolation that sets in early in the race. "You really are alone after about three days. The only communications are VHF and 90 per cent of the time there is no-one on your VHF and no information about the others." Being out of the public scrutiny has some benefits, however, as Thomas Coville, 11th in 1977, confirmed. "There are times when you think, if people could see me now – wandering around on the boat, naked, bearded, in a right state!"

Routes vary slightly from year to year, but generally the first leg is about 1600km (1000 miles) to the Canaries followed by a 4800km (3000 mile) second leg to the Caribbean. That translates roughly into at least 28 days on the water for the fast boats – up to 40 days or more for the slow ones. By that time most skippers will have experienced weather ranging from violent storms to complete calm, physical exhaustion from constantly adjusting sails and steering the boat with insufficient sleep, isolation, boredom, and the dreaded "gunwale bum" from sitting out in the cockpit too much.

### Paying for the ordeal

And how much do you get paid to go through this ordeal? Well, you don't. You pay for the pleasure, and it does not come cheap. An up-and-running Mini is likely to cost up to £70,000 while the cost of a fully-fledged campaign can be up to £90,000 – though some do manage on a budget a quarter that size.

The Mini-Transat was launched in 1977 by Bob Salmon. Hooked on singlehanded racing after covering the 1968 Golden Globe challenge, the British photo-journalist decided to enter the 1972 OSTAR. Unable to raise the kind of budget required to compete with the likes of the 39m (128ft) *Vendredi Treize*, he came up with the idea of a transatlantic race aimed at amateur racers and beginners. Whereas the length of OSTAR entries started at 6.5m (21ft) (Jean Lacombe's 1960 entry

below The race's creator, Bob Salmon, who came up with the idea of an "affordable" transatlantic solo race after competing in the 1972 OSTAR.

*Cap Horn*), Salmon decided that nothing over 6.5m (21ft) would be allowed to enter his race. Apart from that, the race rules were minimal: a maximum of five sails was allowed and electronic navigation was banned.

The one major concession Salmon made to the size of the boats was to build in a stopover during the course to reduce the non-stop time at sea to 4800km (3000 miles). It also gave competitors a chance to opt out of the longer second leg should they decide they or their boats were not quite up to speed. The first race started from Penzance, at the southwest tip of Cornwall, and stopped over in Tenerife in the Canary Islands before heading for the finish at English Harbour in Antigua. The timing of the event meant that the fleet caught the first of the autumnal depressions during the first leg before catching the trade winds on the second. Not surprisingly, the first leg soon acquired a reputation as the great leveller.

Some 24 boats gathered for the first start on 8 October 1977. From the outset, the race was dominated by the French – past masters of singlehanded sailing. There were a few British entries, including the organizer himself. Salmon was in optimistic mood and planned to get into harbour first then count the boats in for the final result. In the event, the competition was tougher than he'd imagined and he only made 15th place, leaving earlier boats to count themselves in. The winner of that race was Daniel Gilard, who would later skipper the maxi catamaran *Jet Services V* before being lost overboard during the 1987 La Baule-Dakar race. Other participants would also go on to high-profile racing careers: in fourth place was Jean-Luc van den Heede, later to make his name in the BOC (Around Alone) and Vendée Globe races, and 12th was Bruno Peyron, future Route du Rhum and Figaro star.

## Tragedy strikes

The danger of taking on the Atlantic Ocean in such small craft was forcefully brought home in that very first race with the death of two skippers: the Belgian Patrick van God and Frenchman Maurice Fouguet. Their deaths signalled that this race was no walkover and forced the organizers to take safety precautions ever more seriously. It was an issue that would come back to haunt them again and again, with the media pouncing on every accident as proof that the race was fundamentally unsafe.

Of that 1977 race, Gilard wrote: "Because when a storm blows the ocean becomes covered in dark craters, the sailors of yesteryear would say they were going into 'the skin of the devil'. It was foul weather for men of the sea. I suffered that foul weather for 11 days … Not much was said about that first Mini-Transat. A hostile silence shrouded the race. Everyone was against it… Everyone thought we were running to the abatoire. They foresaw boats sinking and sailors drowning. They said we were mad to confront the Atlantic in our nutshells…" It would take years before the event was fully accepted within the sailing establishment.

Despite its British origins, the Mini-Transat would become increasingly dominated by the French. Indeed, throughout the 1980s and most of the 1990s, no British skippers entered the race at all, and in 13 finishes there have been only two non-French winners: the American Norton Smith in 1979, and the Swiss Yvan Bourgnon in 1995.

After competing in the first two events, Salmon withdrew to devote himself entirely to the shoreside organization. Then, in 1983, after eight years at the helm, he handed over his charge to Frenchman and fellow journalist Jean-Luc Garnier. The Association Voiles 6.50m was formed in 1984, and a programme of races around France was organized alongside the Mini-Transat. At the same time, a one-design production boat was devised, known as the Serie class, which raced alongside, but had separate results from, the development class, or Proto for short.

Not surprisingly, considering the French enthusiasm for the event, the original Penzance-Antigua course was altered in 1985 to start from Brest and finish in the French island of Guadeloupe in the West Indies. Since then the route has changed every few years, starting sometimes in Concarneau or Douarnenez and finishing in St Maarten or Martinique. In 2001 it ran from La Rochelle to Salvador da Bahia in Brazil – the first time it has ventured below the Equator – with a stopover in Lanzarote. Ironically, under French law boats under 6.5m (21ft) are not allowed to sail offshore, and there are stories in the early days of French competitors having to sail up the Channel to get Britain within legal range before making the crossing and sailing back down to Penzance. The authorities eventually saw sense, however, and gave a special dispensation for the race to go ahead from French shores.

## The British come back

But the French domination was not total. By 1995, a third of the competitors flew foreign flags, ranging from Belgium to Argentina and Israel; and in 1999, nearly half the fleet was non-French, representing 12 nationalities from as far afield as the US, New Zealand, and Japan. The Mini class proved especially popular in Italy, which set up its own association in 1994. After a break of nearly 20 years, the British finally mounted a comeback in 1997; this time they were lead by none other than the Route du Rhum/Europe 1 Star/Vendée Globe British heroine-to-be, Ellen MacArthur. She managed a respectable 15th place in the Proto class, while her fellow team-mate and future business partner Mark Turner did rather better in fifth. Their participation seemed to pave the way for other Brits, with 11 *rostbifs* signing up in 1999 and six in 2001, among them British sailor Brian Thompson. He was narrowly pipped at the post in the second leg when the Frenchman Yannick Bestaven slipped inland of him to snatch first place by 27 minutes. But another UK sailor, Simon Curwen, came second overall, giving the best performance of any Brit in the history of the race.

The number of boats taking part, meanwhile, has steadily risen in the past few years back to the highs of the 1980s. From a low of just 39 boats in 1995, the race hit a record 70 boats in 1999. The potential for accidents on such a busy start line and the difficulties in keeping track of so many competitors persuaded the organisers to restrict the fleet to 55 for 2001. That number was swollen to 60 when they decided to include five

> **❝NOT MUCH WAS SAID ABOUT THAT FIRST MINI-TRANSAT. A HOSTILE SILENCE SHROUDED THE RACE. EVERYONE WAS AGAINST IT…❞**
>
> Daniel Gilard on early attitudes towards the dangerous Mini-Transat

**above** Fancy spending 24 hours a day sailing on your ear non-stop with no-one to give you a break? Ellen MacArthur is one of the few British sailors to have competed in the Mini-transat in recent years.

unsuccessful applicants who turned up for the start anyway and were threatening to compete as unofficial entries. One thing you can never accuse Mini sailors of is lack of determination.

But whether there are 39 or 70 boats taking part, racing such a tiny boat singlehanded across 6437km (4000 miles) of ocean is always going to carry a high level of risk. Fatalities are therefore not uncommon. Over the 25 years that the race has been running, the Mini-Transat has claimed an average of one life for every two starts and, despite the organizers' efforts to raise safety standards, the risks remain.

After the two lives lost in the first race, in 1981 Christian Masicot ran aground on the Lizard and was killed *en route* to Penzance. That same year Steve Callahan's yacht *Napoleon Solo* sank two days after leaving the Canaries. The American took to his liferaft and survived for 76 days on a diet of fresh fish before eventually reaching the West Indies. Two more sailors were lost in 1991: Marie-Agnes Peron, whose boat was wrecked off Santander after rescue services failed to reach her, and Philippe Graber, whose boat was discovered off Fuerteventura in the Canaries with no-one on board.

## Fear of falling

The fear of falling overboard is ever present. Antoine Mayerat described how his worst nightmare turned to reality on the 1999 race. "At four in the morning the boat broaches, the autopilot is jammed, I zip on my survival suit and jump on deck. I hear the mast groaning and it cracks sharply! I take the helm, right the boat and go to check the damage. A lower shroud has snapped and the mast is dangerously bent. I quickly go about to ease the strain. Slight panic: what should I do? I'm about 160 miles from land and I can only sail in one direction. I'm tired and I'm having trouble clearing my mind to make the right decision. Eventually I decide to replace the broken shroud with a strop. I head towards the foot of the mast to climb up but a wave bigger than the rest sweeps the deck and makes me slip overboard. I am in the water, connected by my lifeline. Quickly, very quickly, I climb back on board and lean over the stern to vomit with fear…"

But the big watershed in boat safety happened after the 1993 debacle. Soon after the start the fleet was decimated by 50-knot winds and enormous seas. Twelve boats were abandoned and the experienced French skipper Pascal Leys disappeared, presumed to have fallen overboard in the Gulf of Gascoigne. The race was cancelled and most of the boats headed back to port.

The death of yet another sailor and the loss of so many boats (although most of the abandoned yachts were later saved) forced the organisers to tighten up the safety regulations yet again. The following year the minimum stability of the boats was increased, all entrants were required to carry a storm jib, trysail and sea anchor, and the yachts' maximum draught was reduced from 2.5 to 2m (8ft 3in/6ft 7in), based on the theory that deep fin keels are more prone to capsizing. Skippers were also supplied with survival suits, two lifejackets and an ARGOS transponder, which automatically tracked and transmitted their positions. Another development in the wake of 1993 was the creation of La Compagnie de Pascal Leys in memory of the sailor who died during that race. This non-profit making organisation loans safety gear to skippers who can't afford to buy it themselves.

Despite all these precautions, tragedy struck yet again in 1995 when Olivier Vatinet's yacht, *Bout d'Horizon*, was picked up north of Madeira. Vatinet was nowhere to be seen and the last entry in the log was from four days before. A similar fate befell the Italian Roberto Varinelli in 2001 when he disappeared during the first leg. His *Metallurgica Calvi* was discovered sailing under autopilot with no skipper on board. Little wonder that the race has developed a reputation for being one of the riskiest races on the circuit.

But it's not all danger and adrenaline, as Andrew Cape, 17th in the 1999 race, recalls. The routine of singlehanding can become monotonous in the extreme. "To relieve the boredom, I would think of anything and everything. It's amazing the things that come back to you when you are totally alone. Childhood memories that I hadn't thought of for 30 years came back crystal clear. I would sing songs, go through the stories of films I have seen,

## MINI RULES

Maximum length
6.5m (21ft)
Maximum beam
3m (10ft)
Maximum draught
2m (6ft 7in)
Minimum average freeboard
750mm (30in)
Maximum water ballast
200 litres x 2
Minimum height of cockpit floor
150mm (6in) above waterline
Maximum number of sails
eight, including a storm jib
and a trysail
Compulsory navigation gear
compass, hand-held depth
sounder, sextant, binoculars
Compulsory safety gear
liferaft, survival pack, EPIRB,
flares, survival suit, lifelines,
jackstays, harness, lifejacket,
anchor (8kg/25lb), radar
reflector, foghorn, tricolour
masthead light, first aid kit,
sea anchor, sculling oar

anything to keep me awake. At one point I worked out how many times I would push my sunglasses up on my nose if for the rest of the race I did it once a minute every hour!

"I didn't really have a daily routine, everything was on demand. I ate when I needed to, repaired the breakages when they happened, slept when I couldn't keep my eyes open any longer and carried out the daily maintenance and tidying when I could leave the helm.

"Now I am here I can look back and say that I enjoyed the race but it is definitely a one-off for me. I am satisfied that I pushed the boat to its limit and she worked like a dream, but I do need my creature comforts. I wanted to play a game, read a book, watch a video."

### TRANSAT training ground

Like other singlehanded races, the Mini-Transat has to a large extent grown on the back of the big solo races such as the Vendée Globe and Around Alone. It's a great test bed for sailors and sponsors alike, with more affordable budgets and easier access – getting a 6.5m boat across the Atlantic is an altogether more manageable project than sending an Open 60 around the world. It's also an opportunity for skippers to clock up the mileage required as conditions of entry to other races.

The result, according to one Mini sailor, is that the class is to ocean racing "what carting is for Formula 1 racing", with many of the top names starting off on the smaller boats. The Mini-Transat's roll of honour includes Yves Parlier (1985 winner), Jean-Luc van den Heede (raced in 1977 and 79), Loïck Peyron (1979), Lionel Péan (1979), Isabelle Autissier (third in 1987), Laurent Bourgnon (1987), Thierry Dubois (1993 winner), Yvan Bourgnon (1995 winner) and of course Ellen MacArthur - all would go on to carve themselves reputations in the big ocean races such the Vendée Globe, Around Alone and Whitbread, but the Mini was their training ground.

This desire to emulate the great French sailing heroes of yesteryear has kept many a

> ## ❝MY DREAM WASN'T TO DIE HERE AMONGST THE WAVES, OR TO THRASH MY BOAT IN THE WINDS… ❞
>
> Antoine Mayerat on living the dream

Mini-Transat skipper at his self-imposed ordeal. Take Antoine Mayerat again. "I can't handle it any more. The sea is rejecting me, and my boat is giving up on me. My dream wasn't to die here amongst the waves, or to thrash my boat in the winds… I've realised I shouldn't have tried to live this dream… I've come to the end of what I can bear and my dream of imitating Peyron, Bourgnon or Moitessier will have to stay in my head, where I am capable of jumping over waves, fixing every breakage and sailing the boat flat out through the surf…"

The affordability of the class has also meant that it has become a hotbed of development and innovation. Unlike one-design racing, where the design of the boats is strictly controlled and the designer's job is to find loopholes in the class rules, the open concept of the Mini class encourages a much greater degree of experimentation. And, because of the gruelling nature of the race, theories are soon put to the test in no uncertain terms. Conveniently, what works on a 6.5m boat can often be applied to a 60-footer (18.27m), which means the Minis have often been at the forefront of monohull development, whether it is with water ballast, canting keels, twin rudders, Kevlar sails or articulating bowsprits.

Things have certainly moved on from the early days when most of the boats were production cruisers, often radically modified to perform better or to conform to the race rules - including being mercilessly truncated to fit the 6.5m (21ft) length limit. The famous Muscadet class designed by Philippe Harlé was an early favourite, along with the Dufour T7 and the Serpentaires. And if you couldn't afford to buy it, then you could always build it, with plywood and hard-chined hulls being the order of the day among the homebuilders.

### Lighter and faster

But such amateurism was fated not to last long. Boats in the Proto class particularly have become increasingly sophisticated, with bigger and bigger rigs – 50sqm (540sqft) of upwind sail and 100sqm (1080sqft) off the wind are not uncommon – and lighter and lighter hulls (under a ton fully laden is most sailors' target). Norton Smith, winner of the

**above** The Swiss sailor Yvan Bourgnon is one of only two non-French race winners. His 800kg (1784lb) *Omapi-Saint Brevin* was the lightest boat in the fleet in 1995.

1979 race, started the trend with his water-ballasted *American Express* designed by Tom Wylie. Her plumb bow and flat-bottomed hull would soon become the norm, giving maximum waterline length with almost dinghy-like performance. And, as the rule governing the maximum length excluded rudders, twin stern-hung rudders, angled in opposite directions to give better control when heeled, were soon adopted by most boats.

Yves Parlier raised the stakes further in 1985 with his all-carbon fibre *Aquitaine,* which he built to a design by Jean Berret. The yacht had one of the first ever carbon fibre masts and weighed around a tonne – a remarkable achievement at that time. Despite being penalized 16 hours for taking a shortcut through the Raz de Sein, Parlier narrowly won in a dramatic neck-and-neck finish with a double-handed yacht (an experiment first tried in 1983 and abandoned in 1989). It would take another 10 years for Yvan Bourgnon, in 1995, to reduce the winning boat's weight to 800kg (1764lb), with his *Omapi-Saint Brévin.*

Innovation continued in the 1990s, with Michel Desjoyeaux trying out the first ever canting keel to be used for racing in 1991. The idea was soon applied with great success to the Open 60s in the Vendée Globe and elsewhere and has since become virtually the norm. More recently, developments have focused on various types of bowsprits, with Thierry Dubois experimenting with an articulated pole and others with telescopic systems.

The danger with all this cutting edge development was not just that the boats might become unsafe but that many skippers would be priced out of competition. In common with other singlehanded races, the original ideals of unrestricted competition which are so close to most singlehanders' hearts inevitably clashed with the realities of running a successful, and acceptably safe, race. The more successful and high profile the event becomes, greater sums of money become available, and the stakes are raised ever higher. It's a self-perpetuating scenario in which competitors may be willing to take unacceptable risks to

**below** Despite breaking his mast in gales three days before the finish line, Sebastien Magnen won first place in 24 hours and 15 hours in 1999.

succeed and where money can always be used to buy that half knot of extra speed.

The solution for the Mini-Transat, as with other races, was to put further limits on the type of boats allowed to race and, by extension, on the amounts spent on those boats. Maximum measurements for beam and draught were set, along with minimum freeboard height; mast height was restricted; water ballast was limited, first to 300 litres (300kg) and then 200 litres (200kg); watertight bulkheads were made compulsory; titanium keels were banned, as were carbon fibre masts, and, eventually, Kevlar sails.

## Experience required

Over the years the skippers' qualifications and experience have also come under scrutiny.

Initially a minimum of 800km (500 miles) singlehanded racing was required, but in 2001 this was raised to 1600km (1000 miles) of non-race solo sailing plus 1600km (1000 miles) of solo racing, including 800km (500 miles) non-stop. Traditionally, skippers qualify by participating in other Mini events such as the Mini-Fastnet, the Trans-Gascoigne, and the Mini-Pavois. Despite these stringent entry requirements, 120 hopefuls applied for 55 places in the 1999 Mini-Transat and the 2001 race was similarly oversubscribed.

Another attempt to level the playing field and provide a more affordable option for skippers not intent on joining the technology race was the creation of a one-design class specifically designed for the contest. The Coco was introduced for the

**above** Better known for their successful round-the-world designs, Groupe Finot also dabble in the small stuff, including Phlippe Vicariot's 1989 winner, *Thom Pousse*.

1985 event, leading to a race-within-a-race. Designed by Philippe Harlé, some 80 boats were launched. By 1995, however, the Coco had become outdated and was replaced by the Pogo, a design by Pierre Rolland based on Dubois's 1993 winning boat *Amnesty International.*

Although both designs were successful in their own right and provided a high standard of competition within the class, none has ever won the race outright. The best result by a Coco was Laurent Bourgnon's second place in 1987. First Pogo over the line in 2001 was the intriguingly-named *My Workplace* in 9th place – more than two days behind the first placed Proto – followed by two more Pogos in 10th and 11th places.

In an attempt to broaden the race's appeal, in 1983 two-man teams were allowed to compete. Nearly a third of the entries in that year's race were doubles, with the Thelier brothers finishing second on the first leg. But despite this early success, no double team ever won overall first place and the idea was abandoned after 1989.

In its 25-year history, the Mini-Transat has enjoyed its fair share of drama and hilarity, and 1987 was no exception. That was the year that future BOC (Around Alone) and Vendée Globe star Isabelle Autissier proved that even the best sailors can make mistakes. Despite leading at the end of the first leg to the Canaries, Autissier couldn't find the finish line and lost her first place to a two-handed Coco crew who could! Three weeks later, Laurent Bourgnon, sailing an ultra-lightweight Coco, slipped over the second leg finish line just ahead of Gilles Chiorri and his *Proto Exa.* Chiorri's combined leg one and leg two results were better, however, and he became the first overall winner not to have won either of the legs outright.

## A close run thing

Six years later, it was not only the bad weather that made the news. While most of the 1993 Mini-Transat fleet were either being airlifted to safety or recalled back into harbour, one lone sailor plugged on regardless. Thierry Dubois, on his *Amnesty International,* did not hear the recall

**❝…WHAT CARTING IS TO FORMULA 1 RACING…❞**

A sailor compares the Mini-Transat to the big ocean races

and battled through the storm to the first stop in Madeira. It must have been a close run thing, but it did win him first place. The second leg was the fastest in the race's history, with a force five wind pushing the fleet to St Maarten at an average speed of nearly eight knots. Dubois would not fare so well in the 1996–7 Vendée Globe, when he was plucked from his sinking yacht in the same rescue mission that saved Tony Bullimore.

Another man who proved he had the Mini spirit was Antonio Pedro Da Cruz. Having lost a rudder in the early stages of the 2001 race, he pulled into Portugal for repairs. A few days later he set off in chase of the rest of the fleet, only to collide with a freighter. Miraculously, he was unharmed and carried on to Lanzarote regardless, arriving less than 24 hours before the start of the next leg. Halfway across to the finish in Brazil, however, Da Cruz was dismasted and had to set up a jury rig. Despite meeting headwinds 800km (500 miles) from land, he made it into the port of Belem in Portugal unaided – albeit somewhat further south than he had intended.

Devised by a sailor for sailors, the Mini-Transat is in every sense a salty race. It has also reflected the concerns of sailors everywhere, for their environment, working conditions and the plight of others. This in turn has been echoed in the names of their boats. As well as the usual colourful medley of sponsors' names, many of the names emblazoned on the boats' hulls carry more socially and environmentally aware messages. Thus in 2001 the fleet included: *Pour Enfants 2000, Children Action, Marins Sans Frontieres, Lighthouse Life Foundation, Pour Que l'Ocean Reste Bleu* (So That the Sea Stays Blue) and *Reduction du Temps de Travail* (Reduction in Working Hours). Commercial sponsors included longstanding Mini backers Aquarelle.Com with no less than three boats in the top 10, several French regions, *Jazz Magazine,* builders Pierric Taffet and the French Public Works bureau.

While the big, round-the-world singlehanded races make the headlines, the Mini-Transat is often where those within the sport look for innovation and cutting-edge developments. For it is a race that pushes the limits of boat technology and human endurance to the extreme – and often beyond.

**above** The fleet leaves La Rochelle at the start of the 2001 Mini-Transat, destination Brazil. Leading the group is Grégoire Comby's *Calle Ocho Café Cubano* which finished 46th out of 60 starters.

Dismasted in the 1990–1 solo round-the-world race, forced to abandon ship in 1994–5, retired in 1996–7 and capsized in 1998–9 – Isabelle Autissier is nothing if not persistent. Her sailing career looks like a series of disasters punctuated by brief glimpses of genius. Yet, despite completing only one of her four attempted round-the-world races, the former engineer has impressed with her fortitude in the face of adversity, and become one of France's best known sailing figures.

Autissier is one of a long line of famous French single-handers who cut their teeth racing on the Mini-Transat. She won the first leg and came third overall in 1987, 10 years before Ellen MacArthur claimed an undistinguished 15th place.

For Autissier, as for many others, the Mini-Transat was the first step in what seemed a predestined path to the two big ocean races. It was there, too, that she found her sponsors, the Caisse d'Epargne bank and French region of Poitou-Charentes, who would stay with her from small beginnings through to the big time. "It was during the Mini-Transat that I became hooked on ocean racing," said Autissier. A year later she competed in the Figaro, that other great test bed of French solo sailors, finishing as the fourth newcomer in 1988 and 12th overall in 1989. The BOC was only a few feet of boat away.

Her first race set the tone. Dismasted off Tasmania in the 1990–1 BOC (Around Alone), Autissier limped into Sydney under jury rig. Her eventual seventh place was a testament to her tenacity – it also made her the first woman ever to complete a singlehanded, round-the-world race. It was not an experience she would have the pleasure of repeating. Although her radical Jean Berret design for the next race proved its potential soon after its launch, when it beat the New York to San Francisco record by a massive 14 days and went on to finish the first leg of the

1994–5 BOC in record time, Autissier's hopes of victory were dashed when the boat was dismasted twice during the second leg. Her new Finot-designed *PRB* was no luckier during the 1996–7 Vendée Globe. A damaged rudder forced her to pull in at Cape Town and, although she completed the course, she was disqualified from the official results. Disaster struck again in the 1998–9 BOC (Around Alone) when, despite starting the third leg in first place overall, *PRB* capsized in the Southern Ocean. She was lucky to escape with her life.

It's all a long way from the city childhood Autissier experienced in Paris with her architect father and four sisters. Family holidays in

## THERE ISN'T TIME TO BE AFRAID

Brittany gave the young Isabelle her first taste for sailing, and it seemed natural enough when she took up her studies in agricultural engineering that she should specialize in fisheries. Natural enough, too, that she should build her own aluminium monohull and take it to the West Indies in 1986 – sailing back across the Atlantic singlehanded. Three years and three singlehanded races later she gave up her job and committed herself to a full-time sailing career.

One of only three women to compete in the solo round-the-world circuit (the others are Catherine Chabaud and Ellen MacArthur), Autissier is adamant that it is no longer a male domain: "Of course ocean racing is a sport for women nowadays, even singlehanded racing. Technology has made so much progress that it's no longer necessary to have big muscles to sail a boat to its limits," she said. "Then, it's just a race... Even in the toughest moments you're not afraid, because there isn't time to be afraid." She, more than anyone, should know.

# ISABELLE autissier

# ROUTE
# du rhum

**left** After racing in every Route du Rhum, Florence Arthaud became the first woman to win a major single-handed ocean race in 1990.

# THE FREEDOM RACE

❝ Everything will be allowed, everything. In a few years' time, amateur yachtsmen will press a button and know their precise location. This will prevent many an accident. But first, we must throw open the windows of creation, which for decades a blinkered establishment has kept quite shut. ❞

Michel Etevenon, founder of the Route de Rhum, 1978

It is 28 November 1978. Two boats are approaching Guadeloupe at full pelt after sailing some 5633km (3500 miles) across the Atlantic. Frenchman Michel Malinovsky is on board the powerful 21m (70ft) monohull *Kriter V*, having taken the northern route from St Malo, while Canadian Mike Birch is sailing his diminutive 10.7m (35ft) trimaran *Olympus Photo*, a beneficiary of the trade winds further

**right** The French skipper Michel Malinovsky came second in a nail-bitingly close finish in the 1978 race.

south. Both have survived a series of gales during the first few days of the race which have decimated the fleet and killed one skipper. As they approach the island, Birch stays well offshore to climb upwind while Malinovsky cuts inside him and pulls into the lead in the light airs. As they near the finish line, the breeze picks up. *Olympus Photo* eases her sheets, rapidly gathers speed and starts gaining on *Kriter V*. Less than two miles from the finish, the trimaran romps past the monohull and goes on to cross the line to a wildly cheering crowd. After 23 days at sea, and despite taking totally different routes on totally different craft, just 98 seconds separate the two boats.

It was the perfect way to end the inaugural Route du Rhum race of 1978. The sensational closeness of the finish guaranteed massive publicity, while the disparity between the first two boats gave a clear signal that this was a race open to all – the "free" race the organizers had promised. After all, being well over 17.1m (56ft) long, *Kriter V* would not have qualified for the OSTAR under that race's recently revised rules, and yet she was beaten by the smallest trimaran in the fleet. The excitement of the finish alone made the Route du Rhum an instant popular hit

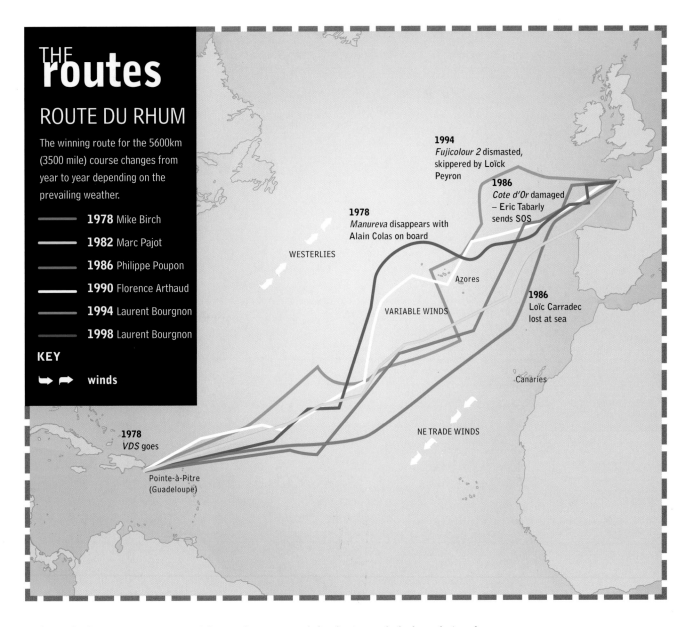

# THE routes

## ROUTE DU RHUM

The winning route for the 5600km (3500 mile) course changes from year to year depending on the prevailing weather.

—— **1978** Mike Birch
—— **1982** Marc Pajot
—— **1986** Philippe Poupon
—— **1990** Florence Arthaud
—— **1994** Laurent Bourgnon
—— **1998** Laurent Bourgnon

**KEY**

➡ ➡ **winds**

**1994**
*Fujicolour 2* dismasted, skippered by Loïck Peyron

**1986**
*Cote d'Or* damaged – Eric Tabarly sends SOS

**1978**
*Manureva* disappears with Alain Colas on board

WESTERLIES

Azores

**1986**
Loïc Carradec lost at sea

VARIABLE WINDS

Canaries

**1978**
*VDS* goes

NE TRADE WINDS

Pointe-à-Pitre (Guadeloupe)

and a media favourite – a reputation it has rarely failed to live up to in subsequent years.

It all started with that most controversial of boats, the four-masted behemoth *Club Méditerranée*, which Alain Colas entered in the 1976 OSTAR. Or even before that, with the 39m (128ft) *Vendredi Treize* that Jean-Yves Terlain brought to the 1972 race. Or the combination of both. The OSTAR organizers decided enough was enough and that competitors would be restricted to 17.1m (56ft) maximum length to maintain the spirit of the event. It was pure coincidence, of course, that this knocked out a large part of the European continental fleet.

The French were incensed. "*Liberté!*" they cried – freedom to sail whatever size boats they wanted; freedom to push the boundaries of technological innovation however far they would go; freedom to be the very best, without limits. Freedom to win. It was also what the sponsors wanted, it seemed. Bigger was better as far as they were concerned, as long as it caught the public's imagination – and if helped win a few races, too, then so much the better.

## Enter Mr Fixit

None was more aware of this than France's "Mr Fixit" Michel Etevenon, the man behind the high-profile campaigns of the various *Kriter* boats and, in particular, of the emerging star Olivier de Kersauson. Although not himself a sailor, Etevenon knew how to make an event attractive to competitors and media alike. It was clear to him that the more outrageous the boats, the greater the spectacle, and the greater the spectacle, the more the sponsors, and the more the sponsors, the more outrageous the boats, and so on. Why derail such a perfectly self-generating system?

The answer, Etevenon decided, was to come up with a new race, without limits. *Liberté* indeed, and *fraternité*, of course – and *égalité*, too, providing you could find the sponsors.

The route would be 5633km (3500 miles) from the port of St Malo in Brittany to Pointe-à-Pitre in the French *département* of Guadeloupe. "Too easy," said some. "Too French," said others. But Etevenon had the backing of a solid group of single-handers, also fed up with the increasingly constrained OSTAR regulations. Thus La Route du Rhum was born.

Some 38 Atlantic breaknecks gathered for the first start of the "transat of freedom" on 5 November 1978. Monohulls mixed it with multihulls, amateurs with professionals. All raced

in one class, without handicap system, regardless of size. Nearly half the entries bore the name of sponsors on their hulls, which was one in the eye for the OSTAR officials and their attempts to tone down the level of advertising. And whereas the OSTAR had banned shore-based routing, regarding it as a form of outside assistance, the new race allowed it – to the consternation of some of the skippers. As routing methods became more sophisticated, this would become an increasingly significant factor in a boat's success – or failure.

Many of the great names of ocean racing were there for the first event: Alain Colas on the legendary *Pen Duick IV* (re-named *Manureva*); Chay Blyth on *Great Britain IV*, on which he had won that year's Round Britain race; Olympic medallist Marc Pajot on the 22.9m (75ft) catamaran *Paul Ricard*; and future OSTAR winner Phil Weld on *Rogue Wave*. And there was the relatively unknown 20-year-old Florence Arthaud, who would go on to figure much more prominently in the history of the race.

**below** The controversial Alain Colas became the first victim of the Route du Rhum when he disappeared on board his legendary *Manureva* (ex-*Pen Duick IV*) in the very first race.

Significant, too, that Mike Birch was there, with his *Olympic Photo* (ex-*A-Cappela*). It was the slightly surreal sight of his modest trimaran *The Third Turtle* slipping into harbour just hours after the multi-million-franc *Club Méditerranée* in the 1976 OSTAR that put the last nail in the coffin of the big boats in that race. Birch has since become one of the most respected veterans of the Route du Rhum and the only skipper to have taken part in every race to date, recording one first, one third, two fourths, and one retirement.

The race got off to a dramatic start, with Pajot losing control of *Paul Ricard*'s spinnaker and mowing down a spectator yacht. Luckily no-one was hurt, but it was the end of the race for Pajot who was unable to make up the time lost making repairs. With a series of depressions hitting the fleet almost immediately with winds of over 50 knots, several other yachts retired with gear failure, among them Blyth on *Great Britain IV* and Pierre Fehlmann on *Great Britain III* (renamed *Disque d'Or*).

But the greatest drama of the race was yet to come. On 17 November the race office received an alarming message from Alain Colas. He was at the helm of the 20m (67ft) *Manureva*, Eric Tabarly's old trimaran in which he had won the 1972 OSTAR and had made his round-the-world record attempt in 1973–4; a trusted boat which he knew intimately. But Colas had still not fully recovered the use of his foot, almost torn off in an accident three years before. His radio message, although not an actual Mayday, suggested he was in trouble. "I am at the centre of the cyclone," he said. "There's no longer any sea; there's no longer any sky." And that was the last anyone heard of him. Despite a belated but extensive search by four Bréguet Atlantic aircraft, Colas and his beloved boat were never found. It was the end of a legend – and the start of many a myth.

### Where did you go *Manureva*?

As is often the case when a sailor disappears without trace, all kinds of stories have sprung up about what really happened to Colas, a man with many enemies and considerable financial problems. Could it have been a cover-up, some suggest, for him to escape his past and start a new life, incognito, elsewhere? Was he run down by a passing ship which either didn't realize what had happened or didn't report it? Or, more mundanely but more likely, was *Manureva* simply worn out from all her heroics and gave up after passing through the eye of the storm?

"Where did you go *Manureva*?" is the question many French sailors have been asking themselves ever since – all the more since the question was turned into the lyrics of a hit song by Alain Chamford and Serge Gainsbourg.

The race made the news again a few days later when Eugène Riguidel drove his *VSD* onto a reef near Antigua in the West Indies. And then there was that memorable finish. Although Etevenon could never have wished for that amount of carnage, let alone any loss of life, the tension of the race and its many dramas were a publicist's dream. La Route du Rhum had arrived – with a splash.

Not surprisingly, after the enormous publicity generated by the first race, an even larger fleet of yachts gathered for the start of the second Route du Rhum on 7 November 1982: 52 boats, more than half of which were catamarans. All the boats were fitted with the new ARGOS tracking system, and most of them bore the name of a sponsor on their hulls. And this time they were divided into classes according to length – already the much-vaunted freedom was being tempered by a few sensible rules. Even so, some 19 boats, more than a third of the fleet, would be forced to retire before the end of the race.

Many of the great names of ocean racing again came to test their mettle, including the legendary Eric Tabarly and a small but distinguished British contingent lead by Robin Knox-Johnston and Chay Blyth. Among those also entered was a man who was to make a mark far beyond the rarified world of solo racing: Marc Pajot. Success had come to him early when, aged 19, he won a silver medal at the 1972 Olympics in Kiel racing a Flying Dutchman. Two years later he and his brother Yves won the 505 world

> **I AM AT THE CENTRE OF THE CYCLONE…THERE'S NO LONGER ANY SEA; THERE'S NO LONGER ANY SKY**

Alain Colas during the first Route du Rhum

championship. And, just in case he became bored, in between the two, Pajot joined Eric Tabarly on *Pen Duick VI* for the 1973 Whitbread Round-the-World race.

Despite his disastrous start in the first Route du Rhum, he had devoted his energies to mounting a credible (though ultimately unsuccessful) challenge for the America's Cup in Fremantle in 1986.

With Paul Ricard now backing Tabarly and his revolutionary hydrofoil trimaran, Pajot turned up in *Elf Aquitaine*, a 20.1m (66ft) catamaran that had already garnered several trophies and had been fitted with an innovative carbon fibre wing mast for the Rhum.

And once again the race got off to a spectacular start. One of the more unusual entries was a 18m (60ft) long by 24m (80ft) wide proa sailed by Guy Delage. Instead of having an outrigger on the downwind side of the main hull like a conventional proa, *Rosières* had one on the windward side which could be filled with water to act as ballast. It was an ingenious arrangement and attracted a great deal of attention before and during the start. Unfortunately, though, a control line slipped just after the start and *Rosières* simply folded up and sank. Delage was rescued unharmed, but it was a poor – albeit somewhat comical – advertisement for his cause.

Meanwhile, strong winds ensured that the leaders belted past the first buoy off Cap Fréhel at up to 22 knots, with Englishman Rob James (Naomi James's husband) getting an early lead on his *Colt Cars GB*, only to be knocked back by Pajot. In fact, it was a promising start for all the Brits, with James, Blyth, and Knox-Johnston in the top five. But it was not to last. After injuring his arm, James suffered rig problems – and, on top of everything, he was feeling seasick for the first time in his life! He retired on the fifth day. He was followed two days later by Blyth, whose autopilot was playing up, and then Knox-Johnston announced he would have to pull in to Madeira to sort out some battery-charging problems. The British challenge was dead.

It was not all plain sailing for the French either. Barely past the start line, Florence Arthaud had to turn back for 48 hours to fix her autopilot

and sort out mast problems. The original "Mr Controversy", Jean-Yves Terlain – who had introduced the concept of jumbo-yachts to the world in the shape of *Vendredi Treize* – was dismasted on the second day. Even Tabarly had to pull in at Camaret to sort out his electrics.

It's an indication of how much boat technology had developed – and how dependent sailors had become on it – that so many of the retirements in 1982 were due to gear failure rather than structural breakages. Whereas in the 1960s and '70s Tabarly twice sailed half way across the Atlantic without autopilot and Knox-Johnston completed most of his circumnavigation with his Admiral self-steering gear out of action, modern sailing machines are more delicate and less forgiving creatures. Manhandling a 20-metre (65ft) catamaran for more than a few hours at a time is no joke and, unlike Knox-Johnston's sluggish but amenable

**left** After 23 days at sea, just 98 seconds separated *Olympus Photo* and *Kriter V* as they stormed into Guadaloupe at the end of the first race.

**below** The seemingly indestructible Eric Tabarly sent out the first SOS of his career durng the second Route du Rhum.

old ketch *Suhaili*, they will not self-steer for weeks on end. By definition such high-tech craft also cost a lot more to replace – a fact that skippers who have struggled for years to obtain sponsorship are no doubt acutely aware of.

## Bucking bronco

But there was also perhaps a human factor at play here. The great heroes of the 1960s and '70s no longer boasted quite the same degree of endurance – you might say masochism – that they once did. No-one seems to have told Figaro veteran Philippe Poupon any of this however. Despite losing part of *Fleury Michon VI*'s rudder, making the trimaran almost uncontrollable, Poupon manhandled his bucking bronco most of the way to Guadeloupe, leaving his hands and arms horribly bruised.

Even the meticulously prepared and well-funded Pajot was having his share of problems. Comfortably in the lead by the end of the first week, *Elf Aquitaine* developed major cracks on her main crossbeam where holes for the inspection hatches had been cut. At first it seemed as if Pajot would have to abandon the race – yet again – but, having made a temporary repair by winding a spare length of wire around the beam, he got his liferaft ready and carried on without telling anyone of this potentially fatal damage.

Pajot's decision to stay silent was a tactical one. With increasingly sophisticated communications between competitors and the race officers – and thus to other competitors and the media – it was all too easy for rivals to decipher each other's tactics and exploit them to their own advantage. And, just as wild animals tend to round on a wounded member of the pack, so competitors will push harder to beat a boat that shows signs of weakness. It's part of the psychological battle of any race, and in the case of ocean racing much of it is waged on the airwaves.

> ❝ I AM PERMANENTLY STRESSED OUT ABOUT CAPSIZING. IT'S HARD TO KEEP THE BOAT IN A GROOVE AMONG THESE ENORMOUS WAVES ❞
>
> Lionel Péan on his experience in the 1986 Route du Rhum

Pajot took the view that if the skippers snapping at his heels realized he had a serious structural problem they might be encouraged to push harder, which in turn would force him to push *Elf* harder and possibly lead to the boat collapsing. He only announced his problem publicly as he neared Martinique, where he pulled in for 35 minutes to attempt a repair. In fact, little more could be done in the time available and he carried on regardless to a convincing 18 day, one hour and 38 minute win – five days faster than Birch the year before.

And the speedy Canadian, where was he? Birch had performed a remarkable comeback on his 15m (49ft) catamaran *Vital* rising from 19th position by day eight to third place by the end of the race. But the biggest shock of the race was Bruno Peyron's 17.7m (58ft) catamaran *Jaz*. With her identical, parallel rigs on each hull, she was much mocked before the start of the race and written out of serious contention by most commentators. Peyron used her downwind ability to advantage, finishing second, just 10 hours behind Pajot's much larger *Elf*.

## Bigger and bigger

1986 was the year of the giants. Only 27 boats lined up for the start but, of those, 13 were over 22.3m (75ft) – nearly half the fleet as opposed to three of that size the previous year. Etevenon's strategy of allowing overt sponsorship was clearly working – all too well. For as the sponsorship levels increased, the leading boats grew bigger and bigger and more and more expensive, while the smaller boats were left behind, literally. And, as the stakes increased, it became harder and harder to find sponsors prepared to put in the amount of money needed for a credible (ie visible) campaign. As for the amateurs, they had dropped out of sight almost completely. No surprise, then, that the fleet had dwindled to almost half the size it had been in 1982.

Not only that, but the race was acquiring an unhealthy rate of retirements and breakages. As the boats became ever more extreme, it became a question of whether the skippers could make it to the end without breaking something. As author David Pelly put it, by the late 1980s, "the sport of racing big multihulls singlehanded had become a more dangerous activity than Grand Prix motor racing. Fast, spectacular, and very risky".

And the 1986 Route du Rhum was no exception. Within minutes of the start, Loïck Peyron was dismasted and had to head back to attempt to find a replacement; Tony Bullimore pulled into Brest after hitting a piece of flotsam, only to lose his *Apricot* on the rocks when a salvage vessel failed to appear. And there were many more – in the end, only half the fleet made it to the finish.

Lionel Péan described the conditions in Thierry Ranou's *La Route du Rhum*: "I am permanently stressed out about capsizing. It's hard to keep the boat in a groove among these enormous waves. I spend almost the whole time stuck in the pod helming and have a minimum of sail up to keep the boat manoeuvrable…. I'm expecting to capsize at any moment."

But the most surprising call the race organizers received was from Tabarly, racing his foil-trimaran *Côte d'Or*. "I cannot make any headway," he said. "One of *Côte d'Or*'s floats is damaged, I think someone will have to come and get me." It was the first SOS the hardy Tabarly had ever sent out. Things were looking bad.

Worse was yet to come. Loïck Caradec was reporting gusts of over 50 knots on his 26m (85ft) *Royale*. Unable to reduce the windage of his wing sail, fixed at 60sq m (650sqft), he was in danger of capsizing under bare poles. The following day the ARGOS tracking system showed *Royale* drifting. A French navy aircraft was despatched and discovered the boat upside down. Florence Arthaud, the competitor closest to the scene, sailed back to look for Caradec, but there was no sign of life and, after taking a few photos, she carried on. The Route du Rhum had lost one of its best-loved competitors.

In the end, as the giant cats dropped out of the race one by one, it was Philippe Poupon who clinched victory, setting a remarkable new record of 14 days, 15 hours, and 57 minutes in his 23m (75ft) *Fleury Michon VIII*. It was a sign of the times that this powerful trimaran, designed by British multihull guru Nigel Irens, was by then

regarded as one of the smaller boats. It was significant too that Poupon claimed to have spent most of his time at the navigation table rather than on deck controlling the boat. "Actually, I think I'm lazy," Thierry Rannou quotes him as saying. "That's why I don't helm much. I've spent 70 per cent of my time inside my wheelhouse. In an event like this, preparation counts a great deal. You have to do a lot of work before in order to do nothing during."

**above** Despite his catamaran *Elf Aquitaine* starting to break up in mid-Atlantic, Olympic medalist Marc Pajot won the second race by a convincing margin.

**above** France's most prolific
sailor, Philippe Poupon, smashed
Pajot's record by nearly four
days on his *Fleury Michon VIII*
in 1986.

Indeed Poupon had spent months
overseeing the design and construction of *Fleury
Michon VIII*. With weather routing playing an
increasingly important role, he had also set up a
telex link with his router, weather wizard Jean-
Yves Bernot, to ensure that none of his rivals
could eavesdrop on their exchanges.

Aside from an ever-increasing reliance of
weather advice, one of the most memorable
events of the race itself, however, was the
extraordinary recovery staged by Loïck Peyron.
Despite seeing his mast collapse "like overcooked
spaghetti" at the very start, he headed back into
harbour, fitted a new mast (nicely *"al dente"* this
time), and five days later set off in a helter-skelter
chase after the rest of the fleet. Despite his late
start he finished in fifth place, three-and-a-half
days behind Poupon, and just 16 minutes slower
than Pajot the year before!

## Speed freaks

Ten years after the much-derided OSTAR
decision to limit the size of competing boats, the
organizers of the Route du Rhum bowed to the
inevitable. If their race wasn't to turn into an
elitist gathering of over-financed speed freaks,
they would have to restrict the size of boats
taking part – it was the only way to broaden the
appeal of the event again. The dream of a no-
holds-barred race had run its course. The French
experiment, while it ultimately proved to be a
blind alley, had nevertheless produced a superb
new singlehanded race which now
complemented rather than conflicted with the
ever more regulated OSTAR. It had pushed
technology to its current limit and discovered
what was sustainable and "human". From 1990
onwards, the race would be restricted to boats up
to a maximum of 18.3m (60ft) long.

The next edition of the race would also break another enduring characteristic of singlehanded races: male dominance. After doggedly turning up for every Route du Rhum since its inception, Arthaud finally reaped her reward in 1990. And, unlike Poupon in the previous race, she would win very much at the helm of her *Pierre 1er*.

In fact, her crossing was marked by a series of problems. First her weatherfax broke down, depriving her of detailed weather information, then her autopilot conked out. Determined to keep going, she lashed herself to the helm and steered for two days through a northbound depression. But then her electrical system gave up completely. It was every single-hander's nightmare: no autopilot, no weather forecasts and no contact with the outside world – including that all-important router. Even when she did eventually get her generator and one of the autopilots working again, she had to limit herself to using them for just three hours a day in order to conserve her fuel, which had become contaminated.

On top of all that, Arthaud fell ill. At the start of the race she was already suffering from health problems and halfway across she started to haemorrhage. Not surprisingly, she contemplated giving up and pressing the ARGOS emergency button. Instead, she kept going and in doing so achieved her own kind of "state of grace", as the great Moitessier would have it. Deprived of almost all technical assistance, she resorted to more rudimentary seamanship, steering by hand and reading the weather from the clouds.

She arrived at Pointe-à-Pitre just happy to have survived. Having lost radio contact a week before, she had no idea where she was in the race and could hardly believe her ears when, approaching Guadeloupe, a press plane informed that she was in the lead. Poupon was thundering down from the north having gambled on the higher route, but even a last blast of speed wasn't enough for him to catch up with Arthaud. He would fight it out with Laurent Bourgnon and Mike Birch for the next few places, with Birch throwing away second and then third place by staying too close to land. Bourgnon himself was lucky to be there, having sustained a severe leak through one of his centreboard cases which kept

him bailing out for most of the crossing. Learning from Pajot's example in 1982, he kept quiet about his difficulties to keep the pack at bay. Sadly, Claude Bistoquet, the first Guadeloupean to enter the race, retired.

The race undoubtedly belonged to Arthaud, who became the first woman to win a major singlehanded race. And what a way to have done it. "I was tired at the start, I was still tired in the middle, and by the end I was even more tired," she said. "Even those who knew I was capable of winning must be shocked." Of the race itself she was later to recount: "I won because I have matured in my way of sailing. I thought about things without worrying what the others were up to; I realized it was better to take a reef in half an hour too early than too late. I put in some good tacks because I felt at ease with my boat, with being on the water. It's the most extraordinary of races, and the most complete."

By 1994 the weather routers had become an essential tool in the ocean racers' box of tricks. And they played a particularly crucial part in that year's Route du Rhum, one of the roughest on record. For a start, there was Florence to contend with – not the previous race's winner, who for the first time in its history was not at the startline, but the hurricane which had coincidentally been

**below** Florence Arthaud receives her prize at the end of the 1990 race, which she won despite gear failure and health problems.

**above** Claude Bistoquet, the first skipper from Guadaloupe to compete in the race, proved unlucky. He was forced to retire in 1990, and capsized in 1994.

**right** *Fujicolour II* was one of the most successful examples of the new generation of 18m (60ft) trimarans, but lost it all thanks to a short length of Spectra rigging breaking. during the 1994 race.

given her name. (It was almost as if no Route du Rhum would be complete without a Florence of some description taking part.) Hurricane Florence turned out to be all puff and no stamina (unlike Ms Arthaud) but it was followed by a series of depressions which decimated the fleet. The only way to sail safely was to skirt around the worst of the bad weather in the north without losing all the wind by heading too far south.

Right from the start the two favourites for the race were Loïck Peyron and Laurent Bourgnon. Peyron came fresh from winning the 1992 OSTAR on Mike Birch's *Fujicolor II*, whose performance he had transformed by fitting a wing mast and foils, giving him, he claimed, an additional six knots. Thanks to a ripped mainsail, Bourgnon came second to Peyron in 1992, but with extended hulls and a lighter mast his *Primagaz* was meticulously well prepared – and going faster than ever with its foils removed!

## Flying Fujicolour

As predicted, the two trimarans sped off ahead of the fleet, with Peyron staying narrowly ahead of

Bourgnon. After just three days the pair were already 70 miles ahead of the rest, with *Fujicolour II* seeming to stretch her lead. But then their tactics changed. As the boats approached a depression, under the direction of their routers each took a radically different path. Advised by Richard Silvani of *Météo France* – the French weather station – Bourgnon suddenly headed south while Peyron, routed by Pierre Lasnier, stayed on the northern route with the intention of weathering the storm and maintaining his progress westward. It was a gamble and, like most gambles, it was the unpredictable factor that ultimately decided the outcome.

A few hours after *Primagaz* had headed south to avoid the storm, *Fujicolor II* was in the thick of it when a short length of Spectra cordage on the running backstay gave way. It was enough to bring the whole mast down and, with it, Peyron's hopes of winning the race. A multi-million franc campaign had foundered on a dodgy bit of string. It seemed too ironic to be true.

Bourgnon, meanwhile, was not having an easy time of it: "It's hell here," he told race

**above** With Loïck Peyron and *Fujicolor II* out of contention, Laurent Bourgnon went on to a record-breaking victory on his remarkable *Primagaz* in 1994.

control. "I've just nose-dived under bare poles. Better warn [Paul] Vatine [lying behind him in second place]."

Both men survived, but real doubts were raised as to why Peyron had continued on such a northerly course rather than taking diversionary action as Bourgnon had. The implication was that it had been his router's idea and that, left to his own devices, Peyron would have headed south along with everyone else. The incident highlighted the problems of over-dependence on what, in the final analysis, is theoretical advice coming from people often with no first-hand experience of sailing in such conditions. What may appear reasonable on paper does not necessarily make sense on water. Their judgement is mainly based on theory; they do not have the skipper's nose, the on-board sense of what is actually happening minute by minute on the water. A successful strategy marries the two skills together – though ultimately the judgement on which direction to steer the boat always remains with the skipper. It is the person on the water who pays the price for any mistakes.

Bourgnon went on to win the race convincingly, with the under-rated Paul Vatine on his *Region Haute Normandie* coming second. The surprise of the race was how well the monohulls fared. For the first time since *Kriter V* in 1978, monohulls featured in the top four, with Yves Parlier shadowing Vatine most of the way across in *Cacolac d'Aquitaine* and Alain Gautier coming in soon after with *Bagages Supérior*. It seemed that the heavy weather had favoured the monohulls, which kept ploughing a steady furrow while the multihulls were being thrown about.

After hurricane Florence, it was hurricane Mitch which hit the fleet in 1998. Numbers were up again, with 37 boats taking part – for the first time almost evenly divided between multihulls and monohulls. There was tragedy before the race had even started as the Open 60 *Coyote* was swept onto the rocks off Cherbourg, killing a TV cameraman who was on board at the time. Laurent Bourgnon, Mike Birch, Alain Gautier, and Paul Vatine all made it safely to the start line,

**above** Fresh from his scrape in the 1996–7 Vendée Globe, where he was rescued by Pete Goss, Rafaël Dinelli staged a stunning comeback in the 1998 Route du Rhum, finishing third in the monohull class.

however. And it was the first Route du Rhum for a young British woman who would go on to make a name for herself in the next Vendée Globe. The 22-year-old Ellen MacArthur was the youngest person in the fleet and one of only four women. She was sailing the Open 50 *Kingfisher*, ex-*Aqua Quorum*, in which Pete Goss had saved Raphaël Dinelli's life in the 1996 Vendée Globe. It must have brought back a few memories for Dinelli, who was there on his *Sodebo-Savourons la Vie*, with its revolutionary unstayed wing mast.

After wiping out large tracts of Central America, Hurricane Mitch ploughed its way through the Route du Rhum fleet during the first part of the race, knocking out several of the monohulls. All made it back to land safely, but Eric Dumont cut himself severely with a knife while climbing the mast of his *Le Havre 2000* to make repairs. Despite bandaging himself up, he passed out for several hours and had to be taken on board a British supply ship for medical treatment. He eventually made it back to his boat and sailed it to safety.

### Calm after the storm

After the storm, the calm – and too little wind, most race skippers will agree, is worse than a little too much. Taking advantage of every subtle wind shift and sea current is the key to getting ahead in light weather. That means endless sail changes and sheet adjustments, it usually means helming by hand as autopilots are not able to respond to such nuances, and it means constantly keeping an eye on the bigger weather pattern. It's nervewracking work, as skippers try to squeeze every last tenth of a knot out of a boat. It's also an important time for the routers, whose advice more than ever can make or break a race.

Bourgnon was certainly aware of that, and for his 1998 campaign – prepared with his usual meticulous thoroughness – he set up a 24-hour routing bureau in Paris which processed information from routers on both sides of the Atlantic to ensure a constant flow of information to *Primagaz*. Bourgnon is said to have undergone hypnosis before the race to optimize his sleeping

patterns and apparently told journalists he had sawn down the handle of his toothbrush and cut the label off his oilskin to keep weight down – all apocryphal stories, but which nonetheless go to the heart of a man who leaves as little as possible to chance.

As usual the fleet split into southerners and northerners, with Francis Joyon pushing the idea to an extreme by sailing *Banque Populaire* straight to Morocco, then through the Canaries, and west to Guadeloupe. He succeeded in avoiding the worst of the calm weather high

> ## " IT'S HELL OUT HERE. I'VE JUST NOSE-DIVED UNDER BARE POLES "

Laurent Bourgnon and his *Primagaz* have a rough time during the 1994 race

pressure area, but the extra speed he gained never made up for the extra distance he had to cover.

In the race for first place Alain Gautier and his brand-new trimaran *Brocéliande* were giving Bourgnon and the eight-year-old *Primagaz* a run for their money. Unbeknown to his rival, Gautier's boat had collided with a whale, and the time lost trying to make a repair would cost him dearly. He staggered over the finish line, exhausted, just three hours after Bourgnon.

There was a scuffle in third and fourth place as it emerged that Franck Cammas had overtaken Marc Guillemot under cover of darkness as the two skippers passed Terre Basse. The race rules state that all boats must switch their navigation lights on at night – not only to be safe but also because unlit boats have an unfair advantage in not being seen by their opponents. Although Cammas was given a 15-minute penalty, it was not enough to change the finishing order.

Back among the monohulls, another low pressure system was ripping through the fleet, flattening Thomas Coville's *Aquitaines Innovation* and ripping *Kingfisher*'s sails. Coville and his boat

**below** Despite setting a new 24-hour speed record, Francis Joyon's extreme southerly route proved too long in the 1998 race.

picked themselves up, shook themselves, and carried on to be the first monohull over the line. Despite problems with her canting keel, Ellen MacArthur also steered her damaged yacht to a popular first place in the smaller monohull class, ahead of several much faster Open 60s and multihulls.

A record number of boats entered the 2002 race, requiring the start to be spread across two days, with the 18 ORMA (Ocean Racing Multihull Association) 18.29m (60ft) trimarans leaving a day after the rest of the 59-strong fleet. Many of the great names of singlehanded racing were there, including the 71-year old Mike Birch, taking part in the race for the seventhth (and probably last) time on Philippe Monnet's old Open 60 the ex-*UUNET*. Also there were Monnet himself, Alain Gautier, Loïck Peyron, Michel Desjoyeaux, Giovanni Soldini, and Yvan Bourgnon in the big trimaran class, with Ellen MacArthur, Mike Golding, and the French favourite Roland "Bilou" Jourdain in the Open 60s.

But storm-force winds turned the first week of the race into a windy rout as almost half the fleet were forced to pull out either through capsize, dismasting, or structural damage. It began on the very first start day when Figaro veteran Sébastien Josse dismasted his Open 60 *VMI* just minutes after rounding the first buoy off Cap Fréhel. The following day Franck Cammas's 18.29m (60ft) trimaran *Groupama* capsized at night and was rammed by Jean Le Cam's *Bonduelle*, taking two race favourites out of contention. It was all too much for Vendée Globe veteran Bertrand de Broc who pulled into harbour and announced he was retiring from singlehanded racing for good.

Meanwhile, the carnage continued, with two monohulls colliding with passing freighters, Francis Joyon's 18.29m (60ft) tri capsizing off Cape Finisterre and *Gitana X* losing the top of her mast. They were followed by two more big tris with big names (Monnet and Bourgnon) which both capsized, while Peyron's top-billed *Fujifilm* broke up due to the power of the waves. Others (including Soldini and Gautier) retired with damage to the boats. And it didn't stop when the bad weather stopped: just 1213km (754

miles) from the finish and leading the fleet, Stève Ravussin capsized his big tri *TechnoMarine*.

The total number of "abandons" was 28, and of the original fleet of 18 big tris which wowed the crowds at St Malo, only three made it to the finish at Guadeloupe. Not surprisingly, in the aftermath of such mayhem, questions were being asked about why these expensive multihulls had succumbed so quickly to the bad weather.

## A landmark victory

The monohulls fared much better, with Jourdain, Golding, and MacArthur forging ahead of their rivals. Once "Bilou" was forced to pull into Madeira for sail repairs, however, it was left to the two Brits to fight a close duel, with MacArthur eventually pulling ahead as Golding struggled with capricious spinnakers.

MacArthur's victory in Class 2 made her not only the first British sailor to win the race but also set a new monohull record. Her time of 13 days, 13 hours and 31 minutes was 53 hours faster than the previous record set by Yves Parlier in 1994, and prompted the race committee president Sylvie Viant to describe her as "the greatest female solo sailor of all time".

Meanwhile, despite having made a "pit stop" at Madeira to repair damage to one of his floats, Desjoyeaux was the first of the remaining three Class 1 trimarans to reach Pointe à Pitre, in a time of 13 days, seven hours and 53 minutes — only six hours faster than MacArthur and nearly 24 hours slower than the 1998 record. It was truly a win by attrition.

Following the death of Michel Etevenon in the summer of 2001, the 2002 race was dedicated to the memory of the man who created one of the great success stories of singlehanded racing. For it was undoubtedly his combination of visionary inspiration and PR acumen that, from that very first start 25 years ago, established the Route du Rhum as one of the classic ocean races. The race that eschewed rules may have collected a few along the way, but it still remains a triumphant celebration of that ultimate freedom: the freedom of the oceans.

**❝THE GREATEST FEMALE SOLO SAILOR OF ALL TIME❞**

Route du Rhum Committee President, Sylvie Viant, on Ellen MacArthur's victory in the 2002 race

**left** Ellen MacArthur's win in the 15m (50ft) monohull class in 1998 confirmed her position as one of the rising stars of singlehanded racing.

Mike Birch's racing career proves two things: that size doesn't count and that size does count. Let me explain. What astonished the pundits at the end of that landmark OSTAR in 1976 was the relative size of the little trimaran that slid into Newport harbour under the towering masts of Alain Colas's jumbo-yacht *Club Méditerranée*. How could the 9.5m (31ft) *Third Turtle* have come so close to beating the mighty 72m (236ft) four-master?

Two years later, when Birch reappeared at the first Route du Rhum and performed the same trick again – only better this time, beating Michel Malinovsky's powerful monohull *Kriter V* with his diminutive catamaran *Olympus Photo* by a mere 98 seconds – the same pundits threw up their hands and said: "Where the hell did he come from?!"

The moral of the story is that while David might beat Goliath, it's still Goliath who makes the headlines. Especially when Goliath is a megalomaniac Frenchman and David is a mild-mannered Canadian.

Birch came to sailing late, having already lived several other lives. Born in Vancouver in 1931, after university Birch worked in a gold mine, then on an oil rig, before trying his hand as a cowboy. His first taste of the ocean was working as crew on various cargo ships, travelling to Europe and Africa, before settling in Britain. There he met his wife Josephine, with whom he had two children, and started working as a delivery skipper.

He was over 40 when he entered his first race, the Aurore (Figaro), in 1972. Bitten by the bug, he bought a fibreglass trimaran designed by rising multihull star Dick Newick. His astonishing performance in the 1976 OSTAR made him the hero of singlehanded aficionados who felt he embodied the true spirit of the race – as opposed to the much-demonized Alain Colas.

It was a little extreme, of course, and Birch went on to show that he appreciated a big, powerful sailboat as much as anyone – notably when he raced the 24.3m (80ft) *TAG-Heuer* into fourth place in the 1986 Route du Rhum. Throughout this time, Birch worked closely with British multihull designer Nigel Irens, perhaps best known for the 18.3m (60ft) trimaran *Apricot* raced by Tony Bullimore. Their most spectacular collaboration was the 24.3m (80ft) *Formule TAG*, built for the 1984 Quebec–St Malo race. Although she didn't win the race, the catamaran did set a new world record by sailing 843km (524 miles) in 24 hours, a standard that would remain

## " A MAN WHO TALKS TO FLYING FISH "

unbroken for over 10 years.

Despite taking up sailing so late in life, in the past quarter of a century Birch has made the Atlantic his playground. As well as taking part in every Route du Rhum and most of the OSTAR/Europe 1 Star races, he has been at the start of every Quebec–St Malo race, proving equally adept at skippering a crewed boat as sailing singlehanded.

But as his race successes mounted and his boats grew in size and complexity, Birch always remained the same: quiet, efficient and warm-spirited. More than most singlehanded sailors, he seemed to stay true to the spirit of the sport espoused by OSTAR-founder Blondie Hasler way back in 1960. Thus when fellow competitor Olivier de Kersauson asked him why he had sailed so far south during the 1978 Route du Rhum, Birch replied: "Because I was looking for the trade winds. The sea was blue, not green. And there were no flying fish, so I went after them."

As Kersauson concluded: "How can you compete with a man who talks to flying fish?"

# MIKE
# birch

AROUND alone

**left** Extreme boats for an extreme race. By the third BOC Challenge in 1990–1, the Finot design concept had established an unstoppable momentum. At the start of the first leg off Cape Town, Christophe Auguin was already in the lead.

# THE routes

## AROUND ALONE

With its four (now five) legs, the BOC Challenge/Around Alone is raced as a series of grand prix races, arguably faster and closer to the edge than it's non-stop equivalent. At 43,200km (27,000 miles) long (now 46,000km (28,755 miles)), it is the longest individual race in the world.

———— **2002–3 route**

———— **1982–3 & 1986–7 route**

### KEY

▲▲▲▲  Icebergs

● ● ● ●  The Doldrums

➤ ➤  Currents

➤ ➤  Winds

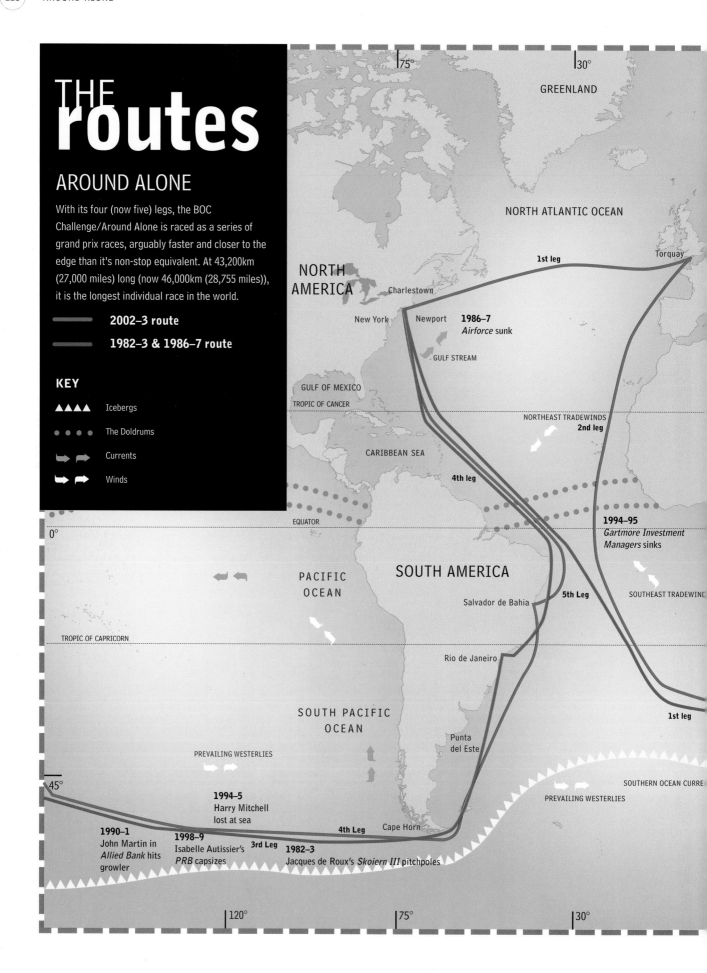

GREENLAND

NORTH ATLANTIC OCEAN

NORTH AMERICA

Charlestown

New York

Newport

**1986–7**
*Airforce* sunk

GULF STREAM

GULF OF MEXICO

TROPIC OF CANCER

**1st leg**

Torquay

NORTHEAST TRADEWINDS

**2nd leg**

CARIBBEAN SEA

**4th leg**

EQUATOR

0°

**1994–95**
*Gartmore Investment Managers* sinks

PACIFIC OCEAN

SOUTH AMERICA

Salvador de Bahia

**5th Leg**

SOUTHEAST TRADEWIND

TROPIC OF CAPRICORN

Rio de Janeiro

**1st leg**

SOUTH PACIFIC OCEAN

PREVAILING WESTERLIES

Punta del Este

45°

SOUTHERN OCEAN CURRE

PREVAILING WESTERLIES

**1994–5**
Harry Mitchell lost at sea

**1990–1**
John Martin in *Allied Bank* hits growler

**1998–9**
Isabelle Autissier's *PRB* capsizes

**3rd Leg**

**4th Leg**

Cape Horn

**1982–3**
Jacques de Roux's *Skoiern III* pitchpoles

120°

75°

30°

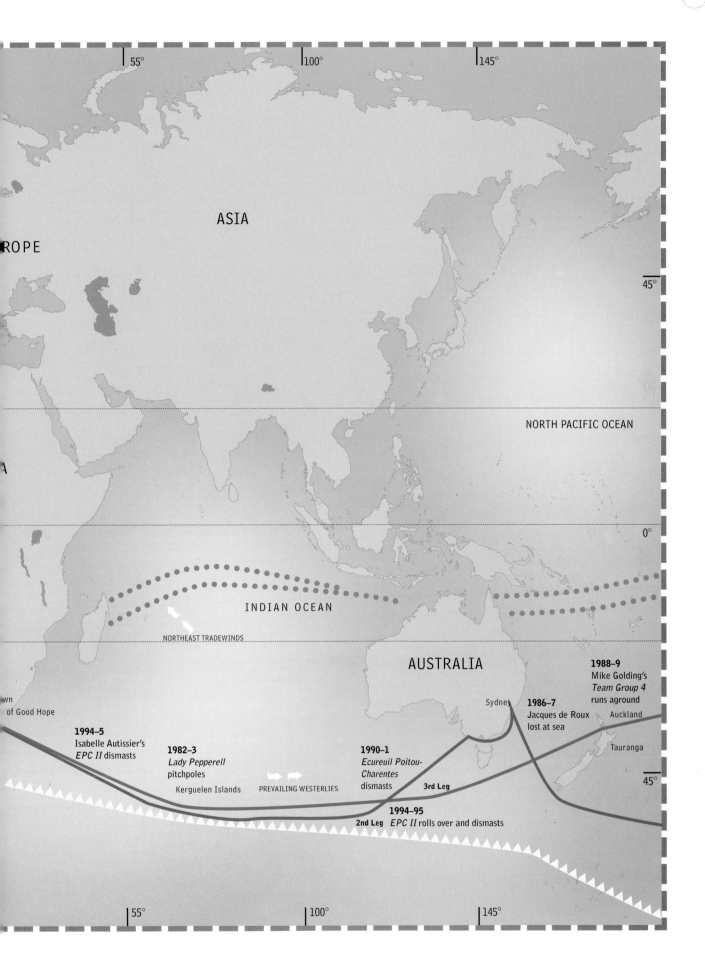

55°    100°    145°

ASIA

EUROPE

45°

NORTH PACIFIC OCEAN

INDIAN OCEAN

0°

NORTHEAST TRADEWINDS

AUSTRALIA

**1988–9**
Mike Golding's
*Team Group 4*
runs aground

Sydney

**1986–7**
Jacques de Roux
lost at sea

Auckland

of Good Hope

**1994–5**
Isabelle Autissier's
*EPC II* dismasts

**1982–3**
*Lady Pepperell*
pitchpoles

**1990–1**
*Ecureuil Poitou-
Charentes*
dismasts

**3rd Leg**

Tauranga

45°

Kerguelen Islands    PREVAILING WESTERLIES

**1994–95**
**2nd Leg** *EPC II* rolls over and dismasts

55°    100°    145°

# THE WORLD IN THEIR HANDS

❝ We expect casualties. We hope there will be no fatalities. We believe some will drop out. But there can be no chance of triumph without the possibility of tragedy, and no ultimate challenge without ultimate demands. Many will be frightened near to death, but they will live with that fear and master it alone. They will push themselves past their own personal limits and as a result get a personal sense of satisfaction that I can only describe as sheer ecstasy. ❞

Robin Knox-Johnston on the extremes of ocean racing

**below** David White played a crucial role as one of the co-founders of the BOC Challenge/Around Alone, but he fared less well in the first race in 1982–3, and retired soon after the start of the second leg.

Race chairman Robin Knox-Johnston was uncompromising in his language at the start of the second BOC Challenge (or Around Alone as the race became known in 1998) in August 1986. And he had reason to be. The first solo non-stop circumnavigator knew what the 25 skippers setting off to race around the world were letting themselves in for. He was proven almost eerily accurate. By the end of the race, six boats had retired, one had sunk, one had gone aground, and one skipper had been lost at sea. Only a very few of them, however, are likely to have experienced "sheer ecstasy". It was in many ways a typical BOC race.

The idea of a round the world singlehanded race was first dreamt up by a small group of OSTAR aficionados over the inevitable pint of beer at the Marina Pub on Goat Island off Newport, Rhode island. OSTAR veteran David White committed himself to building a boat for the race, while Goat Island manager Jim Roos agreed to help manage the event. The all-important sponsorship came indirectly and almost by chance after White and Roos had unsuccessfully approached a host of American companies. Englishman Richard Broadhead meanwhile was trying to raise funds for his own

entry and, after contacting around 800 UK firms, eventually got some interest from the British Oxygen Company (BOC). To Broadhead's disappointment, but to the sport's lasting benefit, BOC decided that rather than just sponsor one sailor it would like to sponsor the whole race. Thus the BOC Challenge was born. At 43,200km (27,000 miles) it is the longest solo race in the world.

The race was conceived from the start as a four-leg event, although the original course, which took in Hobart and Mar del Plata, was altered to reflect BOC's overseas interests. The eventual course was Newport–Cape Town–Sydney–Rio de Janeiro–Newport, and it remained that way for the first two races. Following the OSTAR formula, boats were entered without handicap in two classes, 44–56ft (13.4–17m) and 32–44ft (9.7–13.4m) – although the maximum lengths were increased for the next race to 60ft (18.27m) and 50ft (15.2m) to reflect the new OSTAR set-up. The winner in each class stood to win a $25,000 cash prize.

Thanks to the race's multi-leg structure, the sailors not only sail in company, but also spend time at each of the stopovers fixing their boats, socializing and developing a bond that is often later tested out at sea in the most extreme circumstances. For, beyond the very real competitive edge that exists between them, there is a supportive ethos that only comes from engaging in an extreme sport thousands of miles from terra firma. After all, if you're stuck in the middle of the Southern Ocean on a sinking ship, your best chances of survival are your fellow competitors – providing you've kept up with the fleet. For this reason the race has developed a reputation for fostering camaraderie, and competitors are soon made to feel part of the BOC family.

## Cutting edge

The first BOC Challenge had most of the elements that would characterize the race throughout its history: cutting edge yacht design; charismatic (or at least eccentric) skippers; extreme weather; and daring rescues at sea. The first fatality would not come until the next race.

But while most of the 17 boats which gathered in Newport on 28 August 1982 were seaworthy craft, few were serious race contenders. Most were production cruisers which had been adapted for long-distance racing, and even the custom-built racers were mostly, on the whole, fairly long in the tooth. Only one boat had been specially designed for the race, and it showed.

Philippe Jeantot appeared literally out of nowhere. The French oil rig diver, who held the record for the world's deepest dive of 500m (1642ft), returned from a meandering, 40,000km (25,000 mile) solo cruise with no experience of ocean racing and persuaded the bank Crédit Agricole to fund a brand new boat to the tune of 800,000 French francs. Singlehanded racing had, by then, become a high profile sport in France and could attract sums of money only dreamed of in other countries.

Jeantot chose up-and-coming designer Guy Ribadeau Dumas to draw him a state-of-the-art 56-footer (17m) for the new race. *Crédit Agricole* was the only boat on the start-line of the first BOC to be fitted with water ballast, an idea first developed by Eric Tabarly for *Pen Duick V* – within a few years it would become commonplace. She also had twin daggerboards

aft to steady her on downwind legs and twin headsails for when conditions got too hairy for a spinnaker, as well as a proper wheelhouse (complete with Renault car seat) and reliable roller furling. Not only did *Crédit Agricole* look the part, she was at least a generation ahead of any other boat there. And Jeantot had the financial and logistical back-up to match.

The boat's superiority was all too evident during the race. *Crédit Agricole* finished the first leg 1920km (1200 miles) ahead of the next boat, giving Jeantot an impregnable six and-a-half-day lead over South African Bertie Reed in his *Altech Voortrekker* (a 14-year OSTAR veteran, for goodness sake!). By the time he reached Newport again Jeantot was more than 11 days ahead of Reed and 33 days ahead of Richard Broadhead with a total time of 159 days, two hours and 26 minutes.

## Jeantot supreme

Jeantot had beaten the solo circumnavigation record set in 1974 by Alain Colas on his 21.3m (70ft) trimaran *Manureva* (ex-*Pen Duick IV*) as

**above** The last of Francis Chichester's famous line of *Gypsy Moths* was wrecked on Gebo Island, 250 miles from Sydney, during the 1982–3 race. Her skipper, Desmond Hampton, fell asleep at the helm.

well as the record for the longest seven-day run, covering 2480km (1552 miles) in one week during the second leg. Curiously, though, the record for the longest 24-hour run was broken not by Jeantot but by the Czech, Richard Konkolski, in Class II on his 13.4m (44ft) sloop *Nike II*, who clocked up 395km (247 miles) one noon to noon on the same leg.

Jeantot's main threat during that first race came not from the other modern racers but from a boat from another era, as his log heading into the Indian Ocean on leg two shows: "The whole day is spent trying to make the boat go faster. I am tacking to windward always trying to be on the good side, but that was a mistake. I should have gone south. I would have got some speed rather than heading into the wind. *Gipsy Moth* and *Voortrekker* have both caught up with me and *Gipsy Moth* is even ahead. I had better put some coal in the furnace!

"It can't go on like this. I like *Gipsy Moth* – but behind me… Let's get going *Crédit Agricole*…"

Francis Chichester's last boat, the 10-year-old Robert Clark-designed *Gipsy Moth V*, had

been chartered for the race by Desmond Hampton and, with 380mm (15in) chopped off her stern to fit the size limit, she was in her element. Tragically, a few weeks later she ran aground on rocks on the approach to Sydney after her exhausted skipper fell asleep at the helm. Although Hampton managed to scramble ashore, all that remained of the historic yacht was a pile of fittings retrieved with the help of a chainsaw as the yacht was breaking up.

Not all attempts at innovation were as successful as *Crédit Agricole*. In the same race, Greg Coles's futuristic-looking *Datsun Skyline* sported a revolving wing mast and carbon fibre hull. After starting 11 days late, she trudged across the Atlantic, finally arriving in Cape Town six weeks after the leader. A brief foray into the second leg ended when the New Zealander's self-steering packed up and he retired.

Tony Lush's experiment with an unstayed cat rig also ended in disaster when his 16.5m (54ft) schooner *Lady Pepperell* pitchpoled two weeks out of Cape Town. He was lucky to escape alive as the boat began to ship 10 litres (2 gallons) of water per minute through her keel. The ensuing rescue set the template for future BOC rescues, as ham radio operators ashore provided the crucial link between the boats and the race organizers. Francis Stokes's *Moonshine* was the nearest competitor and was directed to take Lush on board for the rest of the leg to Sydney – under the strict race rules that rescuee must not help rescuer in any way, other than to provide company and act as occasional galley slave. It was the first of many rescues to come during BOC races, although not all of them would be quite as straightforward.

## Perseverance to the rescue

The system was put to the test in the very next leg when Jacques de Roux's *Skoiern III*, in first place in Class II after two legs, pitchpoled in 60-knot winds half-way between New Zealand and Cape Horn. The boat eventually righted itself, but water filled the cabin to within 100mm (4in) of the deck. Thanks to the Argos tracking system and a network of ham radio operators, Richard Broadhead on *Perseverance of Medina* was contacted and beat back into the storm to find de Roux. By the time he tracked down *Skoiern III*, her luckless skipper had been pumping for his life in freezing conditions for nearly three days. The boat sank four hours later. De Roux transferred to a French naval vessel after three days aboard, and Broadhead went on to reap well-deserved acclaim, including being named Yachtsman of the Year in the UK. He was also awarded a 145-hour time allowance from the race committee to make up for the time lost saving de Roux.

The most marked leap in boat technology came in the run-up to the 1986–7 race, when the so-called BOC boat began to emerge. Pointy bows gave way to plumb stems to gain the maximum waterline length and twin rudders, angled outwards, were fitted to give better control while heeling. Water ballast, which could be pumped to the windward side of the boat to help stabilize it, became *de rigueur*. Fully-battened mainsails produced bigger sail areas and reduced wear and tear, while windvane self-steering was largely replaced by electronic systems powered by solar panels and generators. Whereas *Crédit*

*Agricole* had been the only purpose-designed boat in the first race, there were 10 at the start-line in 1986.

Jeantot himself came with another Ribadeau Dumas design, *Crédit Agricole III*, in which he succeeded in slashing 25 days off his previous race record. Three other Frenchmen with growing reputations also came with maxi-sized yachts: Jean Yves Terlain with *UAP Médécins Sans Frontières*, Guy Bernadin with *Biscuits Lu* and Titouan Lamazou with *Ecureil d'Aquitaine* – all would finish well within Jeantot's 1982–3 record. In fact, the average speed of the fleet as a whole increased that year by an amazing 20 per cent, an indication of how quickly yacht design and technology had moved on.

Probably the most innovative boat at the start-line was *Thursday's Child*, raced by Hunter Boats chairman, Warren Luhrs. Used as something of a test bed by her builders/owners, the 18.3m (60ft) yacht boasted a pivoting rudder, lightweight rig, and an advanced water ballast system. She was first monohull over the line in the 1984 OSTAR and the 1985 Round Britain Race, but fared less well in the BOC when she was dismasted approaching Sydney and had to complete the second leg under jury rig. Repairs to the mast were unsuccessful, and Luhrs was forced to retire.

As Knox-Johnston forewarned, the second BOC, in 1986, was marred by its fair share of accidents. Several start-line collisions were followed by the sinking of *Airforce* in mid-Atlantic; *Neptune's Express* was dismasted on the equator; and Harry Mitchell's *Double Cross* was beached while he attempted to pull in at New Zealand for repairs. Canadian John Hughes was dismasted in the Southern Ocean 2400km (1500 miles) from New Zealand but sailed the remaining 7000km (4400 miles) to the Falkland Islands under jury rig – an achievement which earned him a place in the Singlehanded Hall of Fame in Newport. After re-rigging his yacht

> **IN THE EVENT THAT I AM WASHED OVERBOARD, I WOULD PREFER TO SPEND MY FINAL FOUR MINUTES IN QUIET CONTEMPLATION, RATHER THAN BEING TOWED AGAINST 14 KNOTS**
>
> David Scully in *Yachting World*

*Joseph Young* with the help of the Royal Navy, Hughes carried on to Rio, eventually arriving 92 days after leaving Sydney.

But the most tragic event of 1986–7 happened at the end of the second leg when Jacques de Roux, the popular French sailor so valiantly saved by Broadhead in the previous race, went missing. His boat was found sailing itself a few miles away from Sydney with a half-eaten meal on the table. It was assumed de Roux had rushed on deck to check something and fallen overboard. His body was never found.

Safety issues were inevitably raised. Was he wearing a harness? Probably not, as David Scully, skipper of *Coyote* in a later race, would explain so chillingly. "I do not usually wear a harness on deck while sailing solo. In the event that I am washed overboard, I would prefer to spend my final four minutes in quiet contemplation, rather than being towed against 14 knots."

## Quantum leap

If the second generation BOC boats represented a quantum leap of development, the third generation was even more extreme. Rather than all-round racers, many designers focused on producing boats that could perform well in the mostly downwind legs in the Southern Ocean, where just over half the race takes place. The result was extremely beamy, flat-bottomed craft,

with towering rigs and deep, narrow keels – described by some as surfing sleds. Meanwhile, the cost of a top end 60-footer had soared to between $120,000 and $900,000. Long-distance singlehanded boat design had come of age.

At the forefront of the new type were the French designers Groupe Finot, whose first experiment with a boat in that vein had been Alain Gautier's *Generali Concorde* in the 1989 Vendée Globe. Gautier brought the same boat to the 1990–1 BOC, while Christophe Auguin came with another Finot boat, *Groupe Sceta*. Both had 5.8m (19ft) beams – pretty extreme compared to Isabelle Autissier's pencil-like *Ecureil Poitou-Charentes* (ex-*36.15 Met*) at 3.4m (11ft 3in) wide. The only beamier boat there was John Martin's BOC-type *Allied Bank*, at 6m (19ft 7in).

The new breed proved itself beyond doubt, with Gautier, Auguin, and Martin alternating in the top two places in the first two legs and, after Martin struck a growler in the Southern Ocean, Gautier and Auguin shadowing each other for the last two legs. In the end, Auguin triumphed, setting a new course record of 120 days, 22 hours and 36 minutes, nearly two days ahead of Gautier and two weeks ahead of the previous record. Jeantot's 5.6m- (18ft 3in-) wide *Crédit Agricole IV*, by contrast, was regarded as too conservative, and he finished nine days behind the leader.

**far left** Better known for his epoch-making *Vendredi Treize,* Jean-Yves Terlain came third in the 1986–7 BOC on his *UAP Médecins sans Frontières.* She was dismasted in the first Vendée Globe two years later.

**left** Alain Gautier's *Generali Concorde* was the first of the "southern ocean surfers" that would come to dominate the solo round-the-world races.

There was innovation in Class II as well, with Yves Dupasquier's *Servant 4* being dubbed "a 60-footer in disguise". With her streamlined cabin and uncluttered deck, she certainly gave the illusion of size. The ultra-lightweight 50-footer (15.2m) was fitted with an outsize mainsail and carried a minimum of equipment – even her sail wardrobe was limited to three foresails plus mainsail. The stretched Mini-Transat boat won every leg in her class, finishing with a 12-day lead, and was snapping at the heels of the Class I boats most of her way around the world, even beating two of them on the second leg.

## Away with Rio

For the 1990 race, the organizers had decided they'd had enough of the Brazilian factor (not to mention the dreaded Rio's Revenge, which kept skippers glued to their sea-toilets for the first couple of days out of harbour) and had moved the third leg finish to Punta del Este in Uruguay – making the final leg 1600km (1000 miles) longer (or the third leg 1600km (1000 miles) shorter,

depending upon how you looked at it). Mark Schrader, a former social worker who had competed in the 1986–7 race, had by then been appointed race director and would increasingly become the voice of the BOC.

One of the most popular sailors from the first BOC was the Tokyo taxi-driver, Yukoh Tada who, as well as being an experienced sailor, was also a keen musician and an accomplished artist. Despite cramming his 13.4m (44ft) *Koden Okera V* full of electronic gadgetry in the 1982–3 race, he still found room for his tenor saxophone and electric keyboard, plus his paintbrushes and easel – the idea being to hold an exhibition at each port of call. Tada arranged for a Buddhist monk to travel from Japan to bless the fleet, and *Koden Okera* went on to win first place in Class II. Tada came back in 1990 with a 15.2m (50ft) yacht to his own design but fared less well, suffering five knockdowns in the Indian Ocean. He retired during the Sydney stopover and the fleet later heard the tragic news that he had taken his life. The BOC had lost one of its most ebullient and best-loved characters.

**right** The most significant development in Class 2 was the arrival of the "mini-60" *Servant IV*, which even beat some of the 60-footers on some legs in 1990–1.

**below** Jean Luc van den Heede received a rude awakening when he woke up on an Australian beach in 1994–5. He managed to get refloated and still clinch a second place in that leg.

The concept of the Southern Ocean surfers was taken a stage further in 1994–5 with Auguin's *Sceta Calberson*, again designed by Groupe Finot. Although about the same beam as her predecessors, the yacht was built entirely from ultra-light materials, using pre-preg carbon fibre with a Nomex honeycomb core. As a result, she weighed in at just 8.5 tonnes – 1.5 tonnes lighter than *Groupe Sceta*. Auguin went on to set a new 24-hour record during the race of 562km (351 miles).

But the fat girls didn't have it all their own way. BOC and Vendée Globe veteran Jean-Luc van den Heede (known as VDH) stuck steadfastly to his belief in sometimes worryingly skinny boats. He sailed his 2.6m- (8ft 4in-) wide *Let's Go* to second place in Class II in 1982–3, while his 3.4m- (11ft 3in-) wide Class I boat *36.15 Met* achieved third place in the 1989–90 Vendée Globe (with VDH) and seventh in the 1990–1 BOC (with Isabelle Autissier).

Van den Heede was back in 1994–5 with another pencil-boat, this time the 3.8m- (12ft 6in-) wide ketch *Vendée Entreprises* which frequently outperformed the surfers to windward. But it was sailing to windward that VDH nearly lost the race. Tacking up the east coast of Australia at the end of the second leg he fell asleep at the helm for a few minutes. When he woke up *Vendée Entreprises* was on the beach, just 50 miles south of Sydney. Although he might not have thought so at the time, he was lucky: most of that coast is lined with cliffs, yet his boat had cleverly managed to find a soft place to land. Within a couple of hours *Vendée Entreprises* had been pulled off by a police tug and, with the help of various BOC crews, she was sailing again. Despite this mishap, VDH still managed to clinch second place on that leg and went on to a comfortable third place overall – more than three days ahead of David Scully's decidedly buxom 6.4m- (21ft-) wide *Coyote*.

## Isabelle's back

Meanwhile, in the same race Autissier was experimenting with a hydraulic canting keel on her Jean Berret-designed *Ecureuil Poitou-Charentes II*. A canting keel has much the same effect as water ballast but is faster to transfer from one side to the other when tacking. Theoretically, it can also help right a capsized boat although, as Autissier was to discover to her cost in 1999, this does not always work in practice. Although frowned upon at the time for being too complex for singlehanded ocean racing, canting keels have since been adopted by many BOC boats.

Autissier's gamble seemed to have paid off when she won the first leg – this time staged from Charlestown, USA, Newport having apparently become too complacent about hosting the event. The former engineer wowed the yachting fraternity by hammering across the Atlantic in just 35 days – two days faster than the record set by Alain Gautier in 1990–1 and five days ahead of the second-placed *Hunter's Child*. As a result Autissier, who in 1990–1 became the first woman to complete a full BOC circuit, became the first woman ever to win a leg of the race.

But that's as far as her luck went. Six days out of Cape Town her 25.9m- (85ft-) tall carbon fibre mast came down when a shroud sheared in 50-knot winds. Coincidentally, Autissier had been dismasted on the same leg of the race in 1990–1 – only that time she had been 800km (500 miles) away from Sydney and had managed to sail to the finish line under jury rig. But this time *Ecureuil Poitou-Charentes II* was in the middle of the Indian Ocean, 2080km (1300 miles) away from Cape Town and 7200km (4500 miles) away from Sydney. Using her spare spinnaker pole as a mast, she set up a jury rig and sailed to the French-owned Kerguelen Islands, 1920km (1200 miles) away to the east. There, thanks to a fortunate combination of circumstances, a temporary rig had been shipped for her to install and enable her to continue to race.

But her troubles were only just beginning. Less than two weeks after setting off from the Kerguelens, *Ecureuil* was again struck by a violent gale. After suffering two knock-downs, the yacht was hit by an enormous wave which rolled her through 360°, demolished the temporary rig and ripped open the cabin top. As the boat was buffeted by 60-knot winds and a sea to match, Autissier rigged a temporary cover over the gaping hole and started bailing for her life. Then she triggered her EPIRB, or emergency position indicating rescue beacon.

## Rescued!

With the only two nearby competitors experiencing difficulties of their own, a traditional BOC rescue was deemed impossible and a major air and sea rescue operation was launched. The 160-man Australian frigate HMAS *Darwin* set off from her base 2560km (1600 miles) away and, with the assistance of several military aircraft, picked up an exhausted and frightened Autissier three days later. It was one of the biggest such operations ever mounted.

The cost of Autissier's rescue was put at AUS$1.5–2 million, sparking a frenzied debate in the Australian media over who should foot the bill. Under the 1974 international convention for the Safety of Life at Sea (SOLAS), of which Australia is a signatory, all countries are obliged go the rescue of a vessel in distress within their territorial waters. Many Australians, however, felt that the country's tax-payers were being taken for a ride and that the French government, or even the race sponsors, should pay up.

The issue of race safety came to the fore again a few weeks later when the BOC suffered its second fatality at sea. It was Harry Mitchell's third attempt at completing a BOC and achieving his lifelong ambition of rounding Cape Horn. The first time he didn't even make it to the start-line; the second time he ran onto a beach at Buff in New Zealand; and his third and final attempt finally ended 2400km (1500 miles) from the Cape. Having come eighth and 10th in legs one

**below** Marc Thiercelin arrives in Cape Town at the end of the first leg of the 1998–9 race. The Frenchman was later robbed of first place when he dismasted after rounding Cape Horn.

and two respectively on his 12.2m (40ft) *Henry Hornblower*, the charismatic 70-year-old was within days of achieving his goal when, for reasons which have never been discovered, he triggered his emergency signal. Despite an extensive search of the area, no trace of him or his boat was ever found.

## Spiralling costs

By the time of the 1998–9 race the shape of the archetypal Around Alone (ex-BOC) boat had been firmly established: enormously beamy, low on the water and shallow under water but with a deep, pendulous bulb keel. With the principal dimensions decided, the main developments henceforth would be in the materials used to build the boats, with increasingly lightweight, stiff hulls and durable, high-performance sails. The cost of a top flight BOC/Around Alone campaign had soared to over $3 million, while, at $12,500, the entry fee alone was worth half the prize money of the inaugural race. Pressure from sponsors for a return on their investment rose in proportion, as American solo sailor Brad Van Liew came to learn for the 1998–9 race. His

sponsors, the manufacturers of the health snack Balance Bar, only agreed to pay him every time the boat's name was mentioned or shown in the media. As a result, Van Liew spent much of the race banging out copious press releases in an attempt to keep the cash flow running.

Such pressure from sponsors to perform has been a blessing and a curse from the earliest editions of the race. For instance, after his mediocre performance in the first leg of the 1986–7 race, when he came fifth, Titouan Lamazou's backers, Ecureuil d'Aquitaine, informed him they would withdraw support unless he won the next leg. Surprise, surprise, he not only won the next leg but came second in the next two, and was only beaten overall by Jeantot's unstoppable momentum.

With Groupe Finot responsible for the previous two wins in both the BOC and the Vendée Globe, their name tag not surprisingly featured heavily in the fleet assembled for the 1998–9 race – which by then had been re-christened simply Around Alone, the BOC Group having withdrawn its sponsorship of the event. Seven of the 16 boats at the start line were by

**below** The first in Isabelle's hat-trick of diasters. Dismasted 800km (500 miles) off Sydney in 1990–1, she managed to sail into harbour and re-rig her boat. She was not so lucky in her next two BOCs.

Finot – five in Class I and two in Class II – including all three British boats.

Once again Autissier flew ahead in the first leg to what seemed like another record-breaking lead. Less than 1600km (1000 miles) from Cape Town, however, as the leaders vied for pole position, Englishman Mike Golding on *Team Group 4* read the weather a little better and rode in to the finish line on the front of a low pressure system. His time of 34 days and 18 hours – more than a day ahead of Autissier – set a new record and made him the first British sailor to win a leg of the Around Alone.

British hopes were high as the fleet roared across the Indian Ocean, with Golding 240km (150 miles) behind the leader, Giovanni Soldini. Even a second place at the new leg two finish line in Auckland, New Zealand would guarantee *Team Group 4* a comfortable first place overall. With PR high on the agenda of any modern racer, however, Golding decided it would be a good idea to get some aerial shots of *Team Group 4* as she sped through the sparkling clear waters off northern New Zealand. In order to make his rendezvous with a photographer in a helicopter, he sailed closer to shore – a little too close. Within a few minutes he had hit a shoal and his boat started to fill with water. Britain's brightest hope ended as Golding was unceremoniously towed into Auckland the following day. "It was the stupidest thing I have ever done," said the humbled hero. It was hard not to agree.

With Golding out of the race, Autissier was propelled into first place overall. It was the first time she had completed leg two without any major accident and she might have been forgiven for thinking 1998–9 would be third time lucky. But Poseidon had other plans. To keep up with the leader, Marc Thiercelin on *Somewhere*, Autissier dipped down to 55° South on the third leg – much further than any of the other boats other than *Somewhere* – and was averaging 603km (375 miles) per day. Then, half-way between New Zealand and South America, the unthinkable happened. Autissier's *PRB* was knocked on her side and capsized. No amount of movement with her canting keel would right the boat – a situation not helped by *PRB*'s flat decks,

which created a suction with the surface of the water. (Later Finot boats have cambered decks to get around this problem.)

Stuck on an overturned boat in near-freezing conditions, at least 3200km (2000 miles) from land and 960km (600 miles) from the nearest shipping lane, Autissier had no choice but to set off her EPIRB alarm. This time, however, two Around Alone competitors were within striking distance: Thiercelin was 160km (100 miles) ahead and Soldini was 320km (200 miles) to the north. Both boats were asked by the race office to stand by to go to the lone yachtswoman's rescue, but while Soldini immediately altered course and beat into 30-knot winds to try and reach Autissier, after consulting his shore crew Thiercelin carried on.

Soldini sailed through the night and early the next morning, despite visibility being down to half a mile, spotted the upturned hull of *PRB*. Autissier was saved, but once again had to wave goodbye to a much-loved boat.

Back on course for Cape Horn, there was some controversy about how much of a time allowance *Fila* would be given for diverting course. Thiercelin was understandably concerned about protecting the 640km (400 mile) lead he had over Soldini when the incident occurred, while the Italian still hoped to improve on his second place. In the end it was all immaterial as *Somewhere* was dismasted off the coast of Argentina and *Fila* slipped ahead into the lead. Thiercelin eventually arrived in Punta del Este 12 days after *Fila*, having re-rigged his boat in the Falklands, only to be greeted with criticism at his decision to carry on racing after Autissier's accident.

## Soldini slips away

As if to add insult to injury, Soldini flew over the Doldrums while Thiercelin drifted across in light airs, giving *Fila* a massive 14-day lead overall. Soldini's time of 116 days, 20 hours and seven minutes was not only a new race record, it also made him the first non-French winner of the race – and the first non-French competitor to win a

> ❝ IT WAS THE STUPIDEST THING I HAVE EVER DONE ❞

Mike Golding after sailing too close to shore during the 1998–9 race

singlehanded round-the-world race since Robin Knox-Johnston in 1968.

It was the Italian who came closest to experiencing the state of ecstacy described by the veteran British single-hander. "I was transfixed by the sight of *Fila* as she slid down the waves," he said in a message to race control. "When her bow hit bottom, she threw up a huge cloud of spray and almost half the boat disappeared under the water. For a time I thought that the reason we're here on earth is to experience sights like that. You forget that your hands are frozen by the water temperatures of three degrees [Celsius, 37°F] and the stress of the vibration and the fact that the autopilot cannot withstand the impact. The only important thing is that you're racing on the water."

There was good and bad news for the British contingent. After Golding's sudden departure from Class I, all eyes were fixed on Josh Hall on his *Gartmore*. This was Hall's third BOC in increasingly high-profile campaigns: in 1990–1 he came third in Class II on the 15.2m (50ft) *Spirit of Ipswich*, finishing the race with a surgical brace on his leg after dislocating his knee on the second leg [sic]; in 1994–95 his race came to an abrupt end on the first leg when the 18.3m (60ft) *Gartmore* (ex-*Ecureuil d'Aquitaine*, ex-*Lada Poch III*) struck a container and sank mid-Atlantic. He was back in 1998–9 with the new, all-singing all-dancing *Gartmore*, but disaster struck again when he was dismasted 1280km (800 miles) from New Zealand. For a time it looked as if the same boat that had rescued Hall in 1994–5, *Newcastle Australia* now renamed *Balance Bar*, would have to rescue him again, but in the end Hall fashioned a jury rig and sailed unaided to the nearby Chatham Islands.

Class II developed into a war between the crusty Brit Mike Gartside on *Magellan Alpha* and the Franco-American ex-knife thrower JP Mouligne on *Cray Valley*. Mouligne seemed to have forgotten he was on a 50-footer, however, and even beat several Class I boats, coming in nearly four days ahead of Hall on the second leg. Gartside reaped his revenge on the final leg when he became the second British skipper to win a leg of the race, though Mouligne was the undoubted overall champion in the class.

Overall, 1998–9 was remarkable for its high rate of attrition: of the 17 boats that started, only seven made it to the finish. The drop-out rate was particularly high in Class I, where only two boats completed the race – just 30 per cent. The inevitable question was, were these boats really safe or were their designs just too extreme? Had the margins of safety been eroded too far in the search for those extra couple of knots?

But winning the BOC/Around Alone isn't just about having the fastest boat. Tactics, and in particular being able to read the weather, are all-important, too, and each leg of the race has its particular quirks and pitfalls ready to trip up the unwary sailor. With little precedent to refer to, most of the skippers of the first race in 1982–3 opted for the traditional clipper route across the Atlantic. By keeping to the west side of the Atlantic after passing the north-east corner of South America, they avoided the calms associated with the South Atlantic High (pressure area) and hopefully more than made up for the extra distance covered compared to the more direct rhumb line route. On the whole, it has proven the right course to take.

## Into the void

Once in the Southern Ocean, the idea is to keep as much as possible between the high pressure systems in the north and the low pressure systems in the south. In between the two, the trade winds blow in an easterly direction, giving a fast though sometimes hair-raising ride. Balanced against that is the fact that the further south the boats head, the less the distance they have to travel, as the circumference of the earth shortens nearer the pole. Too far south, though, and you're into icebergs.

The tendency in recent years has been for boats to head further and further south, risking collision with icebergs and growlers but cutting hours and even days off their times. Whereas only two boats in each of the 1982–3 and 1986–7 races dropped to the danger zone below 60° South, in 1990–1 nine boats followed that course - no doubt influenced by the fact that three out of the four boats that had tried that route in previous races had ended up as class winners. Many simply

**left** In 2000–1, Giovanni Soldini became the first non-French to win a singlehanded round the world race since 1969, on board his Open 60 *Fila*.

appeared intoxicated by what one referred to as the "Scotch on the rocks".

It was thus inevitable that disaster would strike sooner or later. In 1990-1 John Martin struck a growler 1800 miles from Cape Horn in his *Allied Bank* and had to be picked up by Bertie Reed on *Grinaker* in yet another classic BOC/Around Alone rescue. For the following race the organizers bowed to the inevitable and, despite objections from several competitors, introduced a theoretical mark at 59° South 130° West which all boats had to round.

Brad Van Liew described his experience of these unforgiving waters in this extract from *Into the Wind*, by Tony Bartelme and Brian Hicks.

"18 February 1999: I'm screwed…I am in no-man's land, bobbing around in a tiny boat and a giant storm is bearing down on me. No one in the world can help me except maybe my fellow competitors…

"22 February: It's ugly. Everything is white. Snow, hail, and sea-foam all blowing horizontally across my field of vision. I am surrounded by the most fearsome seas. I am not feeling good about the boat's ability to survive such abuse. It feels like I am seeing something very few people survive to see.

"26 February: I am really getting my ass kicked now…we are now sailing at 7 knots under bare poles. Even without an inch of sail up, I am overpowered and there's not a damn thing I can do about it. Does anyone know how to reef a mast?

"27 February: We are in the death zone. Things are out of control. I can do no more…It's too rough to even think about preparing a meal. I'd have to duct tape the food down the pot to cook it. I am living on Balance Bars…

"My personal condition is deteriorating alarmingly. I haven't eaten anything for so long now I can't remember. I am covered in cuts and bruises…Both the boat and I are undergoing a slow but steady degradation. We are both being beaten down, beaten down, beaten down."

Heading back up the Atlantic, the fleet once again has to negotiate the South Atlantic Low and the Doldrums before crossing the east-going Gulf Stream. Because the conditions are so much less predictable in the Atlantic, tactics become more important than plain boat speed. As a result, many sailors believe that races can be won or lost on these legs. Christophe Auguin proved that in 1990–1 when he set off on the final leg with a 21 and-a-half-hour deficit over Alain Gautier. Making the most of an extra-large mainsail bent on during the Punta del Este stopover, Auguin stayed a little closer to the Brazilian coast and passed through the Doldrums a critical few hours ahead of his rival. The more favourable conditions he encountered as a result meant his *Groupe Sceta* ended the leg nearly three days ahead of *Generali Concorde* – more than enough for him to snatch overall victory. For Gautier, it was devastating. As he put it: "It was the hardest 48 hours of my life."

## Politics and the solo sailor

The BOC wasn't immune to the changing political landscape of the world it so nonchalantly girdled. Launched towards the end of the Cold War, it managed to transcend the crumbling East-West divide. Richard Konkolski was a 39-year-old Czechoslovakian engineer who, when the Czech authorities refused to let him take part in the race, escaped the Eastern Bloc with his wife and son and a friend on board his 13.4m (44ft) sloop *Nike II*. After crossing the Atlantic to Newport via the UK, all four applied for political asylum in the United States. Once at sea, there was concern that the communist navy might try to settle scores with the West's latest protégé and Konkolski's position was kept deliberately vague throughout the race.

By 1998–9 the Soviet Union was no longer, and it was a plain Russian who entered the Around Alone aboard *Wind of Change*. Viktor Yazykov wrote one of the more gruesome chapters in the history of the race when he had to perform painful self-surgery to get rid of an abscess on his arm. Despite following a set of instructions emailed to him from the race doctor, the operation almost went horribly wrong and Yazykov lost nearly a litre of blood over his chart table and cabin floor. Rather cruelly, after his

> ❝ I'M SCREWED…I AM IN NO-MAN'S LAND, BOBBING AROUND IN A TINY BOAT AND A GIANT STORM IS BEARING DOWN ON ME ❞

Brad Van Liew describes the treacherous waters off Cape Horn during the 1998–9 race ordeal, when the former Afghanistan vet arrived in Cape Town second to last, he was grilled mercilessly by the Russian media about his poor performance.

At the start of the 21st century, not the Cold War or the disintegration of the Soviet Union but the threat of global terrorism was to make its impact on the race. To help mark the anniversary of the 11 September bombings in 2001, the start of the 2002–3 race was moved to New York. After a feeder race from Newport, the Around Alone fleet joined the one-off Sail For America event taking place in New York in memory of those killed by the terrorist attacks.

With the race now in the hands of Clipper Ventures, the marine events management company headed by, now Sir, Robin Knox-Johnston, the course took on a slightly more anglicized feel, with different stopovers and a whole new leg thrown in. The first leg took the fleet to Torbay in the UK, before heading south to Cape Town, followed by Tauranga in New Zealand, then Salvador da Bahia (the new Brazilian base used by, among others, the Mini-Transat), and finishing once again in Newport.

Many of the skippers from previous races were back, including Brad Van Liew on the 15.2m (50ft) *Tommy Hilfiger Freedom America* (ex-*Magellan Alpha*). Italy's Simone Bianchetti, veteran of the 1994 BOC and 2000–1 Vendée Globe was sailing the Open 60 *Tiscali Global Challenge*, while France's Thierry Dubois was flying the flag for Amnesty International with *Solidaires*. Following Yazykov's success with his Open 40 in 1998–9, three more of these smaller boats signed up for 2002–3 race. A new prize, the Harry Mitchell Trophy, was awarded for the winning 40-footer (12.2m) in memory of the English sailor lost off Cape Horn in 1994–5.

By 2002, over 100 skippers from nearly 20 countries had taken part in the BOC/Around Alone. A little over half have made it to the end of the course. Contained in these simple statistics is a richly-woven fabric of human experience; individual triumph; dashed hopes; personal awakening; intense fear; and every other emotion that can be felt racing a fragile craft through the most dangerous seas in the world – all shared between an elite group of strong-minded individuals. For, danger and challenges aside, what the race does more than any other is to foster a sense of comradeship. In that sense, Around Alone is a misnomer, for these sailors sail around the world not alone, but together.

**below** The start of the 2002 race was moved to New York to pay tribute to the victims of the September 11 attacks the year before. New Zealand skipper Graham Dalton sails across the line with his new Open 60 *Hexagon*.

## CAREER PROFILE

Christophe Auguin is the world's most successful singlehanded sailor. The only person ever to have won three round-the-world races, he deserves a place among the greats of the sport. Yet, despite this unique record, there are still some who would deny Auguin hero status. "Alain Gautier would have won in 1991 if his mainsail hadn't ripped," they say. "Isabelle Autissier would have won in 1995 if she hadn't capsized," they say. "Autissier or Yves Parlier would have won in 1996 if they hadn't broken their rudders."

# "I LEAVE IT TO OTHERS TO GO AS FAST AS POSSIBLE"

What rankles with these cynics is that Auguin has won his three titles not through spectacular acts of seamanship or by taking undue risks, but through clever positioning, keeping his boat safe, and exploiting the circumstances. His wins have been by stealth and cunning rather than through power and bravery. As he puts it: "There are times when my objective is to save my skin, and I leave it to others to go as fast as possible."

Auguin started sailing at the age of five aboard his father's 6.4m (21ft) Muscadet cabin sailer. At 16, the family moved to Granville and the young sailor soon joined the local dinghy racing circuit. He was soon competing in RORC races, Cowes Week and the Fastnet (including the disastrous 1979 race) and eventually bought his own 4.9m (16ft) Micro on which he won second place in the 1981 world championship.

Then, in 1984, the Figaro came to town. Although more of a team player, Auguin was persuaded to take part by a friend. It proved to be a portentous move. Sailed on identical one-design boats, the Figaro is one of France's top sporting events and its winners are guaranteed star status. Auguin came a promising ninth that year, and fifth the year after. In 1986 he won.

Riding the wave of his success, Auguin left his job teaching technology and entered the high-profile crewed Formula 40 multihull circuit. Ironically, the man who claims to prefer sailing with crew proved less successful as team captain. But although his venture into the big time failed, Auguin didn't come out of the experience empty handed. A lucky connection with the transport and tourism company Groupe Sceta gave him the break he needed to enter the top-flight singlehanded league. Groupe Sceta funded his first Around Alone campaign in 1990-1 and has stood by him ever since.

Besides his undoubted sailing skills and an indulgent sponsor, Auguin has had the good fortune of sailing the top boats in each of the races he has won. The innovative *Groupe Sceta* was one of Groupe Finot's very first Southern Ocean surfers and was only matched by Alain Gautier's *Generali Concorde* in the 1990–1 race. She was followed by the even more radical, super-lightweight *Sceta Calberson* in 1994–5 which, renamed *Geodis*, was updated and fitted with a canting keel for the 1996–7 Vendée Globe. The result was not only an unprecedented three wins in a row, but new race records during his first BOC and the Vendée Globe.

A small, cheerful man, Auguin is not the hardy hero of seafaring legends. Back in harbour his first concern is to be with his wife Véronique Martin and their son Erwan. You can't help but feel that, given half a chance, he'd rather be out sailing with a bunch of friends than battling it out on his own on the other side of the world. But, while some yachting folk might unkindly describe him as "winner by default", the French public don't seem to share this view. In a recent *Paris Match* poll, they voted him among the top 10 sporting personalities they would most like to clone – alongside the likes of Eric Cantona. Now that is hero status.

# CHRISTOPHE augin

**left** The typical shape of a modern Southern Ocean racer – enormously beamy, flat-bottomed, and with insect-like protrusions to help support the mast. Britain's *Group 4* staged a stunning recovery in the 2000–1 Vendée Globe.

# THE route

## VENDÉE GLOBE

Dissatisfaction with the BOC Challenge (now Around Alone), with its compulsory four stops, led a group of competitors to come up with the idea of a non-stop, round-the-world race. The result, 40,000km (25,000 miles) from the west coast of France, single-handed and without assistance is arguably the ultimate sailing challenge.

——— route

**Start** Les Sables d'Olonne, France

**Finish** Les Sables d'Olonne, France

**Passage points**

- The Canary Islands
- Antarctica to starboard
- Heard Island, Southern Ocean, to starboard
- Marker at 50° S 90° E to starboard
- Marker at 57° S 180° to starboard
- Marker at 57° S 120° W to starboard
- Marker at 57° S 67° W to starboard
- Cape Horn, South America, to port

## KEY

▲▲▲▲ Extreme limit of icebergs

●●●●● The Doldrums

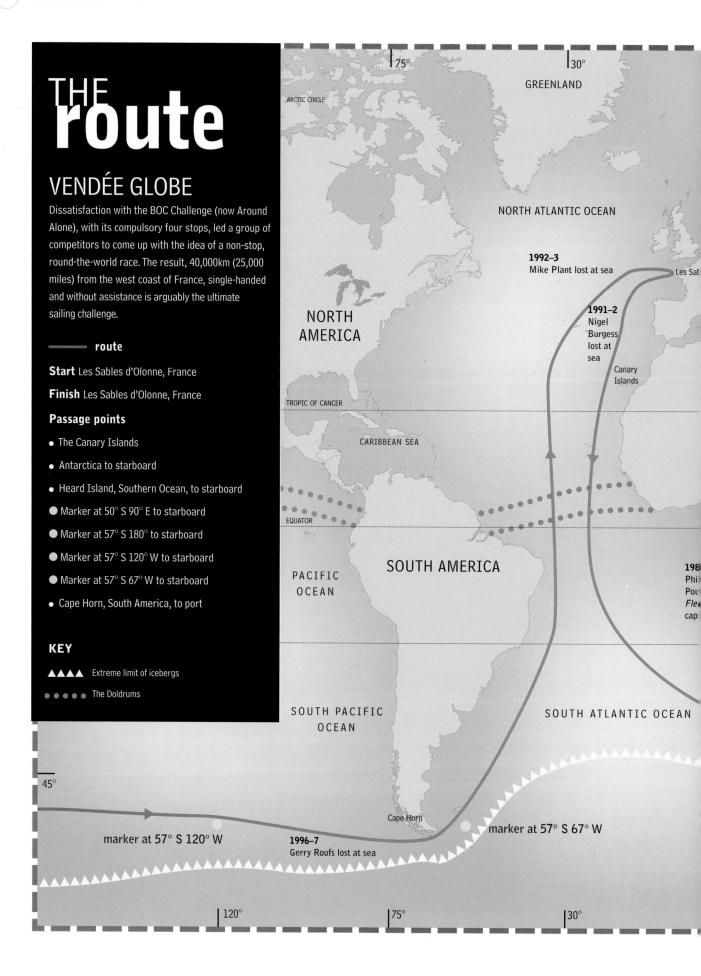

ARCTIC CIRCLE

75°          30°

GREENLAND

NORTH ATLANTIC OCEAN

**1992–3**
Mike Plant lost at sea

Les Sab

NORTH
AMERICA

**1991–2**
Nigel
Burgess
lost at
sea

Canary
Islands

TROPIC OF CANCER

CARIBBEAN SEA

EQUATOR

198
Phil
Pou
*Fle*
cap

PACIFIC
OCEAN

SOUTH AMERICA

SOUTH PACIFIC
OCEAN

SOUTH ATLANTIC OCEAN

45°

Cape Horn

marker at 57° S 120° W

**1996–7**
Gerry Roufs lost at sea

marker at 57° S 67° W

120°          75°          30°

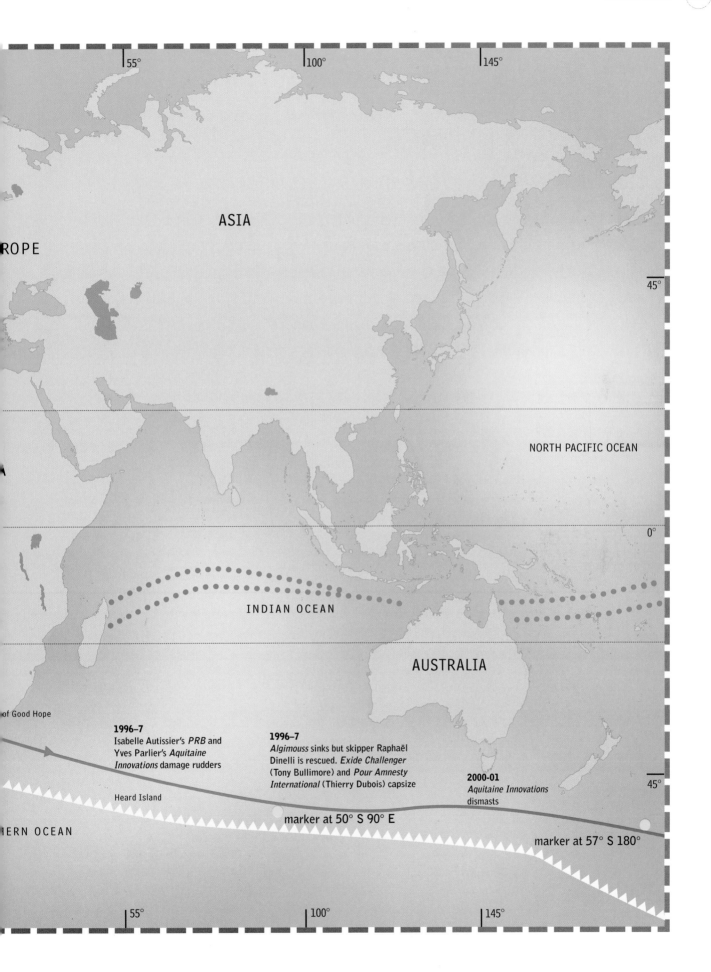

55°

100°

145°

ASIA

ROPE

45°

NORTH PACIFIC OCEAN

0°

INDIAN OCEAN

AUSTRALIA

of Good Hope

**1996–7**
Isabelle Autissier's *PRB* and
Yves Parlier's *Aquitaine
Innovations* damage rudders

**1996–7**
*Algimouss* sinks but skipper Raphaël
Dinelli is rescued. *Exide Challenger*
(Tony Bullimore) and *Pour Amnesty
International* (Thierry Dubois) capsize

**2000-01**
*Aquitaine Innovations*
dismasts

45°

Heard Island

marker at 50° S 90° E

HERN OCEAN

marker at 57° S 180°

55°

100°

145°

# THE BEAUTIFUL RACE

**"** During the BOC I was aware of the limitations imposed on this human adventure by the stopovers. The bonds that a sailor makes with his boat day after day are brutally broken coming back to land. After each stopover you had to re-establish the relationship which had been forged between the man, his boat, and the sea. The intensity of the experience depended on how long it went on for. Moitessier, who inspired hundreds of sailors to follow in his footsteps, spoke about this. The Vendée Globe was born of this observation. **"**

Philippe Jeantot in the official Vendée Globe book by François Mousis

The upturned yacht is a white dash in the water – an insignificant piece of flotsam in an enormous, inhospitable seascape. The distance between the waves tells you that this is no ordinary sea but a large ocean, almost certainly a very, very long way from land. You can imagine the albatrosses skimming the waves in their near-endless flight across one of the world's last great wildernesses. The boat's hull is low in the stern, the twin rudders pointing pathetically skywards, like the fins of a dying fish. Whatever it is – boat, fish, bird – it is clearly mortally wounded. And there in the middle is a sight that sends a shiver down the spine of any sailor: the jagged stub of a keel, broken where it joined the hull; it is cause and effect bleakly staring you in the face, and you only need to have a very basic knowledge about boats to work out what happened. In one glance you have the whole story: broken keel, capsize, life in peril.

The photographs of Tony Bullimore's *Exide Challenger* capsized in the Southern Ocean during the 1996–7 Vendée Globe race are among the most compelling pictures of human endeavour ever published. For a few days in January 1997 the images were on the front page of newspapers around the world, capturing the imagination of millions in a way that few other sailing pictures have.

They were made all the more powerful by the fact that a mystery was attached to them. For, apart from the fact that the boat should have been the right way up, none of the pictures showed any sign of human life. For several days the question was: where is Bullimore? Could he still be on board? Or was he drifting around in his liferaft somewhere in that vast marine desert? Or, perhaps more realistically, had he drowned and was his body floating somewhere beneath its wind-torn surface?

Simultaneously, just a few miles away, Thierry Dubois had capsized in the same storm and the images of the bearded Frenchman clinging to the rudders of his sinking yacht are the stuff of nightmares. Suddenly, half the world was on the edge of its seat, wondering when these unfortunate sailors would be rescued – and whether it was even possible to rescue them.

While military aircraft located the boats and fed the world with those extraordinary images of seafaring disaster, an Australian warship manned by a crew of 143 sailors travelled the 2240km (1400 miles) from Perth to try and rescue one

man and locate the other. Dubois had managed
to swim from his upturned yacht to one of the
liferafts dropped by a rescue plane and was
picked safe and well. But by the time HMAS
*Adelaide* found Bullimore's *Exide Challenger*, five
days after it had capsized, there was still no sign
of life – other than a faint tapping sound picked
up by an underwater sound device – and most
observers assumed Bullimore must be dead. But
the wily old sailor caught them all by surprise
and wrote himself into yachting history when he
swam out of his prison and unexpectedly popped
up next to his stricken yacht. There was a
collective gasp of surprise and delight.

## But where is Roufs?

The dramatic rescue of the two single-handers in
the depths of the Southern Ocean brought a race
that already had a passionate following in France
to a world-wide audience. Only two weeks before
the news had been full of British sailor Pete
Goss's audacious rescue of fellow competitor
Raphaël Dinelli, during which he had battled
256km (160 miles) in hurricane-force winds to
pluck the Italian off his sinking yacht. Goss was
being called a hero and had been recommended
for France's top honour, the Légion d'Honneur.
Less widely reported was the fact that another
competitor, the popular Canadian sailor Gerry

**above** The Vendée Globe shot
into the global spotlight when
four boats capsized or sank in
the Southern Ocean during the
1996–7 race. Thierry Dubois
was one of the lucky ones: after
clinging on to the rudders of his
upturned craft for two days, he
was rescued by the Australian
air force and navy.

Roufs, was missing and would later die in the same race.

Although, as we shall see, there were those within the yachting establishment who felt that such a spate of accidents only proved that the notorious Southern Ocean surfers designed for these races were unsafe and damaged the reputation of the sport, the truth was that the media coverage raised a level of interest in sailing not seen since the very first solo round-the-world race, the Golden Globe, in 1968–9. It was the moment the Vendée Globe moved from mere race into legend.

Perhaps not surprisingly, the original idea for the race had its roots in that great fountainhead of solo racing, the BOC Challenge (now named Around Alone). Three 1986–7 competitors – two-times winner Philippe Jeantot, Bertie Reed, and Guy Bernadin – discussed the concept during the race's Sydney stopover, but it was Jeantot who made the race happen.

The solution to the hiatus of the stop-overs experienced in the BOC, he decided, was to return to the original Golden Globe concept: to sail around the world, leaving the three capes (Good Hope, Leeuwin, and Horn) to port, singlehanded, without stopping and without assistance. Only this time it would be a conventional race with a start and finish line at Les Sables d'Olonne in the Vendée region of France – the *département* which was the race's principal sponsor. The 38,400km (24,000-mile) adventure was billed as the race "to answer the needs of sailors to reach their utmost limits", and Jeantot bet Reed and Bernadin that he would finish a week ahead of everyone else.

The only other compulsory waypoint in that first race was a passage through the Canary Isles - Jeantot, the arch-media manipulator, had realized that getting some interim results and pictures of the fleet early in the race was important to keep the press interested, before the boats all disappeared from sight for three months. Later, once the risks that competitors were willing to take a short cut through the Southern Ocean became apparent, further waypoints were introduced to keep the boats away from possible iceberg areas.

Most of the top names in the world of singlehanded racing signed up for the first Vendée Globe, including BOC veterans Jean-Luc van den Heede, Bertie Reed, Mike Plant, Jean-Yves Terlain, Titouan Lamazou, and, of course, Philippe Jeantot, plus Figaro stars Alain Gautier and Pierre Follenfant and transatlantic race skippers Philippe Poupon and Loïck Peyron.

Several competitors brought innovative new boats, but none which would have as much influence as Alain Gautier's 60-footer (18.27m) *Generali Concorde*. French designers Groupe Finot started with a clean sheet when they designed their first Open 60, producing the most extreme boat in the fleet. With her 5.8m (19ft) beam and 3.5 tonnes of ballast combined with a 4.25m (14ft) draught, *Generali Concorde* provided a stable platform for her enormous 239sqm (2566sqft) of working sail. Compromised by her relatively heavy aluminium hull construction and by rig failure, she never reached her full potential during that race – achieving a modest sixth place in 132 and a half days – but went on to prove herself in the next BOC, coming second behind Christophe Auguin's even more extreme Finot design *Groupe Sceta*. *Generali Concorde* provided the basis for the new generation of Southern Ocean breaknecks which would come to dominate all the future around-the-world races.

There was a sense of foreboding as Eric Tabarly fired the starting gun for the first race on that bitterly cold afternoon of 26 November 1989 and the 13 skippers sailed off into the haze. The last race of this kind, the Golden Globe, had taken place over 20 years before and only one of the eight skippers in that race, Robin Knox-Johnston, had made it back to the finish. The others had either retired or had had to be rescued; one, Donald Crowhurst, had disappeared in strange circumstances. Notwithstanding all the solo races that had taken place since then, no-one had raced non-stop around the world. There was therefore a very real sense that these skippers were launching themselves into the unknown, and the question was not who would come first but rather how many of them would make it back. The silence after the boats had left was deafening.

**below** The man who started it all. Sailing legend Philippe Jeantot won two BOCs before deciding to launch his own non-stop, solo round-the-world race.

## Stuff of media legend

It wasn't long before the drama that would come to typify the Vendée Globe was enacted on TV screens throughout France. A month after the start Philippe Poupon capsized crossing the southern Atlantic and three of his fellow competitors were diverted to his rescue. First on the scene, Loïck Peyron not only managed to right the stricken *Fleury Michon* but captured the whole episode on film. With its themes of inter-dependency and ingenuity in the face of adversity, and blessed by a happy ending, the rescue was a PR gift; the first step towards the race becoming a media legend.

It was a reputation which was confirmed by the end of that very first circumnavigation. Of the 13 boats entered, only seven finished within the simple rules of the race. Terlain was dismasted soon after Poupon capsized and, like him, pulled in to Cape Town. A month later Bertie Reed also retired and three other skippers were disqualified after pulling into harbour for repairs.

The organizers were lucky it wasn't worse. With no course limits in the race rules, several of the fleet headed far south into the Southern Ocean in an attempt to shorten the route. It was a move Jeantot would later condemn, even though he was one of the skippers who had taken that option. "For eight or 10 days we were in a field of icebergs, heading through under spinnakers, with the risk of hitting one at any moment. There weren't any accidents, which was a miracle, but it didn't improve the standing of the Vendée Globe which could exist without that," said Jeantot. "We agreed we'd never do that again – it was too much of a Russian roulette."

**below** The shape of things to come. Alain Gautier's 5.8m- (19ft-) wide *Generali Concorde* raised a few eyebrows when she entered in the first Vendée Globe. Her then-radical design would soon become the norm.

right Artist, novelist, bohemian, and school-girl heart-throb, Titouan Lamazou proved he could sail, too, when he won the 1989–90 Vendée Globe.

The next race included a waypoint at 59° 30' South, 130° West to keep the boats away from the ice (as latitude is measured from the equator, the greater the number of degrees south the nearer the point is to the south pole and, therefore, the greater the likelihood of finding ice). But even that proved insufficient, as skippers dipped down before and after rounding the mark. So, the number of waypoints was increased until in 2000–1 there were four: three at 57° South and one at 50° South where the ice reaches furthest north. As Jeantot explained, with no apparent trace of irony: "The object of the Vendée Globe is to be a beautiful and difficult race – not to be a dangerous race."

The first race ended in an exciting chase up the Atlantic with Titouan Lamazou on *Ecureuil d'Aquitaine II* finishing first and setting a new solo circumnavigation record of 109 days, 8 hours, and 48 minutes. Although banned from subsequent Vendée Globes, weather routing was allowed in this first race and doubtless helped Lamazou avoid some of the pitfalls which Loïck Peyron fell into on board his *Lada Poch III* (Lamazou's former BOC steed) while the boats negotiated the South Atlantic High. Despite Peyron's 14-and-a-half hours' time allowance for assisting Poupon, he finished 17 hours behind Lamazou with Jean-Luc van den Heede (otherwise known as VDH) on the unfashionably narrow yawl *36.15 Met* in third place. Jeantot, meanwhile, was still struggling with a broken gooseneck, the fitting between boom and mast, and, far from finishing a week ahead of the fleet, came in four-and-a-half days behind the leader to take fourth place. He had lost his bet but had nevertheless succeeded in launching a race that had already made the record books and captured the public's imagination – albeit mainly the French public at this stage.

## Mike Plant goes missing

Tragedy marked the 1992–3 Vendée Globe even before the start gun had been fired. The only American entry, Mike Plant and his yacht *Coyote*, disappeared on their way from the US to the start-line. Preparations for the race continued apace but the mood on the quayside was more sombre than usual as a search was mounted for the missing skipper. Eventually, on 22 November, as the 13 competitors headed off, news came that *Coyote* had been found upside down with her mast broken 1.2m (4ft) above the deck. A partially inflated liferaft was found nearby, but of her skipper there was no sign.

The bad news continued as storm force winds hit the fleet in the Bay of Biscay. Four days after the start, the race office received an emergency signal from Briton Nigel Burgess, the Monaco-based yacht broker-turned ocean racer who the French had dubbed "the gentleman skipper". A French naval vessel rushed to the scene and within a few hours discovered his yacht drifting off Finisterre with storm jib and triple-reefed main set. Divers later recovered the sailor's body – he had been wearing a survival suit and carrying two portable ARGOS beacons and had sustained an injury to the back of his head. Although it's still not clear exactly what happened, it seems likely that Burgess was preparing to abandon ship when he was struck by the boat's boom and thrown over the side into the water, where he died of hypothermia.

It was a grim start to the race and instilled in Burgess's fellow sailors an understandable sense of foreboding. If two skippers had died before the fleet was even out of the Bay of Biscay, what did the next 40,000km (25,000 miles) hold in store?

In fact, the first week was the most eventful of the whole race. Not only did the competitors mourn the passing of two of their colleagues, but six yachts were forced to turn back into harbour with storm damage. The carnage started on day two when Yves Parlier's *Cacolac d'Aquitaine* (the former BOC winner *Groupe Sceta*) was dismasted; Philippe Poupon sprang a leak on *Fleury Michon X* and VDH broke a spreader on the boat they called his "*cigare rouge*" (red cigar), *Groupe Sofap-Helvim*. Day three saw three more skippers return, including Loïck Peyron, whose boat's hull began to delaminate. Three of the six were able to restart within a day or so, but it took Parlier a week to re-rig his boat, by which time he

> ❝ THE OBJECT OF THE VENDÉE GLOBE IS TO BE A BEAUTIFUL AND DIFFICULT RACE – NOT TO BE A DANGEROUS RACE ❞
>
> Philippe Jeantot, founder of the race

faced even stronger winds when he set off from Les Sables than at his first attempt.

The story of the race became how the late starters caught up with the rest of the fleet. Despite setting off four days after the official start, VDH and Poupon made remarkable progress chasing their rivals across the Indian Ocean. As they entered the Southern Ocean at the end of December they were less than 1440km (900 miles) behind the race leader, Alain Gautier, having overtaken all but the first three boats and with Poupon having managed to "*manger le grand barbu*" ("eaten up the big bearded one" – in other words, overtaken VDH). By the time they reached Cape Horn, Poupon was in second place and VDH in third, with Poupon less than 640km (400 miles) behind Gautier and on track to beat Lamazou's 1989–90 record.

Poupon's luck ran out on the final run up the Atlantic. Not only did Gautier stretch his lead once again, but 2080km (1300 miles) from the finish *Fleury Michon X*'s rig collapsed in relatively gentle conditions. Far from being beaten, Poupon set up a jury rig attached to his mizzen and managed to sustain an average of around 8.5 knots for the remaining distance. It wasn't fast enough to keep VDH at bay, however, and he slipped in 12 hours ahead of Poupon to claim second place.

## Peyron powers on

Meanwhile, Peyron was following the comeback skippers' example and "eating up" the rest of the fleet. Unfazed by his nine-day delay, he came up from the rear to overtake the backmarker Jean Yves Hasselin after just over a month at sea. Less

**below** While everyone else converted to the beamy Finot concept, Jean-Luc van den Heede stuck with his unfashionably narrow yawls. He achieved his best result when he came second on his "red cigar" *Groupe Sofap-Helvim.* in 1992–3.

than two weeks later Peyron rounded Cape Horn in fourth place and on track to beat Lamazou's record, having sustained an average speed of over nine knots since his re-start. Like Poupon, however, he was thwarted by the unpredictable Atlantic weather and, although he held on to his fourth place over the Hungarian Nandor Fa, he finished well outside the record.

They were the fortunate ones. Bertrand de Broc, on the other hand, seemed unable to shake off his run of bad luck. Dismasted during the 1990 Route du Rhum, he was eliminated from the La Baule–Dakar race the following year after hitting a buoy. For the 1992–3 Vendée Globe he persuaded his sponsors Groupe LG to buy Lamazou's former BOC boat *Ecureuil d'Aquitaine* (*Lada Poch III* in the 1989-90 Vendée), which he lightened by 1.5 tonnes and modified the keel.

With *Groupe LG* taking an early lead and then settling comfortably into second place as they raced across the Southern Ocean, it looked as if de Broc's luck had finally turned. But a week into the new year his devils struck again. The mainsail sheet caught him in the face causing a nasty cut in his tongue which, following instructions faxed from the race doctor, he had to stitch together himself. It took him several days to clean up all the blood. Two week later, his sponsors ordered him to pull into New Zealand because of fears about the boat's keelbolts. When *Groupe LG* was eventually pulled out of the water nothing untoward was found but de Broc's race was destroyed – as was his relationship with his sponsors.

But the race really belonged to Alain Gautier and his innovative yacht *Bagages Superior*. Gautier led the race from the moment he overtook de Broc on the Equator, and although Poupon closed the gap in the Southern Atlantic, Gautier finished the race nearly 1600km (1000 miles) ahead of him. A development of two previous Finot boats, *Generali Concorde* and *Groupe Sceta*, *Bagages Superior* was the latest incarnation of the Southern Ocean surfer concept. Unlike most, however, she was ketch rigged to capitalize on the predominantly downwind sailing conditions expected during the race. Built with a composite hull and carbon fibre deck, she weighed two tonnes less than *Generali Concorde*.

*Bagages Superior* was described by *Yachting World* magazine as "the benchmark for all future [round-the-world] designs" (May 1993), and on the following page Jeantot defended the race's safety record. "How many other boats are required to have three watertight bulkheads and compartments?" he was quoted as saying. "The boats carry three ARGOS beacons, an EPIRB and plenty of survival gear. Their design is up to ABS or Bureau Veritas [international boat building] standards and often stronger." Jeantot would be singing a very different tune by the end of the next race in 1996.

Several records were set during the 1996–7 Vendée Globe, including the fastest solo 24-hour passage. Less salubriously, it was also the race in which, of the 16 competitors, seven retired or were disqualified, five boats capsized or sank, and one skipper died. Two years later a similar spate of attrition afflicted the Around Alone (former BOC Challenge) race, with only seven out of 17 competitors finishing. Suddenly the safety record of all the round-the-world races came under scrutiny and, in particular, the design of the more extreme Open 60s was called into question.

## Canting keels and wing masts

There were six Finot boats at the start line of the third Vendée Globe in 1996, including three built specially for that race, but the most extreme of them by far was Yves Parlier's revolutionary *Aquitaine Innovations*. Weighing in at just 7.6 tonnes, she was two thirds the weight of *Bagages Superior*. Instead of a fixed keel she sported a pivoting wing mast with booms extending on either side of the hull to which the shrouds, the wires holding up the mast, were attached. Her designers estimated this would give her a two-day advantage over a conventionally rigged vessel – as opposed to the one-and-a-half-day advantage attributed to a canting keel. In practice, the mast had already collapsed during that year's Europe 1 STAR and Parlier had barely had time to try out the replacement rig.

The start of the race was played out like the first act of a play, during which the *dramatis*

**above** Sailing the latest development of the Southern Ocean surfer concept, *Bagages Superior*, Alain Gautier easily led the way in 1992–3, finishing nearly 1600km (1000 miles) ahead of his nearest rival.

# ❝ THE BENCHMARK FOR ALL FUTURE DESIGNS ❞

*Yachting World* on *Bagages Superior*

*personae* are sent on stage in a carefully ordered sequence as the plot unfolds. Stage direction in this case came from the seasonally inclement Biscay weather. On the second day out Didier Munduteguy was dismasted and had to head back to Les Sables d'Olonne under jury rig, while Tony Bullimore returned to repair his autopilot. They were followed on day three by Thierry Dubois who had hit some flotsam, and Nandor Fa who was having trouble with his keel. But while Munduteguy and Fa both suffered further damage on their second outings and were eventually forced to retire from the race, Bullimore and Dubois were eventually able to head off in pursuit of the fleet. Now tailenders, their vulnerable position at the rear – far from the help of their fellow competitors should things go badly wrong – would be a crucial factor in the drama that was about to be played out on the vast stage of the Indian Ocean.

Meanwhile, Parlier was heading hell for leather down the Atlantic, treating the race more like one of the Figaro sprints which had made

him famous than the marathon everyone else took it to be. Isabelle Autissier sailing her new Finot-designed *PRB*, and Christophe Auguin with his revitalized *Sceta Calberson*, now renamed *Geodis*, followed anxiously in his wake. The inevitable happened two-and-a-half weeks after the start when *Aquitaine Innovations*'s forestay broke and Parlier was finally forced to slow up a little. Auguin and Autissier slipped into the lead, racing neck and neck into the Southern Ocean well ahead of the rest of the fleet. Auguin's customary caution paid off when first Autissier struck a piece of flotsam and then Parlier hit some ice and both were forced to pull out of the race with damaged rudders. Although the two sailors would continue the race as unofficial contestants, Auguin had by then established a huge lead which only gear failure or a major disaster could overturn. As if to assert his dominance further, he succeeded in breaking his own singlehanded monohull record, established in a previous BOC race by sailing 598km (374 miles) in one 24-hour period – an average speed of 15.6 knots.

Behind Augin, Gerry Roufs was pushing hard to catch up, while behind him the chasing pack was just entering the Southern Ocean almost within sight of each other. Meanwhile tailenders Dubois and Bullimore were still well behind, with Dubois suffering a further setback when one of his rudders was damaged by flotsam, forcing him to pull in to Cape Town for repairs.

Christmas Day 1996 brought 60-knot winds and waves as tall as a six-storey building. Towards the back of the fleet, Raphaël Dinelli was having trouble controlling his yacht *Algimouss,* Jeantot's former *Credit Agricole IV*, as he surfed down the mountainous seas under bare poles. Dinelli, an unofficial entry in the race having failed to complete the required 3200km (2000-mile) qualifying passage, was below decks using his autopilot to steer the yacht. After surviving several knockdowns *Algimouss* eventually succumbed to the sheer power of the elements and capsized. The shock forced the mast through the deck and water poured in as the boat slowly righted herself. Within a few hours she was almost flooded, only kept afloat by the watertight compartments – those that hadn't been destroyed by the force of the waves. Dinelli clambered onto the almost-awash deck and lashed himself to the stump of the mast where, with nothing to eat or drink, he stood for two days and a night buffeted by freezing cold winds, praying that someone would reach him before *Algimouss* sank.

## Goss to the rescue

Dinelli was lucky to be one of that tightly-bunched third group of yachts. The two competitors nearest to him were Patrick de Radigues and Pete Goss, with de Radigues tantalizingly close, just 60 miles away upwind. It would have taken him a few relatively painless

**❝ I'VE GOT NO MORE CIGARS LEFT, NO MORE WINE AND HARDLY ANY CLOVES OF GARLIC FOR THE PASTA, AND ON TOP OF THAT NO SEX…I'VE TURNED INTO THE MOST MONASTIC MAN ON THE PLANET ❞**

Didier Mundutuguy on life after 116 days at sea

**below** The most radical design in 1996–7 was Yves Parlier's *Aquitaine Innovations,* with her pivoting wingmast. Rig problems and a collision with some ice forced him to retire from the race off Australia.

hours to alter course and pick up the French sailor. But de Radigues's electrics were playing up, putting him out of radio contact, and he sailed on oblivious of Dinelli's plight. Goss was at that time 256km (160 miles) downwind, also sailing under bare poles in survival mode having himself been knocked down three times. His moment of truth came when he was asked by the race director, Philippe Jeantot, by radio from France to turn around and try to rescue his fellow competitor. His immediate response, raising a storm jib and turning his boat around to face the full fury of the storm, would change the course of his life. At that moment Goss became, as proclaimed by newspapers around the world, a true sailing hero.

But running with the wind and sea in such conditions is one thing; beating into them to make progress upwind is quite another and there was some doubt whether Goss's boat would be able to withstand the strain. Fortunately, however, *Aqua Quorum*, the only 50-footer (15.2m) in the fleet, benefited from the rather more conservative shape drawn by her British designer, Adrian Thompson. Her relatively narrow beam of 4.6m (15ft) – compared to 5.9m (19.4ft) of the 18.2m (60ft) *Aquitaine Innovations* – stood her in good stead as she tacked back upwind to the helpless Dinelli.

The Frenchman's life was hanging by a thread when a Royal Australian Air Force plane pinpointed him and dropped a liferaft. It was just in time: his yacht sank 10 minutes later.

Thirty hours after turning back Goss found Dinelli and performed a textbook rescue in the still horrific conditions. Once back on course Goss famously made his new shipmate a reviving cup of tea – a gesture so typically English that it has gone down in the annals of sailing folklore in France. The pair then sailed on to Hobart together, after which Goss continued on alone, finishing the race in fifth place with a time of 126 days, 21 hours, and 25 minutes (including a 318-hour allowance for rescuing Dinelli) – becoming the first British sailor to finish the Vendée Globe. He received a hero's welcome back at Les Sables and was later awarded the Légion d'Honneur in France and an MBE in the UK. A lifelong

friendship was established between the two sailors, with the pair racing together in a two-handed transatlantic race the following year. Goss was also best man at Dinelli's wedding.

## Double trouble

It was a very different matter for Bullimore and Dubois when their boats capsized almost simultaneously on 4 January 1997. Thanks to the sequence of events which started with Bullimore's autopilot failing at the start of the race and continued through to Dubois rejoining the fleet after fixing *Pour Amnesty International*'s rudder, the two skippers found themselves within 64km (40 miles) of each other, 2240km (1400 miles) from land and 1920km (1200 miles) from their nearest fellow competitor, Catherine Chabaud. With no chance of Chabaud being able to sail into the wind to reach them in time, the Australian navy's HMAS *Adelaide* was dispatched and, with the support of several Australian air force planes, succeeded in rescuing both sailors in an operation that had people throughout the world on the edge of their seat.

The race organizers were still helping co-ordinate the Bullimore/Dubois rescue when a new emergency began to emerge. Gerry Roufs was over 2560km (1600 miles) behind the race leader, Auguin, on 7 January when his ARGOS beacon suddenly stopped transmitting. The race office was unable to contact him by radio and Isabelle Autissier, back as an unofficial competitor after having *PRB*'s rudder repaired in Cape Town, couldn't raise him on VHF despite being only about 32km (20 miles) away. By the time the alarm was raised, she faced a Goss-like mission to sail 240km (150 miles), into near-hurricane force winds to reach Roufs's estimated position. Except that Autissier's yacht, a classic Finot Southern Ocean surfer fundamentally unsuited to tacking into a gale, was already damaged and its skipper exhausted from coping with the extreme conditions. After 24 hours she had made only 80km (50 miles) to windward and, amid some controversy, Autissier was relieved of her rescue duty.

Almost exactly midway between Australia and South America, there was no chance of

**right** The moment Pete Goss won his Légion d'Honneur. Picking up the shipwrecked Raphaël Dinelli after battling through 30 hours of horrific seas on the valiant *Aqua Quorum*.

**above** Three shipwrecked sailors were rescued in the 1996–7 race, but a fourth was never found. The remains of Gerry Rouf's yacht, *Groupe LG*, were eventually found on the coast of Chile.

mounting a Bullimore/Dubois type rescue – for a start, none of the aircraft available had that kind of range. Instead, a passing ship, the Panama-registered *Mass Enterprise*, diverted her course and began searching the area on 9 January. Marc Thiercelin, sailing the former *Groupe Sceta*, joined the search the next day, followed by another passing freighter, the Indian ship *Aditya Gaurav*. But despite receiving satellite pictures of the area which identified 18 possible targets, nothing was found. Roufs's great friend, Eric Dumont, sailing the former *Bagages Superior*, was last on the scene but with the wind rising to 50 knots he, too, had to give up the search.

The upturned hull of Roufs's yacht was eventually found six months later drifting 480km (300 miles) off the Straits of Magellan, its keel and rudders intact but with no sign of the skipper. It was almost a month before Roufs's family was informed, by which time the boat had vanished again. Nine months after the accident a few fragments of wreckage were recovered on the Chilean coast but the mystery surrounding Roufs's last hours remains.

The final piece of bad luck in this rollercoaster of a race struck that most unlucky of singlehanders, Bernard de Broc. Having fallen out with his sponsors following the 1992–3 debacle – after which Groupe LG had switched its allegiances to the tragic Roufs – de Broc found a novel new way of raising money for his next campaign. For 250 French francs, members of the public and companies alike could put their names on the side of his boat, appropriately named *Votre Nom Autour du Monde* ("Your Name around the World"). He left Les Sables with 6000 subscribers, including the French President, Jacques Chirac, to keep him company on the voyage.

## The luck of de Brock

As de Broc approached Cape Horn, however, he noticed that the floors of his yacht were delaminating and reluctantly decided to pull in at Ushuaia in Tierra del Fuego. Although this would rule him out of the official finish list it would at least ensure that he completed his circumnavigation. Or so he thought. In fact, his

keel dropped off completely 480km (300 miles) from the finish line, his boat turned turtle and he had to be rescued by a French naval helicopter. De Broc's luck, it seemed, hadn't changed that much after all.

Seemingly immune to his fellow competitors' misfortunes, Auguin sailed a charmed path through the string of depressions in the Southern Ocean, at one point riding for three days on the edge of a slow-moving cold front, clocking up over 1600km (1000 miles). He finished his near-perfect race in 105 days, 20 hours, and 31 minutes – four days faster than Titouan Lamazou's record, set in the first race. Not only that, but he was also the first person to win three round-the-world solo races. At the other end of the fleet, Catherine Chabaud sailed a steady, safe race to become the first woman to complete the Vendée Globe and the fastest woman to complete a non-stop solo circumnavigation, beating Kay Cottee's record, set in 1988, by 49 days.

The events of the 1996–7 Vendée Globe sent shock waves through the yachting fraternity. It wasn't just the fact that so many boats had capsized but the horrifying fact that they had remained upside down. The behaviour of Dubois's *Pour Amnesty International* was of particular concern. Despite losing her rig and being fitted with a canting keel, which can usually be used to help right a capsized vessel, the yacht remained inverted – a phenomenon largely attributed to her flat decks. Whereas traditionally decks are gently cambered, or curved, to help shed water more quickly, several of the newest round-the-world racers were fitted with flat or even concave decks which created a suction with the surface of the water when they capsized. Autissier would go on to experience precisely this phenomenon with her *PRB* when it turned over in the Southern Ocean during the 1998–9 Around Alone (former BOC) race.

The media was appalled. "I don't think we can send another race into the Southern Ocean with very wide craft which won't right themselves until a satisfactory solution has been found," opined Sir Robin Knox-Johnston in his monthly column for *Yachting World*. "There has to be a

**above** The Canadian sailor Gerry Roufs was a multihull sailor who had raced on some of the top crewed yachts on the circuit. He was lost at sea during his first Vendée Globe.

limit to what we can ask the…rescue authorities to undertake."

The Vendée Globe organizers responded swiftly, and before the last boat was even home held a meeting with the skippers and designers to decide what to do. The result was that the rules for the 2000–1 race were the most stringent ever, combining the standards set by the professional skippers' and the race organizers' respective associations. For a start, boats had to be self-righting from at least 125° and have at least 130 per cent buoyancy. In practice this meant that many of the older boats had to be fitted with heavier keels – three tonnes, as opposed to as little as two tonnes on some of the more extreme 1996 boats – and a dome over the aft deck to make them less stable when capsized. Several of the newer boats had longer cabins for the same reason, while Dubois's new boat *Solidaires* stood out both for her stripey colour scheme and her marked deck camber. He was clearly not wanting a repeat performance of his last race.

## Record entry

The enormous world-wide publicity generated from the previous race meant that far from scaring off potential competitors there was a record number of entries: 24 skippers from seven countries. And, even more remarkably, almost half of them were sailing boats built specially for the event. This time Groupe Finot accounted for six of the 11 new boats, including two-times Figaro winner Michel Desjoyeaux's new *PRB*, America's Cup sailor Thomas Coville's *Sodebo*, and British star Mike Golding's *Team Group 4*. Marc Lombard, the designer of Jeantot's *Crédit Agricole IV*, had two new boats at the start line: Catherine Chabaud's *Whirlpool* and Roland Jourdain's *Sill*, both also highly ranked. Several historic yachts were back dressed up in new livery, including Poupon's old *Fleury Michon X* which, after racing in 1996–7 Vendée as de Broc's *Votre Nom*, had gone on to set a new westabout world record with Philippe Monnet at the helm in 2000 and the boat was back for a fourth circumnavigation as Simone Bianchetti's *aquarelle.com*. Pete Goss's much-venerated *Aqua Quorum* was being skippered by Patrice

Carpentier, and Auguin's old *Sceta Calberson/Geodis* had metamorphosed into Bernard Gallay's *voilà.com*.

One of the more puzzling entries to some was British newcomer Ellen MacArthur, at 24 the youngest skipper ever to enter the race. MacArthur had won her class in the 1998 Route du Rhum and had just had a new, state-of-the-art Open 60 built in New Zealand, which she had sailed back to the UK earlier that year. Although she came first in her class on *Kingfisher* during the Europe 1 New Man STAR (the latest appellation for the old OSTAR), this was her first round-the-world race and few rated her chances. After all, how could this "slip of a girl" be expected to beat the experience and strength of French giants such as Yves Parlier, sailing his third Vendée, and Dominique Wavre, veteran of four Whitbread Round-the-World races?

The scheduled start was delayed until 9 November due to strong winds but, once off, Parlier again set a frantic pace streaking down the Atlantic, with a pack including the 40-year-old Desjoyeaux and MacArthur in hot pursuit. Heading into the Southern Ocean, Parlier's *Aquitaine Innovations* showed that she was still as competitive as when she was first launched in 1996 by setting a new 24-hour record of 670km (419 miles), sustaining an average speed of 17.46 knots.

It came as no great shock when two weeks later it was announced that Parlier had been dismasted. As Chabaud put it: "Yves is a mad genius the way he controls his boat, but [the dismasting] doesn't surprise me." More of a surprise was that rather than retiring and heading to Perth, the nearest port 2400km (1500 miles) to the north, he decided to carry on under jury rig. His plan: to put into Stewart Island in New Zealand and erect a more permanent rig to complete the race with.

Parlier certainly painted one of the more colourful pages in the history of the race by spending nine days anchored off Stewart Island creating an 18m- (59ft-) tall mast, having

**❝YVES IS A MAD GENIUS THE WAY HE CONTROLS HIS BOAT❞**

Catherine Chabaud on hearing that Yves Parlier had been dismasted during the 2000–1 race

**left** Catherine Chabaud became the first woman to complete the Vendée Globe when she finished in sixth place in 1996–7.

improvized with a home-made oven to get the glue to cure and giving a fair imitation of a latterday Robinson Crusoe as he plucked mussels from the seashore. Heading back into the Southern Atlantic, Parlier encountered another problem. Before setting off from Les Sables d'Olonne he had provisioned, somewhat optimistically, for just 100 days. By the time he rounded Cape Horn, he was running out of food and having to supplement his diet with fish and seaweed. Ironically, his eventual finishing time of just under 127 days was only a day or so longer than his 1992–3 result on *Cacolac d'Aquitaine* – and 100 days faster than Francis Chichester's time set in 1966!

## Carnage at the tail end

Further back in the fleet, breakages were coming thick and fast. Patrick de Radigues was the first to retire. The unfortunate Belgian was knocked unconscious after falling onto a winch and woke up to find himself on a beach in Portugal. He managed to get his boat floating again but wrote himself out of the race by having to accept outside assistance. So did Raphaël Dinelli, who struck a whale in the fourth week and had to pull into Cape Town for repairs – although this time he did manage to complete his circumnavigation, albeit as an unofficial competitor.

But the great comeback story of 2000-1 was Mike Golding on *Team Group 4*. The British favourite to win the race inexplicably dismasted just 40 miles from Les Sables and had to limp back into port. Eight days after the official start he set off again, with a new rig, but this time with a different goal: to set a new round-the-world record. Golding astonished everyone by sprinting down the Atlantic, overtaking the Russian tailender, Fédor Konyukhov, off Cape Verde after four weeks and then gradually climbing his way up through the fleet. By the time he rounded Cape Horn he was in eighth place behind fellow Briton, Josh Hall, on *EBP-Gartmore*. Golding finished the race in seventh place with a race time of 110 days, 16 hours, and 22 minutes – or 102 days after he set off, well inside Auguin's 1996-7 record. Unfortunately for him, however, the goal posts had by then completely changed.

## Michel vs Ellen

The race up the Atlantic to the finish line was fought like a series of duels. Desjoyeaux rounded Cape Horn 966km (600 miles) ahead of his nearest competitor, MacArthur, and had every reason to feel supremely confident of victory. The only fly in the ointment was that pesky little girl who had slalomed her way through the icebergs of the Southern Ocean and confounded her critics in the process by showing her transom to most of the established names of singlehanded racing. Ellen MacArthur was on a roll and, as Desjoyeaux fell into a hole, she gradually nibbled away at the miles that separated them. Snapping at her heels were Roland Jourdain and Marc Thiercelin, followed a little way off by Dominique Wavre and Thomas Colville; and even further back Mike Golding and Josh Hall, each pair apparently locked together in mortal combat.

Desjoyeaux meanwhile saw the lead he had hitherto thought unassailable dwindle until *Kingfisher* actually overtook him – briefly – for MacArthur had her own problems to deal with: torn sails, a collision with a submerged container which sheared one of her daggerboards, and finally a broken stay which forced her to slow down for the home stretch. As it turned out, Desjoyeaux finished comfortably ahead in 93 days, three hours, and 57 minutes, smashing the previous record, set by Christophe Auguin in 1996–7 by an amazing 12 days. He received a tumultuous welcome at Les Sables d'Olonne – only surpassed 24 hours later when "*la petite Anglaise*" received a phenomenal reception from an adoring crowd celebrating the achievement of fastest woman to circumnavigate the world singlehanded.

It had been a fast race overall, with the 24-hour record broken several times and finally being claimed by Jourdain when he covered a distance of 696.8km (435.3 miles) at an average speed of 18.14 knots. All six of the first boats home finished within Auguin's race record. Not only that, but not a single boat had been lost. Finally, it seemed, Jeantot's dream of creating a beautiful and difficult race, and not just a dangerous one, had come true.

**right** After 101 days at sea, Mike Golding completed the 2000–1 Vendée Globe, well within the previous round-the-world record, but well outside the new 93-day record set in the same race by Michel Desjoyeaux.

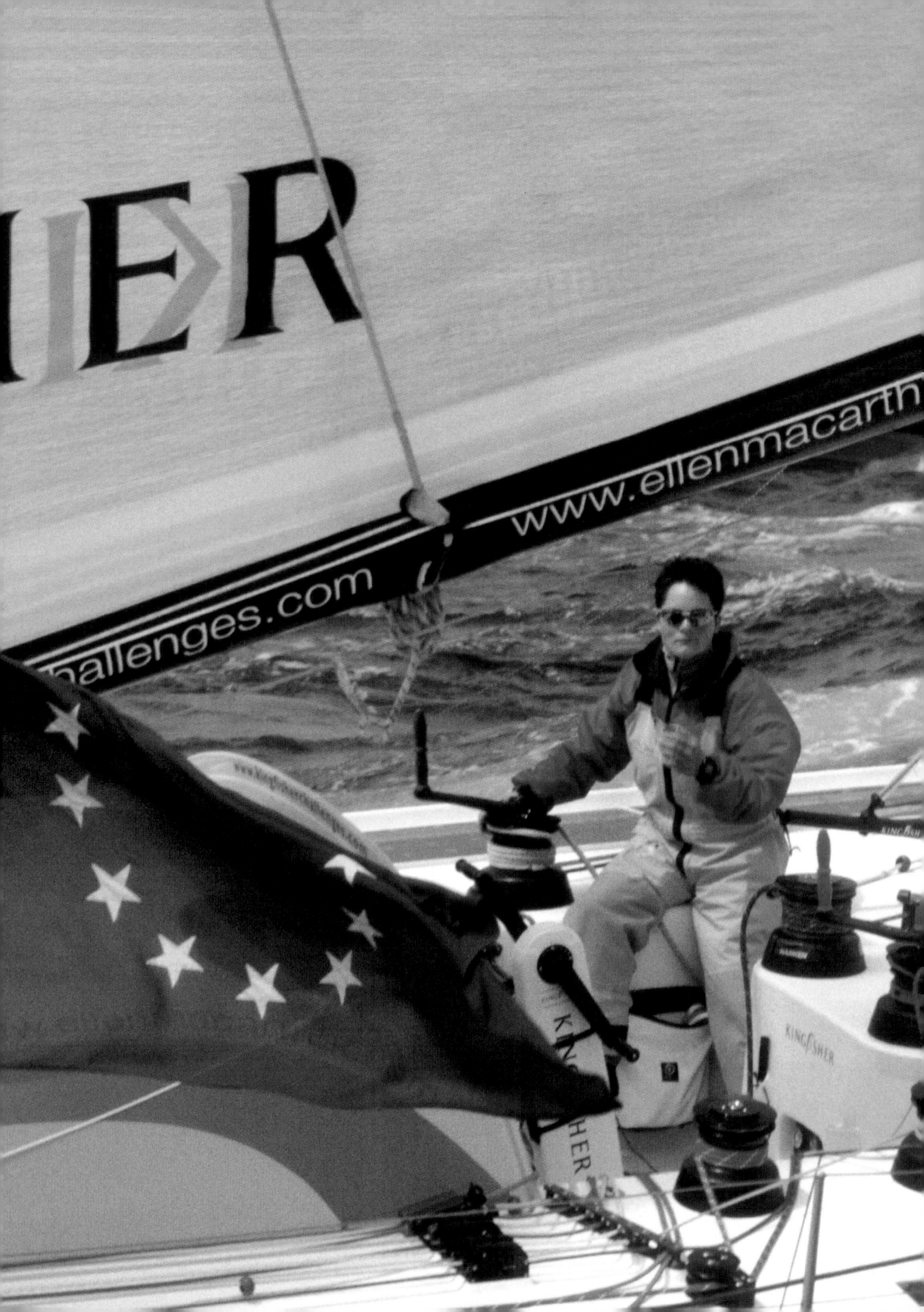
HER
www.ellenmacarth
hallenges.com

## CAREER PROFILE

**1976** Born in Derby, England, on 8 July

**1995** Young Sailor of the Year. Youngest person to pass the Yachtmaster Offshore Qualification

**1997** 14th in Mini-Transat (classification: 7m (21ft) yacht; finishing time: 33 days)

**1998** Yachtsman of the Year. Overall 5th in Route du Rhum, 1st place in class (classification: Open 50 monohull; finishing time: 20 days, 11 hours)

**2000** 1st place in Europe 1 Newman Star (classification: Open 60; finishing time: 14 days, 23 hours)

**2001** 2nd place in Vendée Globe (classification: Open 60; finishing time: 94 days, 4½ hours)

**2002** 1st place in Route du Rhum (classification: OPen 60; finishing time: 13 days, 13 hours)

Rarely has a sportsman received so much adulation for not winning a race. When Ellen MacArthur arrived at Les Sables d'Olonne on 10 February 2001, tens of thousands of supporters cheered her over the Vendée Globe finish line – noticeably more than had greeted the winner of the race, Frenchman Michel Desjoyeux, 24 hours before. MacArthur had become the fastest woman and the youngest person to circumnavigate the globe in a singlehanded race.

To the French, who had already named her "Jeune Espoire de la Voile" ("Sailing's Young Hope"), she was "la petite Anglaise", and even

## ❝ GO FOR IT! ❞

before the start of the 2000–1 Vendée Globe they would boom out her favourite phrase, "Ellen, à donf!" ("go for it!"). She appeared on the front pages of almost every UK newspaper, while sailing magazines devoted countless pages to her achievement. MacArthur-mania had begun.

At 24, she was the race's youngest skipper and, alongside Catherine Chabaud, one of only two women entered. MacArthur herself said, "Realistically, if I can make it to the finish line in good shape I'll be happy. If I sail well I think I can make the top 10 – that would be fantastic." In fact, she was among the leaders from the very start and in second place for most of the race, even overtaking Desjoyeaux for a heart-stopping day after passing the Falklands. Her eventual finishing time of 94 days and four and a half hours was 11 days faster than the previous record.

It was a far cry from MacArthur's childhood in land-locked Derbyshire. After an aunt took her sailing at the age of eight, she saved up her school dinner money for three years to buy her own 2.4m (8ft) dinghy which she sailed on nearby Ogston Reservoir. By the age of 18 she had moved up to a Coribee, a 6.4m (21ft) sailing boat, which she restored and navigated singlehanded around Britain. The same year she became the youngest person to pass the RYA Yachtmaster Offshore exam and was named Young Sailor of the Year.

Despite this recognition, MacArthur struggled to raise the funding to enter her first singlehanded race, the 1997 Mini Transat. She bought a one-way ticket to France and completed the 4320km (2700-mile) race in 33 days on her second-hand boat *Le Poisson*. That was followed by another transatlantic, the legendary Route du Rhum, in which she won her class on Pete Goss's famous Open 50 *Aqua Quorum* (renamed *Kingfisher*).

Her star rose a little higher when she was named Yachtsman of the Year in 1998. Two years later she won the monohull class in the Europe 1 New Man Star transatlantic race (the former OSTAR). Soon after, she secured a £2 million sponsorship deal from retailers Kingfisher to take part in the Vendée Globe. Suddenly, the cash-strapped prodigy was propelled into the big time.

Despite her relative lack of experience, MacArthur's success in the 2000–1 Vendée Globe was no fluke. Preparation with race manager Mark Turner was key. Meteorology guru Jean Yves Bernot gave her advice about weather and strategy; leading chronobiologist Claudio Stampi taught her to regulate her sleep in 20-minute snatches; Olympic dinghy sailor Paul Brotherton lent his experience in match racing. But perhaps the most valuable lessons were learned sailing her state-of-the-art Open 60 *Kingfisher*, from New Zealand, where it was built, to France, giving her invaluable Southern Ocean experience and allowing her to familiarize herself with the boat.

Her second place in the race was a remarkable achievement, but perhaps even more exciting is the potential that that result suggests, confirmed by her 2002 Route du Rhum victory. At 26, MacArthur has plenty more races to win.

# ELLEN macarthur

**left** One of the most popular events for solo sailors is the Azores and Back (AZAB) race from Falmouth. Ronnie Nollett set a new monohull record in 1995 by completing the outward leg in just under eight days.

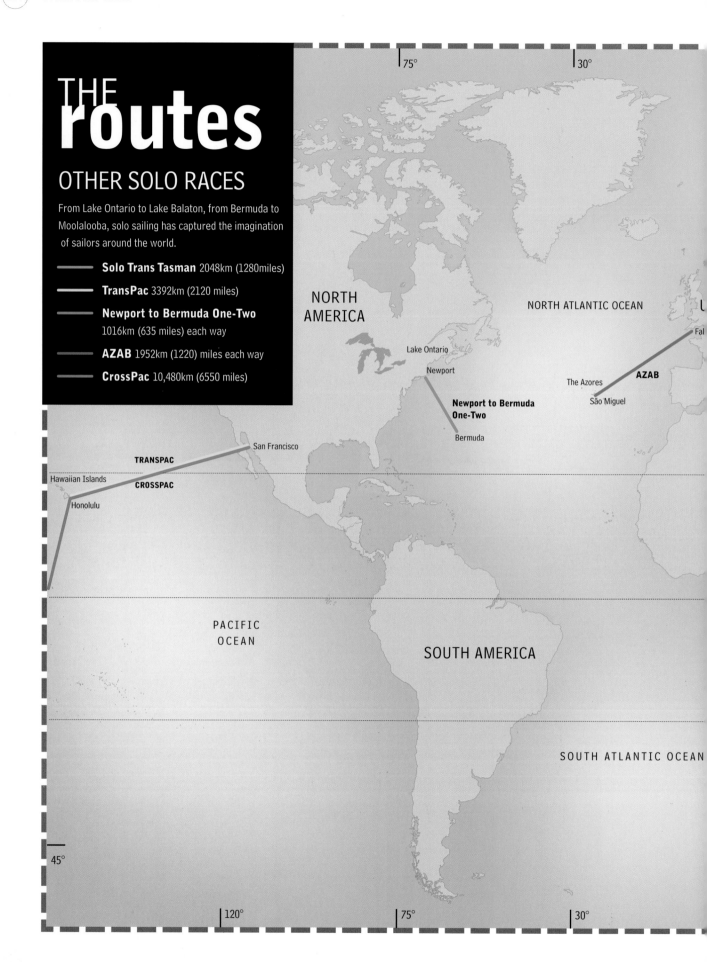

# THE routes

## OTHER SOLO RACES

From Lake Ontario to Lake Balaton, from Bermuda to Moolalooba, solo sailing has captured the imagination of sailors around the world.

— **Solo Trans Tasman** 2048km (1280miles)

— **TransPac** 3392km (2120 miles)

— **Newport to Bermuda One-Two**
1016km (635 miles) each way

— **AZAB** 1952km (1220) miles each way

— **CrossPac** 10,480km (6550 miles)

NORTH AMERICA

NORTH ATLANTIC OCEAN

Lake Ontario

Newport

**Newport to Bermuda One-Two**

Bermuda

The Azores

**AZAB**

São Miguel

Fal

U

San Francisco

**TRANSPAC**

Hawaiian Islands

**CROSSPAC**

Honolulu

PACIFIC OCEAN

SOUTH AMERICA

SOUTH ATLANTIC OCEAN

45°

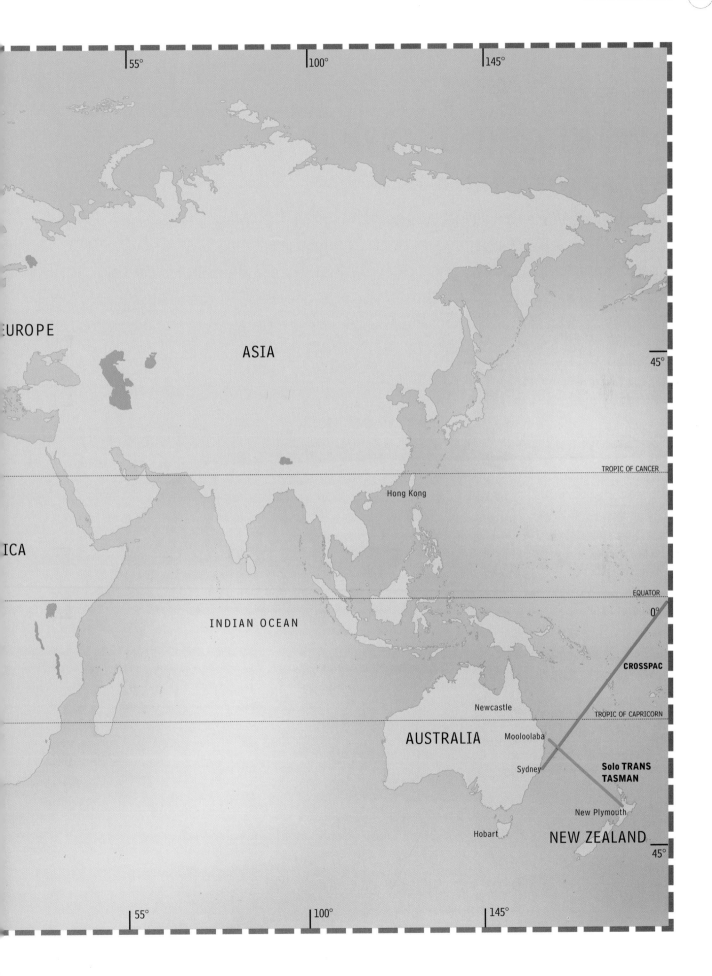

# A WORLD OF THEIR OWN

**❝** His last report was on 1st June at position 32.49 166.14. The radio signal was poor, however he was sailing well … The yacht has just one battery to operate all functions on the yacht … The yacht has sailed through extreme conditions …There are three EPIRBs [distress mechanisms] on the yachts… No EPIRBs have been activated that can be attributed to *Skiddy Too*… The race committee will be monitoring the situation closely for the next two days… **❞**

Extract from the press statement issued by the Solo Trans-Tasman Race organizers, upon the disappearance of Bretten Holland in June 2002

June 2002, the Tasman Sea; singlehanded sailor Bretten Holland has gone missing in his 9.8m (32ft 3in) yacht *Skiddy Too* while racing between New Zealand and Australia. Last spotted on 1 June after sailing through "extreme conditions", he has been out of radio contact for several days, and concern is mounting for his safety. The race organizers are forced to issue a press statement reassuring everyone that "Bretten is a very competent aircraft pilot with good navigational skills" and "*Skiddy Too* has a reputation as being a very strong, capable, and seaworthy yacht". None of the yacht's emergency alarms have been activated, they say, and they expect Bretten back "within this two-day period". They nevertheless issue an alert to the Australian Search and Rescue Centre, just in case.

Northerly winds funnel down from the Pacific to meet weather systems spinning up from the Antarctic, building up a vicious sea between the land masses of New Zealand and Australia. This is certainly not the place to go for a leisurely summer cruise. It was on this stretch of water that seven boats were abandoned, three boats sunk, and six sailors died as the result of a sudden storm during the Sydney to Hobart race in 1998.

Sailors taking part in the Solo Trans-Tasman Race have to cross the full width of this unpredictable sea, starting from New Plymouth on New Zealand's North Island and finishing at Mooloolaba near Brisbane in Queensland. Not surprisingly, several yachts have been dismasted, abandoned, and sunk during the history of the race, although no lives have yet been lost. Concern for Bretten Holland is therefore very real.

## Pushing the limits

This drama on the Tasman Sea has all the hallmarks of a classic Vendée Globe or Around Alone (ex-BOC) type rescue preamble – except without the hype. The sailors taking part in this race usually do it without sponsorship and without media profiles because they love the thrill of sailing alone, of pushing the challenge to the limits for the sake of it. There are no glittering prizes at the end of it; no knighthoods, no books to write and no royalties to be collected. It's pure sport.

For, while the high-profile events steal the limelight, more modest singlehanded races are taking place around the world – sometimes in the most unlikely of places. Take Lake Ontario in Canada, several hundred miles away from the

sea, where the Port Credit Yacht Club claims to have "a long history of nurturing and supporting singlehanded sailboat racing". Or the Royal Hong Kong Yacht Club which runs a series of races for Dragon-class boats in which the rules specifically state "the helm and the crew shall be the same person" (by which delightfully arcane term we are meant to understand that they must be sailed singlehanded). San Francisco Bay has its very own Single Handed Sailing Society which as well as putting on the famous Transpac Race to Hawaii also stages a lively programme of other,

shorter solo races throughout the summer, including the intriguingly-named Three Bridge Fiasco Race held (and here may be the clue) in January. Across the Pacific there are Shorthanded Sailing Associations in both Australia and New Zealand, although both tend to specialize in double- rather than singlehanded races. Among the Australian sailors who have started their careers here are BOC veterans Kanga Birtles and David Adams and circumnavigator Kay Cottee.

Which brings us back to the Southern Hemisphere where, unbeknown to the organizers

**above** The Trans-Tasman covers one of the most treacherous stretches of sea in the world. Amateurs and professionals take part in the 2048km (1280-mile) single-handed race.

and local press waiting anxiously on shore, Bretten Holland is still battling his way across the Tasman Sea on his little yacht *Skiddy Too*. He eventually arrives in Mooloolaba on 8 June, 13 days after setting off from New Plymouth and two days after the race leaders have come into harbour. As the organizers had suspected, the boat's electrics had been playing up, putting his autopilot out of action and forcing him to hand steer for 24 hours a day – as well as closing down his communication system. It's a scenario that's been acted out many times in the major round-the-world races, except that there it's the boats' high-tech satellite systems that get wiped out during a knockdown, or their ARGOS transponder which goes walkabout leaving the race organizers to fret about the boats' whereabouts. No satellite systems or ARGOS transponders for the Tasman fleet though; Holland's sole means of communication was a ham radio, not known for its resistance to water.

Like others of its kind, the Trans-Tasman race was inspired by the growing success of the OSTAR in the 1960s. With its long tradition of yachting and its close links to England, it's perhaps not surprising that New Zealand was one of the first countries to espouse this new form of racing. And with the UK race starting from Plymouth, where better to base its Kiwi equivalent than New Plymouth on the west coast of North Island? Three members of the New Plymouth Yacht Club duly formed a committee in 1968, and adopted wholesale the rules devised for the OSTAR. The race across the Tasman was to be held every four years, during the OSTAR's off years. Mooloolaba, 2048km (1280 miles) away in Queensland, was chosen as the finishing point for its convenience and safety of navigation, well away from the dangerous shoals of Brisbane's Moreton Bay.

### Bullfrog Sunblock

Five boats turned up for the first race in 1970, including the first and only non-antipodean entry, American Marvin Glenn on his trimaran *Rebel*, who rudely grabbed first place by a wide margin in nine days, five hours, and seven minutes – 27 hours ahead of the first antipodean

boat. The eight races that have taken place since then have been fought exclusively between New Zealand and Australian boats, with Aussie boats ratcheting up five wins to the Kiwis' three. The worst year for the race's originators was 1986, when continentals (i.e. Australians) dominated the first nine places. That was the year when Australian Ian Johnston set the record for the fastest crossing on his trimaran *Bullfrog Sunblock* (one of the few fully-sponsored boats in the race) in six days, eight hours, and 50 minutes.

The slowest crossing goes to the Kiwi sailor Roger Taylor who in 1974 took an astonishing 35 days to reach Mooloolaba on his yacht *Roc* – giving an average distance made good of 58.4km (36.5 miles) per day – or under 1.5 knots. Taylor was not so much dawdling or admiring the scenery as just sailing a slow boat. Not only was *Roc* the smallest vessel to ever take part in the race, she was also, as her name suggest, built of ferro-cement, although "concrete" construction was vindicated eight years later when John Sayer won on his *Floating Footpath* in a far more respectable 11 days and 10 minutes.

No singlehanded race would be complete without its stories of disasters at sea, and the Trans-Tasman is no exception. The 1978 race was its nadir, with Cyclone Hal sowing chaos among the record-sized fleet of 15 starters. John Jury had to abandon his *Easterly I* after she was rolled over and dismasted – the yacht was later salvaged off the Australian coast – while Bob Millard had to finish the race under jury rig after his *Witchetty* was dismasted. Millard still made it to the finish line within the time limit. But the real drama of that race was the disappearance of the 1974 winner Bill Belcher and his *Josephine*. The yacht was eventually found by the Australian Navy submerged inside the notorious Middleton Reef, but there was no sign of her skipper. Several weeks later, Belcher was picked up by a merchant ship drifting out to sea in his liferaft. His ordeal was later made into a film.

### Dishing the dirty

And what the Tasman serves up on the outward leg you can be sure it will dish out on the way back. Although not under race conditions, several competitors have come a cropper on the return journey to New Zealand, most notably in 1974, when Tony Allen's *Rebel II* inexplicably capsized, leaving the poor skipper drifting in his liferaft for several days before being picked up by a passing freighter. The same year Ian McBride's yacht *Unique* hit a submerged object off South Queensland and he also had to take to his liferaft. Despite these accidents the Trans-Tasman race has a remarkably good record of safety, considering it crosses such treacherous water.

Less than a month after the antipodean single-handers have made it into harbour, on the other side of the Pacific another bunch of "crazy" solo sailors are setting off on an even longer unassisted race. Unlike the Trans-Tasman, however, the Singlehanded Trans-Pacific race takes place every two years and attracts fleets of up to 38 yachts. When the 3392 (2120-mile) contest from San Francisco to Hawaii was started in 1978, it was variously described as "courageous", "heroic", "insane", and even "suicidal". Since its inception, nearly 200 skippers have successfully made the crossing, sticking two fingers up to the cynics who predicted death and destruction.

The roots of the solo TransPac are inextricably entwined with those of another offshore race sailed out of San Francisco: the Single-handed Farallones Race. Lying 40km (25 miles) out to sea from the Golden Gate bridge, the Farallones Islands have long been a symbolic waypoint for Californian sailors. When businessman George Sigler announced the date for a singlehanded race to Southeast Farallon Island and back in 1977, over 60 skippers turned up at the start line. Most were knocked back by the gale force winds that hit the fleet as it headed out to sea, but 14 plucky sailors made it out there and back to the finish line late that evening. More importantly, the idea of a solo race starting from San Francisco Bay had been born, and the Singlehanded Sailing Society (SSS) was formed soon after.

Inevitably, though, many skippers wanted to go one further, onward to the next island - in this case Hawaii, 3392km (2120 miles) to the west. So the SSS (dubbed by some as the "organization of

people who don't usually join anything – the ultimate un-yacht club") obliged with a race of more challenging proportions. A fleet of 33 yachts set off under reefed mainsails for the first singlehanded TransPacific Yacht Race on 15 June 1978. They were divided into two classes, with 14 boats in the 22-30ft (6.7-9.1m) class and 19 in the over 9.1m (30ft) class, and the final result was calculated using a handicap system which took into account the different characteristics of the various boats taking part.

Strong winds during that first race meant some speed records were set that would stand for another 10 years – in fact, the weather was so wild that only 22 boats made it to the finish line in Hanalei Bay, with the other 38 retiring along the way. Norton Smith and his yacht *Solitaire* set the record in their class and overall with an elapsed time of 13 days, two hours, and 34 minutes (which translated to nine days, 17 hours, and 18 minutes on corrected time). There was no doubt that an exciting new ocean race, in line with what was happening on the other side of the continent, had arrived on America's west coast –

**below** Peter Hogg smashed the previous record for the 3392km (2120 mile) Trans-Pacific race by three days in 1994 on his trimaran *Aotea*, finishing in eight days and 20 hours.

although, unlike the OSTAR, the SSS event was to remain a largely amateur affair. While the Farallones race remained an annual event, the new TransPac was set to take place biennially, on even years.

## Anomalies

As ever the handicapping system produced some interesting anomalies. Despite finishing first on elapsed time in both 1980 and 1982 and setting a new race record, Michael Kane and his speedy trimaran *Crusader* were beaten on adjusted time by monohulls in both races. Four years later, in 1986, even Ian Johnston and his trimaran *Bullfrog Sunblock*, fresh from setting a new record in the Trans-Tasman, couldn't beat the handicap. Despite setting a new overall elapsed time record of 10 days and 10 hours, and a new 24-hour record of 560km (350 miles), he was still beaten on adjusted time by Dan Newland on *Francis Who?*, the first monohull to finish, with a time of 13 days and six hours.

Another interesting first took place during the 1986 race, when blind sailor Hank Dekker made the crossing on his wittily-named 8.5m (28ft) yacht *Outta Sight* using Braille charts, a Braille compass and a talking Loran [navigation system] and clock. Dekker not only finished the race in a respectable 17 days and 19 hours but came third on corrected time.

The monohull record itself stood until 1988 when Bill Stange and his yacht *Intense* set a new time of 11 days and 15 hours, only to have it beaten by Stan Honey on his yacht *Illusion* during the "windy race" of 1994. Honey's record was in turn beaten by Ray Thayer aboard *Wild Thing* during the next race. The 18.3m (60ft) *Wild Thing* was built to take part in the 1994–5 BOC race, but never quite made it due to innumerable teething problems. With her wide beam and enormous rig (including a 409sqm (4400sqft) spinnaker) she looked every bit one of those Southern Ocean surfers so beloved of BOC and Vendée Globe sailors – except that she weighed twice as much as they do. Equipped for cruising at the time, microwave, television and freezer were among the many home comforts that didn't prevent her setting the current TransPac

monohull record of 10 days, 22 hours, and 53 minutes.

One of the windiest races on records, 1994 also saw an impressive new multihull record of just eight days, 20 hours and 16 minutes – that's an average of 10.75 knots over the whole course – set by Peter Hogg and his 12.2m (40ft) trimaran *Aotea*. But even that couldn't survive the onslaught of millionaire sailor Steve Fossett. After beating records in a dozen crewed and singlehanded races around the world, Fossett brought his 18.3m (60ft) trimaran *Lakota* to San Francisco in 1998 to claim another scalp. He duly reduced the multihull record to seven days, 22 hours and 38 minutes before heading off to the

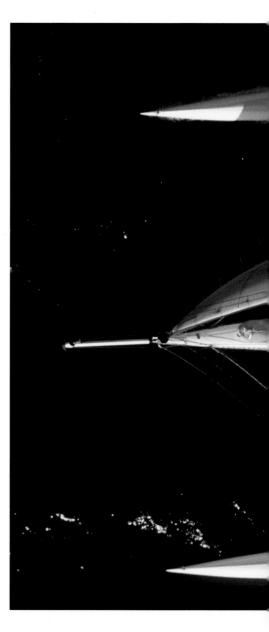

Great Lakes for his next record: the Chicago-to-Mackinac race. His TransPac record still stands.

The race's most persistent competitor, however, is without doubt Ken "the General" Roper who has taken part in seven solo TransPacs, coming first in class in 1998. Roper has sailed over 128,000km (80,000 miles) on his 9.4m (31ft) *Harrier,* much of it singlehanded. He was 72 when his boat was dismasted in the 2000 race. Undaunted, he set up a jury rig and successfully completed the course.

## Rite of passage

Those early descriptions of "crazy" and "suicidal" have long since been discredited by a regular fleet of about 20 boats – 38 was the high water mark in 1980, dipping to as low as 12 in 1994. Over the past 24 years there has been little damage and no loss of life, and the solo TransPac has undoubtedly attracted its fair share of characters. The race has a devoted following, whether it is those who come to it for serious competition or, probably the majority, simply as a personal rite of passage, as one competitor Bob Cranmer-Brown's log from the 1988 race demonstrates. "I lie in my

❝ I LIE IN MY BUNK…WHILE THE BOAT TEARS MADLY THROUGH THE NIGHT UNDER SPINNAKER, LIKE A WILD HORSE SHAKING ITS HEAD WITH SHEER EXUBERANCE OVER ITS SPEED ❞

Bob Cranmer-Brown on conditions during the Trans-Pac race

**left** American millionaire Steve Fossett set new records in a string of races on his trimaran *Lakota,* including the singlehanded TransPac, which he whittled down to seven days and 22 hours in 1998.

bunk and watch the wind instruments at the masthead while the boat tears madly through the night under spinnaker, like a wild horse shaking its head with sheer exuberance over its speed. Every once in a while the keel would give out a loud moaning cry to the whales below as we hit 18 knots and I pray for nothing to break."

On years when the TransPac isn't raced, singlehanded enthusiasts can cross over to the other side of the United States and join the Newport to Bermuda One-Two – though, as the name implies, they will have to compromise on the return journey and take a crew member with them. It's an ingenious concept which allows skippers to test their mettle on their own for the 1016km (635-mile) outward leg, rest for about a week on the island, and then have a slightly more relaxing (and usually faster) journey back. And, bearing in mind the lively social scene in Bermuda and resulting hangovers, that's probably just as well…

The 2032km (1270-mile) race was started in 1977 and has been held biennially ever since. It boasts among its alumni many of America's top single-handers, including the likes of OSTAR veteran Francis Stokes who, sailing with his son on the return leg, set a record on his yacht *Moonshine* which stood for 10 years. Steve Pettengill is said to have won his place on board *Hunter's Child* in the 1994–5 BOC – when he was second in Class I – after sailing with Warren Luhrs, the owner of Hunter Marine, the boat's sponsors, on the return leg from Bermuda. More recently, the Bermuda One-Two's line-up has included JP Mouligne (Around Alone Class II winner in 1998–9), Brad Van Liew (third place in Around Alone Class II in 1998–9 ) and George Stricker (Around Alone in 1998–9). In fact, if you're pursuing a singlehanded career in the United States, the likelihood is that at some stage you'll do the Bermuda One-Two, if only for the invaluable contacts you're likely to make. As Muffin Dubuc, who has been involved with the

**right** Skippers are obliged to take one crew with them for the return voyage of the Newport-to-Bermuda One-Two. Francis Stokes sailed out on his own in 1978, and back with his son, winning both ways and setting a 10-year record in the process.

race since its inception, puts it: "Our little race has started many of the world's finest."

The biggest navigational factor affecting the race is the crossing of the Gulf Stream at the northern part of the course – the first part of the outward leg. With a current of up to four knots, eddies of up to three knots and 160km (100 miles) wide the Gulf Stream needs to be plotted accurately. Its position, however, isn't constant so in the past skippers had to rely on previous experience and nous to make the right decision. Nowadays, thanks to the advent of satellite photography, its position is far easier to predict, but competitors can still get caught unawares. "The Stream is kind of like having a mistress, I guess," says Bjorn Johnson, overall winner of the 2001 race. "It can be wonderful or terrible." On top of that, the interaction between the Stream's warm currents and the cold water to the north often creates unpredictable weather patterns, with periods of light winds interrupted by sudden lightning squalls.

## Barrier reef

Once through the Gulf Stream, it's usually a pleasant ride for the last 480km (300 miles) to Bermuda, with warm southwesterlies prevailing. The barrier reef that guards Bermuda to the north and northeast is the main danger and needless to say has claimed its fair share of craft – particularly in days of yore. After all, navigation hasn't always been as easy as it is now. "The first two races, in 1977 and 1979, were the most challenging," says Juan Perez, at 67 years of age the only sailor to complete every Bermuda One-Two since its inception. "Back then, we had no electronics for navigation. Loran was just beginning. It was hard to find the island."

With GPS, that is no longer a problem, but Perez still carries a sextant on board his 10m (33ft) sloop *Tango*. "I use it occasionally to refresh my memory," he says.

Boats entered in the race range from 9.4m (31ft) to 15.2m (50ft), split into four classes according to size, with prizes awarded for both legs according to real and handicap times. While the faster yachts make it to Bermuda in less than four days, the slower ones can take more than a

week. Several new records were set in the windy year of 1999, but the jewel in the crown went to Jeffrey Siegal who finally broke the three-day barrier on his yacht *Appreciation* by completing the outward leg in two days, 19 hours, and 48 minutes – beating the previous elapsed time record from 1993 by over six hours.

A different kind of achievement was recorded in 1999 when Tristan Mouligne – son of Patrick Mouligne, a long-time supporter of the race, and nephew to the more famous "JP" – became the youngest person ever to enter the race. At just 19 years of age, he was under the official skippers' age limit and had to convince the organizers of his competence by completing a 320km (200-mile) solo passage as well as proving his skills in celestial navigation and other essential seamanship skills.

Tristan was competing on his family's 13.4m (44ft) ketch *Frog Kiss*, in which he had completed the second leg of the race with his father in 1997, only this time it was his younger brother, the 16-year-old John-Jay, who joined him on the return leg. Not only did the pair successfully complete the race but they stunned the old timers by winning first place overall on handicap – proving perhaps that a good bloodline is just as important as a fast boat.

So is tenacity in the face of adversity, or in the case of 2001 winner Jan Brandt, a lack of wind. "It was just flat. I needed to do something to keep my sanity, so I put on a pair of fins and jumped overboard. My boat's pretty light, so I can push it. It wasn't something to get closer to Bermuda. It was just something to keep my sanity and also to cool down. But I did learn that I can push the boat at 0.66 knots, sustained."

But the Bermuda One-Two isn't simply about racing. According to Brandt of *Team Kokopelli*, it has a higher purpose: "Although it is a competitive event," he writes, "the major emphasis of the event is the continued development and appraisal of offshore rigs, sail plans, sail gear, boat design, communications developments, and boat handling techniques for

> **❝ THE STREAM IS KIND OF LIKE HAVING A MISTRESS, I GUESS…IT CAN BE WONDERFUL OR TERRIBLE ❞**

Bjorn Johnson, overall winner of the 2001 Bermuda One-Two race shorthanded passagemakers." It's a mission the race shares with most other singlehanded competitions throughout the world and which makes the sport so valuable to all yachtsmen, whether sailing on their own or with crew.

## Two's company

Another offshore contest that successfully combines single- and double-handed sailing is the Azores and Back Race, known as AZAB for short. The organizers of this race, the Royal Cornwall Yacht Club (RCYC), have gone one step further, however, and allowed competitors to mix and match any combination they like of double- and singlehanded crews over its two legs. This means that a boat can sail to the Azores with two crew and return singlehanded, or vice versa, or go both ways with the same configuration – in race-talk this means that you have the choice of four options: one-one, one-two, two-one or two-two. Not only that, but a completely new crew can take over the boat once it reaches the Azores to sail the return leg, thus up to four people might sail the same boat during the course of the 4000km (2500-mile) race.

Confused? Wait till the prizegiving! In practice the system seems to work well and has produced one of the most enduringly popular races on the short-handed racing circuit. In its heyday in the 1970s the AZAB enjoyed boasted a fleet of up to 89 competitors, and as recently as 1995 some 61 yachts lined up for the start. The lowest turnout was 35 boats in 1991.

Diversity is the essence of the AZAB, with hardcore sailors using it as a qualifier for the OSTAR and other singlehanded races and some just enjoying it as a challenging cruise. As a result, the start-line typically includes everything from out-and-out racers to yachts more akin to floating caravans. There's no room for snobbery here.

## Spark

The spark that set the whole thing off was a letter to *Yachting Monthly* magazine in 1972 suggesting that, following the success of the fourth OSTAR, a shorter race should be held for sailors who could neither afford nor had the time nor the expense of a transatlantic race. The then assistant editor of the magazine, Andrew Bray (currently editor of *Yachting World*) joined forces with OSTAR veteran Andrew "Spud" Spedding, the author of the letter, Chris Smith, and Colin Drummond (current race chairman and RCYC vice-commodore) to set the wheels in motion. The Azores was chosen as the ideal destination, providing sufficient challenge and suitably exotic surroundings while fitting into a reasonable four- to six-week time frame. Like the OSTAR, the AZAB would be raced every four years, 12 months before its transatlantic mentor.

The first race in 1975 got off to a flying start with 52 entries including several up-and-coming names, such as Clare Francis on *Robertson's Golly*, future Route du Rhum star Michel Malinovsky on *Rousslane,* and Nick Keig on the first of his famous *Three Legs of Man* trimarans. The race was ranked on handicap, and although Keig set a real-time record of 7 days, 3 hours, and 58 minutes for the outward leg which would remain unbeaten for 20 years, it was the Belgian Gustaf Versluys on his yacht *Tyfoon V* who won on corrected time.

Several of the competitors in the 1975 AZAB went on to take part in the next year's OSTAR – including co-organizers Andrew Bray and Colin Drummond, who were both forced to retire with damage to their boats – starting a trend which would continue to the present day. Having got themselves and their yachts up to speed for one singlehanded race, for many it's their best ever opportunity to tackle "the big one".

Another key aspect which was evident from that very first race was the benefit of the Azores stopover. Not only did the few days on the island of São Miguel give crews a chance to make repairs and indulge in a little tourism, it also provided a vital social element that was to become a large part of people's enjoyment of the race. It may in part explain why so many sailors come back again and again – the record for attendance is currently held by Brian Dale who has sailed in every AZAB since 1979 and finished third in class on *Lone Shark* in 1999.

As well as chalking up the largest number of entries, 1979 was the first year that double-handed boats were allowed to compete in the race. It was a concept that quickly proved very popular, with 75 per cent of the boats being double-handed in the following race in 1983. By 1999 that figure had risen to around 90 per cent.

Despite sending some 374 yachts off on a fairly hazardous 4000km (2500-mile) ocean adventure, the AZAB has enjoyed a remarkably hazard-free 25-year history. The notable exception was the 1991 race, the year when strong winds enabled several yachts to break the six-day barrier on the return leg. Less fortunate were the 9.1m (30ft) *Minitech,* which lost her keel on the outward leg and capsized, and the 12.2m (40ft) catamaran *Queen Anne's Battery Marina,* which capsized on the windy return leg. Both crews were rescued unharmed.

The crew of *Severalles Challenge* were even luckier during the 1995 race. They sent out a Mayday after their multihull capsized on the outward leg and were picked up, along with their yacht, by a passing Russian freighter on its way to Brazil. As the ship passed the Azores, *Severalles Challenge* and crew were put back into the water and towed into harbour, thereby completing the first leg by default despite their mishap.

## Records broken

Many race records have been set and beaten over the years, but Nick Keig's original seven-day outward leg record has proven one of the hardest to beat. *Cherry Valley Super Duck* (better known as *Panic Major*) trimmed it down to five days, 23 hours, and 11 minutes, in 1987, and the 12.2m (40ft) *Spirit of England* managed an outstanding four days, 22 hours and 14 minutes in 1995 – but both of those were double-handers. The singlehanded record was finally broken in 1995 when Trevor Leek sailed the outward leg in an elapsed time of six days, four hours, and 39 minutes in his trimaran *Mollymawk.* Despite incurring a six-hour penalty for arriving in Falmouth less than the specified 24 hours before the start, his adjusted time was still well inside

**below** One of the monohulls to look out for in the AZAB race is *Hakuna Matata.* Despite being one of the smallest boats in the fleet, she completed the outward leg in nine days and four hours in 1999.

seven days. Most mortal competitors can expect each leg to take between up to twelve days.

Over the years the organizers have experimented with a number of ranking methods – from real time results in separate classes, like the OSTAR, to a two-tier system with prizes for both elapsed and handicap times – eventually settling for the current five-class handicap system. Likewise the size limit has gradually increased over the years, from the original 7.2m (22ft) minimum and 11.6m (38ft) maximum to the current 8.8m (29ft) and 18.6m (61ft).

The results for the AZAB are already complicated by the fact that there are so many possible crew combinations. Combine this with the fact that the yachts themselves are divided into five classes, all of which are awarded prizes for both legs of the race, with some additional prizes for the elapsed time winners, and you have a logistical puzzle of Homeric proportions. Not surprisingly, the prize list is long and bewildering. The oldest trophy is the RCYC

Prince of Wales Cup dating from 1863 and awarded "to the yacht in Class II achieving the shortest corrected aggregate time". Then there is the Henri-Lloyd Challenge Cup awarded "to the yacht in any class taking the shortest aggregate elapsed time". Not forgetting the Visick Perpetual Trophy awarded "to the yacht in any class, the skipper and crew of which are related, achieving the shortest aggregate corrected time," and so on… You get the picture.

As if that wasn't enough, a new prize was introduced in 1999 for the yacht "whose crew are judged by their peers to have contributed most to the Corinthian spirit of the event". The idea was inspired by the Cutty Sark Tall Ships race whose principal award goes not to the first boat over the line or on handicap but to the ship which has given most to the spirit of the event. Great concept, but one which adds to what is an already eye-glazingly long prize-giving ceremony.

Ranking complications aside, the AZAB has proven to be one of the most popular single-/doublehanded races in the world, surviving

**below** Started as a more accessible version of the OSTAR, the 3904km (2440-mile) AZAB attracts a fleet of up to 89 boats. Many competitors go on to sail in the OSTAR or other longer singlehanded races.

several rival races which still struggle to attract the same number of competitors.

## Alone across the Pacific

Less enduring was the transpacific race from San Francisco to Tokyo, which ran every six years from 1969–81 and was famously won by Eric Tabarly in 1969. The idea of a singlehanded race across the entire Pacific is too alluring to go away completely, however, so it's not entirely surprisingly to hear of a new event being launched for 2003. The CrossPac will leave San Francisco on 12 July and arrive in Newcastle, New South Wales (just north of Sydney) about two months later having crossed 10,400km (6500 miles) of the most exposed – and most beautiful – seas in the world. The race is open to single- and double-handed entries and takes in a stopover at Honolulu in Hawaii, breaking the journey into 3360km (2100-mile) and 7040km (4400-mile) chunks. At more than twice as long as crossing the Atlantic, it's an impressive journey and one which race chairman Alan Hebert hopes "will surely turn out to be one of the world's premier shorthanded, offshore races." Only the round-the-world solo races are longer. "I can't think of a better way to cap an offshore sailing career, or to qualify for the Vendée Globe or Around Alone," says Hebert. Plus you'd have 15 months to cruise back from Australia for the start of the next Vendée Globe. Perfect.

## "Bermuda backwards"

Another lesser-known new race uncovered while researching for this book is one proposed by American single-hander Dodge Morgan. For several years Morgan held the record for the fastest solo circumnavigation, completed in 1985–6, which he started and finished in Bermuda. Now it seems he is planning something a little more contrary. He told *Points East* magazine that he and a friend called Tom would be launching a "Bermuda Backwards Two-One" in 2002. It would be just like the Bermuda One-Two, he said, "only Tom and I will team up to do this event in reverse of tradition. With the solo fleet racing to Bermuda, we will doublehand to Newport and, with the pairs racing back to Newport, Tom will solo to Bermuda. There is a certain poetry in this procedure. We will be in both ports without the crush of many sailors jockeying for bragging rights and degrading the service in bars. We will not be fraught by the frayed nerves that come from being amidst a testosterone [pumped] fleet, thus relieved of the attending demand for constant watches and freed of discouraging sightings of competitors. We will, of course, be receiving the starting process via satellite, so our crossing times will have complete and unassailable legitimacy at any protest committee meeting. Racing boils down to just a matter of reading clocks anyway.

"Our major challenge will occur when we must pass through the oncoming fleet. During this scary period, we will mount a loud hailer fitted with an endless loop audio tape (technically known as a Mobius strip) on the bow, repeating over and over the words, 'starboard tack, woman overboard, fresh pizza, stock market crash news on channel 169'." Whatever turns you on, Dodge.

Such a rich variety of singlehanded races points to a healthy and sustained interest in what is by definition a minority sport. Doubtless the enormous publicity generated by the dramatic events of the 1996–7 Vendée Globe has raised the stakes but so, too, has the international recognition received by solo stars such as Christophe Auguin, Ellen MacArthur, and JP Mouligne. But most of the best-known names have honed their skills and built up their sea miles by taking part in the smaller races. The continued prosperity of these is therefore an important factor in the continuing success of the sport as a whole. Although perhaps not enjoying the numbers it did in the peak years of the late 1970s, the overall impression is of a steadily increasing participation. Indeed, racing standards have never been higher nor, particularly since the 1996–7 debacle, have they been safer.

Singlehanders have entered the 21st century still on their own but more certain of the way ahead than ever before.

> **I CAN'T THINK OF A BETTER WAY TO CAP AN OFFSHORE SAILING CAREER, OR TO QUALIFY FOR THE VENDÉE GLOBE OR AROUND ALONE**
>
> Alan Herbert on the CrossPac

## CAREER PROFILE

**1968** Born in Los Angeles, CA

**1980** Newport to Bermuda Race

**1997** Newport to Bermuda One-Two

**1997** US Navy Seamanship Award

**1998–9** 3rd in Class II, Around Alone

When Brad Van Liew entered the 1997 Newport to Bermuda One-Two, he expected a moderately challenging race followed by a week in the sun. Fate had other plans. On the outward leg his rudder broke and he improvised a jury rig with a washboard and spinnaker pole. This act of self-sufficiency not only won him the Seamanship Award from the US Navy but foretold was to come in the following months – only in far more extreme circumstances.

Van Liew started sailing dinghies at the age of six. By the time he was 12 he was crewing off shore on the Newport to Bermuda race, and took part in several crewed offshore races in his teens; but it was singlehanded racing that really caught his imagination. By the age of 21, while still at university, he had decided to enter the BOC Challenge – only a lack of willing sponsors prevented him. It would be eight years before he was able to realize his dream.

But, apart from being a fully-certified boat-nut, Van Liew is also an archetypal American

## ❝ A JACK OF ALL TRADES ❞

entrepreneur. He looked elsewhere for his first career – to the skies. After graduating from the University of Southern California, he qualified as a commercial pilot and by the age of 30 he had set up his own successful air charter company.

While his business prospered, Van Liew continued sailing, delivering yachts on the east coast of America and joining the IOR race circuit. "I started turning more to singlehanded racing as I got tired of some aspects of crewed racing," he said. "All the personalities on board. But mostly because I enjoy being a jack of all trades. I want to do everything on board. I enjoy it all: navigating, foredeck, trimming. But on a crewed boat I would only be doing one of those things and I found it very frustrating."

Eventually he and his wife Meaghan decided to use their savings to fund a BOC campaign. They bought Alan Nebauer's 15.2m (50ft) *Newcastle Australia*, built for the 1994–5 BOC, and renamed it *California Challenge*. Finding sponsors proved much harder until, just a few days before the start of the 1998–9 race, the nutrition snack manufacturers Balance Bar stepped in. They came up with the unusual formula of paying Van Liew according to the amount of media coverage he generated. Van Liew agreed willingly – and then spent much of the race hammering out press releases with copious references to his sponsor's name.

The race proved tougher than Van Liew had expected, particularly the long haul through the Southern Ocean during which he endured nearly two weeks of gales approaching Cape Horn. He eventually made it into Punta del Este, only to be dismasted 50 miles into the fourth and final leg. He improvised again, setting up a jury rig with the spinnaker pole, while on shore his support crew got a replacement mast ready. "It felt like the world picked me up by the scruff of the neck and said, 'You will not stop here,'" he later commented. He finished the race in third place overall in Class II, the only American to finish that year, and the youngest skipper in the race.

During the race, Van Liew struck up a close relationship with British skipper Michael Gartside, finishing the second leg with only two minutes between them – the closest finish in the history of the race. It seemed quite natural, then, for Van Liew to buy Gartside's more modern, Groupe Finot-designed *Magellan Alpha* to enter the next Around Alone in 2002 – only this time with the security of a campaign fully-sponsored by clotheswear manufacturers Tommy Hilfiger. At the age of 33, and with a professional flying career already behind him, Van Liew has finally become the professional sailor he dreamed of being since he was 12.

# BRAD van liew

# THE WINNERS

## EUROPE 1 NEWMAN STAR (EX-OSTAR/CARLSBERG STAR/EUROPE 1 STAR)

| Sailor | Yacht | Finish time |
|---|---|---|
| **1960** | | |
| Francis Chichester | *Gipsy Moth III* | 40d 12h 30m |
| Blondie Hasler | *Jester* | 48d 12h 02m |
| David Lewis | *Cardinal Vertue* | 55d 00h 50m |
| **1964** | | |
| Eric Tabarly | *Pen Duick II* | 27d 03h 56 m |
| Francis Chichester | *Gipsy Moth III* | 29d 23h 57m |
| Val Howells | *Akka* | 32d 18h 08m |
| **1968** | | |
| Geoffrey Williams | *Sir Thomas Lipton* | 25d 20h 33m |
| Bruce Dalling | *Voortrekker* | 26d 13h 42m |
| Tom Follett | *Cheers* | 27d 00h 13m |

| Sailor | Yacht | Finish time |
|---|---|---|
| **1972** | | |
| Alain Colas | *Pen Duick IV* | 20d 13h 15m |
| Jean-Yves Terlain | *Vendredi 13* | 21d 05h 14m |
| Jean-Marie Vidal | *Cap 33* | 24d 05h 40m |
| **1976** | | |
| Eric Tabarly | *Pen Duick VI* | 23d 20h 12m |
| Mike Birch | *The Third Turtle* | 24d 20h 39m |
| Kazimierz Jaworski | *Spaniel* | 24d 23h 40m |
| **1980** | | |
| Philip Weld | *Moxie* | 17d 23h 12m |
| Nick Keig | *Three Legs of Mann III* | 18d 06h 04m |
| Philip Steggall | *Jeans Foster* | 18d 06h 45m |
| **1984** | | |
| Yvon Fauconnier | *Umupro Jardin V* | 16d 06h 25m |
| Philippe Poupon | *Fleury Michon I* | 16d 12h 25m |
| Marc Pajot | *Elf Aquitaine II* | 16d 12h 48m |
| **1988** | | |
| Philippe Poupon | *Fleury Michon I* | 10d 09h 15m |
| Olivier Moussy | *Laiterie Mt St Michel* | 11d 04h 17m |
| Loick Peyron | *Lada Poch II* | 11d 09h 02m |
| **1992** | | |
| Loïck Peyron | *Fujicolour* | 11d 01h 35m |
| Paul Vatine | *Haute-Normandie* | 12d 07h 49m |
| Francis Joyon | *Banque Populaire* | 12d 09h 14m |
| **1996** | | |
| Loïck Peyron | *Fujicolour II* | 10d 10h 05m |
| Paul Vatine | *Region Haute-Normandie* | 10d 13h 05m |
| Mike Birch | *Biscuits La Trinitaine* | 14d 12h 55m |
| **2000** | | |
| Francis Joyon | *Eure et Loire* | 09d 23h 21m |
| Marc Guillemot | *Biscuits La Trinitaine* | 10d 01h 59m |
| Franck Cammas | *Groupama I* | 10d 02h 40m |

# MINI TRANSAT

| Sailor | Boat |
|---|---|
| **1977** | |
| Daniel Gilard | *Petit Dauphin* |
| Kazimierz Jaworski | *Spaniel* |
| Halvard Mabire | *Haro* |
| | |
| **1979** | |
| Norton Smith | *American Express* |
| Jean-Luc van den Heede | *Gros Plant* |
| Daniel Gilard | *Petit Dauphin* |
| | |
| **1981** | |
| Jacques Peignon | *Iles du Ponant* |
| Vincent Lévy | *Pineau des Charentes* |
| Eric Lecotelley | *Forclusion* |
| | |
| **1983** | |
| Stéphane Poughon | *Voiles Cudennec* |
| Bernard Abalan | *Bousbir* |
| Olivier Chapuis | *Supermarché Champion* |
| | |
| **1985** | |
| Yves Parlier | *Aquitaine* |
| Fred Guérin | *La Croix* |
| Sylvain Berthomé | *Isle d'Abeau* |
| | |
| **1987** | |
| Gilles Chiorri | *Exa* |
| Laurent Bourgnon | *Côte de Jade* |
| Isabelle Autissier | *Ecureil* |
| | |
| **1989** | |
| Philippe Vicariot | *Thom Pouss* |
| Fred Guérin | *Les Filles de la Rochelle* |
| Dominic Bourgeois | *Côtes de Bourg* |
| | |
| **1991** | |
| Damien Grimont | *GTM Entrepose* |
| Patrice Carpentier | *L'Intrépide* |
| Dominic Bourgeois | *Alibi* |
| | |
| **1993** | |
| Thierry Dubois | *Amnesty International* |
| Marc Lepesqueux | *Sidel* |
| Yves le Masson | *Port de Trébeurden* |

**above** Mini-Transat 1989, before the start.

**far left** *Jester*, in which Blondie Hasler finished second in the 1960 OSTAR.

| Sailor | Boat |
|---|---|
| **1995** | |
| Yvan Bourgnon | *Omapi-Saint Brévin* |
| Thierry Fagnent | *Santé Rhône Alpes* |
| Bernard Stamm | *Hotel Albana* |
| | |
| **1997** | |
| Sébastien Magnen | *Karen Liquid* |
| Thomas Coville | *Zurich* |
| Jean-François Pellet | *Globe 2000* |
| | |
| **1999** | |
| Sébastien Magnen | *Voile Magazine Jeanneau* |
| Pierre-Yves Moreau | *Sablières Palvadeau* |
| Chris Sayer | *Navman* |
| | |
| **2001** | |
| Yannick Bestaven | *Aquarelle.com* |
| Simon Curwen | *QDS* |
| Arnaud Boissieres | *Aquarelle.com* |

# SOLITAIRE DU FIGARO

**1970**
Joan de Kat
Michel Malinovsky
Pierre Bonnet

**1971**
Michel Malinovsky
Pierre Bonnet
Yves Deborde

**1972**
Jean-Marie Vidal
Michel Girard
Michel Malinovsky

**1973**
Gilles Le Baud
Dominique Lunven
Eugène Riguidel

**1974**
Eugène Riguidel
Bruno Lunven
Bernard Pallard

**1975**
Guy Cornou
Gilles Gahinet
Bruno Lunven

**1976**
Guy Cornou
Bernard Pallard
Gilles Gahinet

**1977**
Gilles Gahinet
Patrick Morvan
Michel Malinovsky

**1978**
Gilles Le Baud
Patrick Eliès
Patrick Morvan

**1979**
Patrick Eliès
Olivier Moussy
Gilles Gahinet

**1980**
Gilles Gahinet
Patrick Morvan
Philippe Poupon

**1981**
Sylvain Rosier
Jean François Fountaine
Gilles Gahinet

**1982**
Philippe Poupon
Gilles Gahinet
Hervé Papin

**1983**
Lionel Péan
Philippe Poupon
Damien Savatier

**1984**
Christophe Cudennec
Damien Savatier
Gery Trentesaux

**1985**
Philippe Poupon
Jean Le Cam
Christophe Cudennec

**1986**
Christophe Auguin
Pascal Leys
Patrick Eliès

**1987**
Jean Marie Vidal
François Lamiot
Antoine Lebec

**1988**
Laurent Bourgnon
Alain Gautier
Antoine Lebec

**1989**
Alain Gautier
Halvard Mabire
Laurent Cordelle

**1990**
Laurent Cordelle
Dominique Wavre
Halvard Mabire

**1991**
Yves Parlier
Michel Desjoyeaux
François Lamiot

**1992**
Michel Desjoyeaux
Jean Le Cam
Damien Savatier

**1993**
Dominic Vittet
Jean Le Cam
Roland Jourdain

**1994**
Jean Le Cam
Hervé de Kergariou
Roland Jourdain

**1995**
Philippe Poupon
Philippe Vicariot
Jean Le Cam

**1996**
Jean Le Cam
Michel Desjoyeaux
Hervé de Kergariou

**1997**
Franck Cammas
Dominique Wavre
Marc Guessard

**1998**
Michel Desjoyeaux
Eric Drouglazet
Jean Le Cam

**1999**
Jean Le Cam
Eric Drouglazet
Gildas Morvan

**2000**
Pascal Bidegorry
Armel Le Cleach
Gildas Morvan

**2001**
Eric Drouglazet
Sébastien Josse
Gildas Morvan

**2002**
Christophe de Pavant
Gilles Chiorri
Charles Caudrelier

**right** Francis Joyon in *Banque Populaire*, Route du Rhum, 1998.

# ROUTE DU RHUM

| Sailor | Yacht | Finish time |
| --- | --- | --- |
| **1978** | | |
| Mike Birch | *Olympus Photo* | 23d 06h 59m |
| Michel Malinovsky | *Kriter V* | 23d 07h 01m |
| Phil Weld | Rogue Wave | 23d 15h 51m |
| **1982** | | |
| Marc Pajot | *Elf Aquitaine* | 18d 01h 38m |
| Bruno Peyron | *Jaz* | 18d 11h 46m |
| Mike Birch | *Vital* | 18d 13h 44m |
| **1986** | | |
| Philippe Poupon | *Fleury Michon* | 14d 15h 57m |
| Bruno Peyron | *Ericsson* | 16d 17h 03m |
| Lionel Péan | *Hitachi* | 17d 07h 08m |
| **1990** | | |
| Florence Arthaud | *Pierre 1er* | 14d 10h 8m |
| Philippe Poupon | *Fleury Michon* | 14d 18h 39m |
| Laurent Bourgnon | *RMO* | 14d 18h 46m |

| Sailor | Yacht | Finish time |
| --- | --- | --- |
| **1994** | | |
| Laurent Bourgnon | *Primagaz* | 14d 06h 28m |
| Paul Vatine | *Région Haute Normandie* | 14d 09h 38m |
| Yves Parlier | *Cacolac d'Aquitaine* | 15d 19h 23m |
| **1998** | | |
| Laurent Bourgnon | *Primagaz* | 12d 08h 41m |
| Alain Gautier | *Brocéliande* | 12d 11h 54m |
| Franck Cammas | *Groupama* | 12d 19h 41m |
| **2002** | | |
| Class I | | |
| Michel Desjoyeaux | *Géant* | 13d 07h 53m |
| Marc Guillemot | *Biscuits La Trinitaine* | |
| | *–Team Ethypharm* | 13d 19h 36m |
| Lalou Roucayrol | *Banque Populaire* | 14d 07h 01m |
| Class II | | |
| Ellen MacArthur | *Kingfisher* | 13d 13h 31m |
| Mike Golding | *Ecover* | 13d 19h 36m |
| Joé Seeten | *Arcelor Dunkerque* | 16d 00h 51m |

## AROUND ALONE (EX-BOC CHALLENGE)

| Sailor | Yacht | Finish time |
| --- | --- | --- |
| **1982–3** | | |
| Class I | | |
| Phillippe Jeantot | *Crédit Agricole* | 159d 02h 26m |
| Bertie Reed | *Altech Voortrekker* | 170d 16h 51m |
| Richard Broadhead | *Perseverance of Medina* | 192d 10h 06m |
| Class II | | |
| Yukoh Tada | *Koden Okera V* | 207d 13h 55m |
| Francis Stokes | *Moonshine* | 209d 01h 32m |
| Richard Konkolski | *Nike III* | 213d 16h 46m |
| | | |
| **1986–7** | | |
| Class I | | |
| Phillippe Jeantot | *Crédit Agricole III* | 134d 05h 23m |
| Titouan Lamazou | *Ecureuil d'Aquitaine* | 137d 17h 36m |
| Jean-Yves Terlain | *UAP Pour Medicins* | |
| | *Sans Frontieres* | 146d 10h 58m |
| Class II | | |
| Mike Plant | *Airco Distributor* | 157d 11h 44m |
| Jean-Luc van den Heede | *Let's Go* | 161d 07h 37m |
| Harry Harkimo | *Belmont Finland* | 168d 09h 21m |
| | | |
| **1990–1** | | |
| Class I | | |
| Christophe Auguin | *Groupe Sceta* | 120d 22h 36m |
| Alain Gautier | *Generali Concorde* | 122d 12h 49m |
| Philippe Jeantot | *Crédit Agricole IV* | 129d 14h 49m |

| Sailor | Yacht | Finish time |
| --- | --- | --- |
| Class II | | |
| Yves Dupasquier | Servant 4 | 141d 15h 49m |
| Don McIntyre | Buttercup | 153d 12h 21m |
| Josh Hall | New Spirit of Ipswich | 157d 04h 08m |
| | | |
| **1994–5** | | |
| Class I | | |
| Christophe Auguin | *Sceta Calberson* | 121d 17h 11m |
| Steve Pettengill | *Hunter's Child* | 128d 04h 03m |
| Jean Luc van den Heede | *Vendée Enterprises* | 129d 17h 59m |
| Class II | | |
| David Adams | *True Blue* | 131d 05h 06m |
| Giovanni Soldini | *Kodak 2* | 134d 00h 46m |
| Chaniah Vaughan | *Jimroda II* | 166d 16h 06m |
| | | |
| **1998–9** | | |
| Class I | | |
| Giovanni Soldini | *Fila* | 116d 20h 07m |
| Marc Thiercelin | *Somewhere* | 130d 09h 23m |
| – | – | – |
| Class II | | |
| Jean-Pierre Mouligne | *Cray Valley* | 132d 04h 03m |
| Michael Garside | *Magellan Alpha* | 138d 12h 10m |
| Brad Van Liew | *Balance Bar* | 150d 20h 22m |

**below** Philippe Jeantot on *Crédit Agricole* in the 1990 BOC Challenge.

## VENDÉE GLOBE

| Sailor | Yacht | Finish time |
|---|---|---|
| **1989–90** | | |
| Titouan Lamazou | *Ecureuil D'Aquitaine II* | 109d 08h 48m |
| Loïck Peyron | *Lada Poch III* | 110d 01h 08m |
| Jean-Luc van den Heede | *36.15 MET* | 112d 01h 14m |
| **1992–3** | | |
| Alain Gautier | *Bagages Superior* | 110d 02h 22m |
| Jean-Luc van den Heede | *Groupe Sofap-Helvim* | 116d 15h 01m |
| Philippe Poupon | *Fleury Michon* | 117d 03h 34m |
| **1996–7** | | |
| Christhope Auguin | *Geodis* | 105d 20h 31m |
| Marc Thiercelin | *Credit Immobilier de France* | 113d 08h 26m |
| Hervé Laurent | *Groupe LG Traitmat* | 114d 16h 43m |
| **2000–1** | | |
| Michel Desjoyeaux | *PRB* | 93d 03h 57m |
| Ellen MacArthur | *Kingfisher* | 94d 04h 25m |
| Roland Jourdain | *Sill Matines & La Potagère* | 96d 01h 02m |

**above** Titouan Lamazou on *Ecureuil D'Aquitaine II*, winner of the **1989–90** Vendée Globe.

# BIBLIOGRAPHY

### The Background

Francis Chichester *Gypsy Moth Circles the World* (International Marine, 2000)

Robin Knox-Johnston *A World of My Own* (Norton & Co., 1994)

Bernard Moitessier *The Long Way* (Sheridan House, 1995)

Peter Nichols *A Voyage for Madmen* (Profile Books, 2002)

Alec Rose *My Lively Lady* (Sheridan House, 1988)

Joshua Slocum *Sailing Alone Around the World* (Adlard Coles Nautical, 1996)

Nicholas Tomalin & Ron Hall *The Strange Voyage of Donald Crowhurst* (International Marine, 2001)

### OSTAR

Gérald Asaria *Challenge: Lone Sailors of the Atlantic* (Smithmark, 1979)

Frank Page *Alone Against the Atlantic* (David & Charles, 1981)

### Route du Rhum

Thierry Rannou *La Route du Rhum* (Éditions du Sport, 1994)

### BOC/Around Alone

Tony Bartelme & Brian Hicks *Into the Wind* (Evening Post, 1999)

Tony Fairchild *The Third Time Around* (Robert Hale, 1991)

Paul Gelder The Loneliest Race (Sheridan House, 1995)

Robin Knox-Johnston & Barry Pickthall *The BOC Challenge 1986-87* (Robertsbridge, 1987)

Barry Pickthall *The Ultimate Challenge* (Orbis Publishing, 1983)

### Vendée Globe

Tony Bullimore *Saved* (Warner Books, 1997)

Pete Goss *Close to the Wind* (Headline, 1998)

Derek Lundy *Godforsaken Sea* (Yellow Jersey Press, 1998)

Ellen MacArthur *Taking on the World* (Michael Joseph, 2002)

Jean-Yves Montagu *Le Grand Souffle* (Albin Michel, 1993)

François Mousis & Serge Messager *Le Vendée Globe – Histoire d'un Mythe* (Éditions des Vignes, 2001)

### General

Jean-Michel Barrault *Des Bateaux et des Hommes* (Éditions Robert Laffont, 2002)

Bob Fisher *The Great Yacht Races* (Orbis Publishing, 1984)

Benoît Heimermann *Seuls Autour du Monde* (Éditions Ouest-France, 2000)

Benjamin Lambert *Les Grands Navigateur en Solitaire* (Bordas, 1989)

David Pelly *The Illustrated Encyclopedia of World Sailing* (AA 1989)

# GLOSSARY

**505** a class of 5m (16ft 6in) long crewed racing dinghy.

**aft** near or towards the stern of a ship.

**America's Cup** an historic yacht race held roughly every four years since 1851 and won by the United States every year until 1983.

**anchorline** rope to hold a yacht to her anchor.

**ARGOS transponder** a positioning beacon which transmits periodic signals several times a day via satellites to a land base in Toulouse, France. Enables race organizers to keep track of a competitor's position, and can be activated in case of emergency.

**ASR** Air-Sea Rescue.

**astern** behind or towards the rear of a ship.

**autopilot** electronic machine which steers the vessel automatically either to a compass course or, if linked to a wind vane, wind direction.

**ballast** heavy material such as gravel, sand, iron or lead, placed in the bilge of a ship to ensure its stability.

**ballast keel** section of a yacht's keel usually made of iron or lead to improve stability.

**bare poles** with no sails raised.

**beam** a ship's breadth at its widest point.

**bermudan sail** a triangular mainsail, without an upper spar, which is hoisted up the mast by a single halyard attached to the head of the sail.

**bilges** the lowest internal portion of the hull of a ship.

**bobstay** a rope used to hold down the bowsprit of a yacht and keep it steady.

**boom** a pivoted spar to which the foot of a vessel's sail is attached, allowing the angle of the sail to be changed.

**bowsprit** a spar running out from a ship's bow used to give extra sail area and/or attaching the forestay.

**bulb keel** a keel where the weight is concentrated in a bomb-shaped protrusion at the bottom of a thin foil.

**bulkheads** a dividing wall or barrier between separate compartments inside a ship.

**canting keel** a keel whose angle can be adjusted to place its weight further to windward and increase its righting moment.

**cat rig** a sail configuration with the mast at the front of the vessel and with no jibs or other headsails.

**catamaran** a boat with twin hulls in parallel.

**centreboard** a pivoted board that can be lowered through the keel of a sailing boat to reduce sideways movement.

**centreboard case** the box that contains the centreboard and prevents water entering the boat.

**chine** the angle where the strakes of the bottom of a boat or ship meet the side.

**chronometer** an instrument for measuring time at sea.

**cockpit** recessed space in the deck where the helmsman and crew stand or sit.

**crossbeam** the girder which hold the hulls of a multihull together.

**cutter** a yacht with a single mast, a mainsail, and two forward sails.

**daggerboard** a kind of centreboard which slides vertically through the hull of a sailing boat.

**depression (weather)** a region of lower atmospheric pressure, especially a cyclonic weather system.

**dismasting** when the mast collapses (usually due to rigging failure).

**displacement** the amount or weight of fluid that would fill a floating ship, used as a measurement of the ship's size.

**doldrums** an equatorial region of any ocean with calms, sudden storms, and light unpredictable winds.

**dory** a small flat-bottomed rowing boat with a high bow and stern.

**double-ender** any vessel with two 'pointy' ends.

**double-handed yacht** a yacht raced with a skipper and one crew.

**downwind** in the direction in which the wind is blowing.

**draught** the depth of water needed to float a particular ship.

**Fastnet** a small island off the south coast of Ireland, or an abbreviation for a famous yacht race starting in Cowes, rounding the Fastnet Rock, and finishing in Plymouth.

**fin keel** a narrow keel, usually made of steel.

**flotsam** the wreckage of a ship or its cargo found floating on or washed up by the sea.

**Flying Dutchman** a 6m (19ft 10in) racing dinghy which has been an Olympic class since 1960.

**foil** each of the structures fitted to a hydrofoil's hull to lift it clear of the water at speed.

**foil-trimaran** a trimaran using the hydrofoil principle to raise the hulls clear of the water to achieve greater speed.

**Folkboat** a class of 7.6m (25ft) long cruising/racing yacht with a worldwide following.

**fore** the front part of a ship.

**forestay** the wire which supports a vessel's mast from the front.

**freeboard** the height of a ship between the waterline and the deck.

**full-rigged ship** a vessel carrying square sails on every mast.

**fully-battened** when the stiffeners used to prevent the sail flogging run the whole width of the sail all the way to the mast.

**fully-decked** when the deck covers the whole boat.

**gaff** a four-sided, fore-and-aft sail mounted on an upper spar, or gaff, which extends aft from the mast.

**gaff cutter** a one-masted boat rigged with a gaff mainsail and two forward sails.

**garboard** the first plank laid on a ship's bottom next to the keel.

**genoas** a large jib or foresail whose foot extends aft of the mast, used especially on racing yachts.

**giro-compass** a digital compass system.

**gooseneck** fitting that attaches the boom to the mast, allowing it to move freely.

**Great Circle** the shortest route from one point to another following the curve of the earth's surface.

**growler** a small iceberg that rises a little above the water.

**Gulf Stream** a warm current which flows from the Gulf of Mexico parallel with the American coast towards Newfoundland, continuing across the Atlantic Ocean towards NW Europe as the North Atlantic Drift.

**gunwale** the upper edge of planking of the side of a boat.

**Half-ton rule** a class of yacht designed within a certain list of parameters set by the IOR.

**halyard** a rope used for raising and lowering a sail, yard, or flag.

**handicapping system** method of adjusting the results to compensate for the different capabilities of yachts racing in a mixed fleet.

**headsail** any sail set forward of a vessel's foremast.

**headwind** a wind blowing from directly in front, opposing forward motion.

**heel** to lean over owing to the pressure of wind or an uneven load.

**helm** a tiller or wheel for steering a boat or ship.

**hull** the main body of a ship including the bottom, sides, and deck, but not the masts, superstructure, rigging, engines and other fittings.

**hydrofoil** a boat whose hull is fitted underneath with shaped vanes (foils) which lift the hull clear of the water at speed.

**inspection hatches** access points to check otherwise inaccessible parts of a boat.

**IOR** International Offshore Rule, a set of criteria created in 1971 to measure yachts as part of a handicapping system.

**jackstay** a rope, bar or batten placed along a ship's yard to bend the head of a square sail to.

**jib** a triangular staysail set forward of the mast.

**junk rig** a type of sail originating in Asia with a complex arrangement of full-length battens and control lines. The sail overlaps the mast and is usually used without foresails.

**jury rig** a makeshift rig used to sail a dismasted vessel to port.

**keel** the lengthwise timber or steel structure along the base of a ship, on which the framework of the whole is built up, in some vessels extended downwards as a blade or ridge to increase stability.

**keel bolts** fastenings used to attach the keel to the hull.

**ketch** a two-masted, fore-and-aft rigged sailing boat with a mizzen mast stepped forward of the rudder and smaller than its main mast.

**Kevlar** a synthetic fibre of high-tensile strength invented by Dupont

**knock down** when a boat is knocked on her side by a sudden gust or squall, especially under spinnaker.

**lashings** rope fastenings.

**lead keel** ballast keel made of lead

**list** to lean over to one side, typically because of a leak or unbalanced cargo.

**lug rig** a traditional, triangular-shaped sail whose top edge is attached to a yard (or pole) which overlaps the mast. Usually used without foresails.

**mainsail** the principal sail of a yacht.

**mainsheet track** a strip of shaped metal running down the back of the mast on which the mainsail runs up and down attached by slides.

**monohull** a boat with only one hull, as opposed to a catamaran or multihull.

**moorings** the ropes, chains, or anchors by which a boat is moored.

**multihull** a boat with two or more hulls.

**Nomex** a lightweight, high-strength modern construction material.

**off the wind** when the front of the boat is at more than 90° to the wind.

**Open 50** a class of racing yacht designed within a limited set of parameters, the main one being a maximum overall hull length of 15.2m (50ft).

**Open 60** same as an Open 50 but with a maximum overall hull length of 18.2m (60ft).

**outrigger** a beam, spar, or framework projecting from or over a boat's side. A float or secondary hull fixed parallel to a canoe or small ship for stability.

**pitch** to rock in a fore and aft direction.

**pitchpoled** a fore-and-aft capsize, where the bow sinks into the water and the stern is lifted into the air.

**planing lines** a shape designed to make a boat move at high speed over the water rather than through it.

**plumb bow** when the front of the boat is vertical to rather than angled to the water.

**port** the side of a ship on the left when one is facing forward.

**pre-pregnated carbon fibre** a high-tech construction material supplied already saturated with adhesives which cure when heated.

**proa** a type of sailing boat originating in Malaysia and Indonesia that may be sailed with either end at the front, typically having a large triangular sail and an outrigger.

**production boat** any mass-produced yacht.

**rhumb line** an imaginary line on the earth's surface, cutting all meridians at the same angle, used as the standard method of plotting a ship's course on a chart.

**ribs** the curved transverse struts of metal or timber in a ship, extending up from the keel and forming part of the framework of the hull.

**rigging** the system of ropes or wires employed to support a ship's masts (standing rigging), and to control or set the yards and sails (running rigging).

**Roaring Forties** stormy ocean tracts between latitudes 40 degrees and 50 degrees south.

**roll** to rock from side to side.

**roller furling** a method of stowing a sail by rolling it around a pivoting stay.

**RORC** Royal Ocean Racing Club.

**running backstay** adjustable wire rigging which supports the mast from the stern.

**running before a storm** sailing with the wind on the stern.

**sampan** a small boat of a kind used in the Far East, typically with an oar or oars at the stern.

**sea anchor** a kite-shaped contraption thrown into the sea on the end of a rope and used to hold a vessel into the wind during a storm to prevent it going side-on to the waves.

**seakeeping** the ability of a vessel to withstand rough conditions at sea.

**self-steering** a mechanism which uses the pressure of the wind against a vane to steer the boat at a constant angle to the wind.

**servo-pendulum rudder** a small fin linked to certain self-steering mechanisms which 'powers' the system.

**sheet** a rope attached to the lower corner of a sail for securing or extending the sail or for altering its direction.

**shrouds** the wire which supports the mast(s) from the sides of the vessel.

**skiff** a light rowing boat or sculling boat, typically for one person.

**sloop** a one-masted sailing boat with a mainsail and jib rigged fore and aft.

**Spectra** a high-strength modern synthetic sail fibre.

**spinnaker** a large three-cornered sail, typically bulging when full, set forward of the mainsail of a racing yacht when running before the wind.

**spinnaker poles** poles used to set and control the spinnaker.

**spreaders** the arms on either side of the mast used to push out the shrouds to give better support to the mast.

**stanchions** the upright rods which hold the lifelines around the deck perimeter.

**starboard** the side of the ship to the right when one is facing forward.

**stay** the wire which supports the mast(s) from the front and back of the vessel.

**stayed/unstayed** with/without standing rigging to support the mast.

**staysails** a triangular fore-and-aft sail extended on a stay.

**stem** the main upright timber or metal piece at the bow of a ship, to which the ship's sides are joined at the front end.

**stern** the rearmost part of a ship or boat.

**stern-hung rudder** a rudder that is attached to the back of the boat visible above water level, as opposed to one that is entirely underwater.

**storm jib** a small, specially reinforced foresail hoisted in very strong winds.

**strakes** a continuous line of planking or plates from the stem to the stern of a ship or boat.

**strop** a collar of leather or spliced rope.

**survival suit** an all-in-one outfit designed to withstand extreme conditions.

**tacking** changing course by turning a boat's head into and through the wind.

**titanium** a hard silver-grey metal used in strong, light, corrosion resistant alloys.

**topside** the upper part of a ship's side, above the waterline.

**trade winds** a wind blowing steadily towards the equator from the northeast in the northern hemisphere, or the southeast in the southern hemisphere.

**trimaran** a yacht with three hulls in parallel.

**trisail** a small, specially reinforced mainsail hoisted in very strong winds.

**twin rudders** two rudders set near each side of the boat, as opposed to a single, central rudder.

**upwind** against the direction of the wind.

**water ballast** a method of increasing a yacht's righting moment by pumping water into tanks located at the outermost point where deck and hull meet

**waterline** the level normally reached by the water on the side of a ship.

**weatherfax** a forecasting service which supplies weather charts by fax.

**wheelhouse** part of a ship or boat serving as a shelter for the person at the wheel.

**windage** the air resistance of a moving object such as a vessel.

**windvane** a revolving wing which shows which way the wind is blowing.

**windward** facing the wind, or on the side facing the wind.

**wing mast** a aerodynamically-shaped mast which revolves to show its best profile to the wind.

**wing sail** a rigid or semi-rigid structure similar to an aircraft wing fixed vertically on a boat to provide thrust from the action of the wind.

**wishbone schooner** a vessel with the foremast as high or shorter than the masts behind it and rigged with a sail (or sails) having an elliptical boom on either side, in the manner of a windsurfer.

**yard** a cylindrical spar tapering to each end, slung across a ship's mast to hang a sail from.

**yaw** the twisting motion of a yacht in a heavy seaway.

**yawl** a two-masted fore-and-aft rigged sailing boat with the mizzenmast stepped aft of the rudder post.

# INDEX

*Numbers in italics refer to captions.*

# PICTURE CREDITS

Front cover PPL/Jon Nash

Back cover DPPI/Benoit Stichelbaut

*in page order*

2 DPPI/Jacques Vapillon

5 DPPI/Jeal-Marie Liot

6 DPPI/Henri Thibault

9 DPPI/Jaques Vapillon

12–13 PPL/Knox-Johnston archive

17 PPL/Bill Rowntree/Knox-Johnston archive

19 PPL/Francois Richard

20 PPL

21 PPL

23 PPL/D.H.Clarke

24 PPL/D.H.Clarke

27 Bettmann/Corbis

28 Corbis/Sygma

29 PPL/Barry Pickthall

31 PPL/Chichester Archive

32 PPL/Chay Blyth archive

33 PPL/Francois Richard

34–35 PPL/Naomi James

36 PPL/Bill Rowntree/Knox-Johnston Archive

38–39 PPL/Jon Nash

42 PPL

43 PPL/Chichester archive

44 PPL/Barry Pickthall

45 PPL/Francois Richard

46 PPL/Jon Nash

47 PPL/Francois Richard

48 Bettmann/Corbis

49 PPL/Francois Richard

50 PPL/Alastair Black

52 PPL/Francois Richard

53 PPL/Alastair Black

54 PPL/Francois Richard

56 PPL/Jon Nash

57 Corbis Sygma/Isabelle Bich

58 Bettman/Corbis

60–61 DPPI/Thierry Bovy

64–65 DPPI/Jaques Vapillion

66 DPPI/Benoit Stichelbaut

68 DPPI/Benoit Stichelbaut

70 DPPI/J.M.Liot

73 DPPI/J.M.Liot

74 DPPI/Benoit Stichelbaut

75 Jean Christophe Marmara

76 PPL/Jason Holtom

78–79 PPL/Francois Richard

80 PPL/Francois Richard

82 DPPI/Jean-Marie Liot

84 DPPI/Jaques Vapillion

87 DPPI/Eric Cattin

88 DPPI/Benoit Stichelbaut

89 DPPI/Benoit Stichelbaut

91 DPPI/Jacques Vapillon

92 DPPI/Billy Black

94–95 DPPI/Jaques Vapillon

96 DPPI/Jean-Jacques Bernard

98 DPPI/Jean-Jacques Bernard

100 DPPI/Jean-Jacques Bernard

101 DPPI

103 Corbis Sygma/ Jean Guichard

104 Corbis Sygma/ Eric Preau

105 DPPI/Jacques Vapillon

106 DPPI/Jaques Vapillon

107 DPPI/Henri Thibault

108 Corbis Sygma/ Philippe Giraud

109 DPPI/Jean Marie Liot

110–111 DPPI/Henri Thibault

112 DPPI DPPI/Jean-Marie Liot

114 DPPI/Jean-Jacques Bernard

116–117 PPL/Barry Pickthall

120 PPL

121 PPL/Ace Marine Photography

122 PPL

124 PPL/Jamie Lawson-Johnston

125 PPL/Barry Pickthall

126 PPL/David Tease

127 PPL/Jamie Lawson Johnston

129 PPL/Billy Black

130 PPL/Jamie Lawson-Johnston

132 PPL/CBO

135 PPL/Billy Black

136 PPL/Jack Alterman

138–139 PPL/Mark Pepper

143 PPL/AFP

144 PPL/Francois Richard

145 PPL/Pierre Saboulin

147 PPL/Francois Richard

148 PPL/Francois Richard

150 PPL/Francois Richard

151 PPL/Francois Richard

153 PPL/J.McDonough

154 PPL/Francois Richard

155 PPL/Francois Richard

156 DPPI/Benoit Stichelbaut

159 PPL/Mark Pepper

160 PPL/Phil Russel

162–163 Graham Snook

167 Andrea Francolini

169 Antrim Associates, Naval Architects/Jim Antrim

170–171 DPPI/Henri Thibault

172 PPL/Chris Cunningham

175 Colin Wharton

176 Anne Hammick

178 PPL/Billy Black

180 PPI/Jon Nash

181 PPL/Francois Richard

183 DPPI/Henri Thibault

184 PPL/Barry Pickthall

185 PPL/Francois Richard